THE SHREDDED CHEF

———

Cover designed by Claire Guigal

Book designed by Claire Guigal

Edited by Andrea Lynn

Photographs by Emily Blumberg

Art direction by Jeremy Blumberg

Published by Oculus Publishers, Inc.

www.oculuspublishers.com

Visit the author's website: www.muscleforlife.com

The
Shredded Chef

120 RECIPES FOR BUILDING MUSCLE, GETTING LEAN, AND STAYING HEALTHY

MICHAEL MATTHEWS

THE PROMISE

___

**No matter how many times you've tried and failed to "diet,"
no matter how hopeless or confused you might feel,
there is one thing the diet and weight loss industry didn't lie to you about.
You absolutely, positively can build muscle and lose fat
eating foods and doing workouts you actually enjoy.**

What if I could show you how to improve your body composition and health by forever abandoning every form of boring, restrictive "dieting" ever devised?

What if I gave you a "crash course" in how to use food to make losing fat and gaining muscle simple and inevitable?

What if I showed you just how flexible you can be with your food choices while still looking the way you want to look and feeling better than ever before?

And what if I promised that everything I'm going to teach you isn't just a quick fix but a true lifestyle that you can enthusiastically embrace and maintain for the rest of your life?

Imagine if you woke up every day looking forward to each meal you're going to eat and enjoying it guilt-free because you knew, with certainty, exactly what is going to happen in your body and why.

Imagine people's surprise when they see you "having your cake and eating it, too"—quite literally! Imagine their continued confusion as you lose fat and improve your health while eating foods strictly verboten by the latest and greatest "diet gurus." Yes, I'm talking about grains, starchy carbs, fruit, red meat, and even the most dreaded molecule of them all, sugar.

Well, you can have all these things! It's not nearly as complicated or tough as the diet and nutrition industry would have you believe. It doesn't matter whether you're 21 or 61, whether you're in shape or not. No matter who you are, I promise that you can change your body into whatever you desire and you can do it without all the mental and physical agony that so many other people have to go through.

So, would you like my help?

If you answered, "Yes!" then you've taken a leap, not a step, toward your goals to become a leaner, healthier you.

Your journey to dietary freedom begins as soon as you turn to the next page.

ABOUT THE AUTHOR

—

"A gold medal is a wonderful thing. But if you're not enough without one, you'll never be enough with one."
IRV FROM THE MOVIE COOL RUNNINGS

I'm Mike, and I believe that every person can achieve the body of his or her dreams. I work hard to give everyone that chance by providing workable, proven advice grounded in science.

I've been training for more than a decade now and have tried just about every type of workout program, diet regimen, and supplement you can imagine.

While I don't know everything, I know what works and what doesn't.

Like most guys, I had no clue what I was doing when I started out. I turned to magazines for help, which had me spending a couple of hours in the gym every day and wasting hundreds of dollars on worthless supplements each month, only to make mediocre gains.

This went on for years, and I jumped from workout program to workout program. I tried all kinds of splits and routines, exercises, rep ranges, and other schemes, and while I made some progress during this time (it's impossible not to if you just keep at it), it was slow going and eventually put me in a rut.

My weight remained stuck for over a year, and I wasn't building any strength to speak of. I had no idea what to do with my nutrition beyond eating "clean" and making sure I was getting a lot of protein.

I turned to various trainers for guidance, but they had me do more of the same. I liked working out too much to quit, but I wasn't happy with my body, and I didn't know what I was doing wrong.

TIME TO GET SMART

I finally decided that it was time to get educated—to throw the magazines away, get off the forums, and learn the actual physiology of muscle growth and fat loss to figure out what it takes to build a muscular, lean, and strong body.

I sought out the work of top strength and bodybuilding coaches, talked to scores of natural bodybuilders, and read hundreds of scientific papers. A clear picture emerged.

The real science of getting into incredible shape is very simple—much simpler than the health and fitness and supplement industries want us to believe. It flies in the face of almost all the crap that we hear on TV, read in magazines, and see in the gym.

As a result of what I learned, I completely changed the way I trained and ate, and my body responded in ways I couldn't believe. My strength skyrocketed. My muscles were growing again for the first time in years. My energy levels went through the roof.

THE BIRTH OF MY CAREER

Along the way, my friends noticed the improvements in my physique and began asking for advice. I became their unofficial trainer.

I took "hardgainers" and put 30 pounds on them in a year. I took people who were absolutely baffled as to why they couldn't lose weight, stripped 30 pounds of fat off them, and helped them build noticeable muscle at the same time. I took people in their fifties who believed their hormones were too bottomed out to accomplish anything with exercise and helped them turn back the clock 20 years in terms of body fat percentage and muscle definition.

After doing this over and over for years, my friends started urging me to write a book. I dismissed the idea at first, but it began to grow on me.

"What if I had had such a book when I started training?" I thought.

I would've saved an untold amount of money, time, and frustration, and I would've achieved my ideal physique years ago. I enjoyed helping people with what I had learned. What if I could write books that would help thousands or even hundreds of thousands of people?

That got me excited.

I acted on the impulse, and the result was the first edition of my book *Bigger Leaner Stronger*, which was published in January 2012. Sales were slow at first, but within a month or two, I began receiving e-mails full of high praise from readers.

I was floored. I immediately started working on my next book and outlined several more.

Here's a picture of me after almost six years of lifting regularly. Not very impressive. Something had to change.

Here's how my body has changed since. Quite a difference.

I've now published several books, which have sold more than 500,000 copies. More importantly, though, every day I get scores of e-mails and social media messages from readers who are blown away by the results they're seeing. They're just as shocked as I was years ago when I learned just how simple building lean, healthy muscle and losing fat—without ever feeling starved or miserable—can be.

It's motivating to see the impact I'm having on people's lives, and I'm incredibly inspired by the dedication of my readers and followers. You guys and gals rock.

WHERE TO NOW?

My true love is researching and writing, so I'll always be working on another book, my website (www.muscleforlife.com), and whatever other literary adventures come my way.

My big, evil master plan has three major targets:

1. Help a million people get fit and healthy.

"Help a million people" just has a sexy ring to it, don't you think? It's a big goal, but I think I can do it. And it goes beyond just helping people look good—I want to make a dent in alarmingly negative trends we're seeing in people's overall physical and mental health.

2. Lead the fight against "broscience" and other BS.

Unfortunately, this industry is full of idiots, liars, and hucksters who prey on people's fears and insecurities. I want to do something about it. In fact, I'd like to become known as the go-to guy for practical, easy-to-understand advice grounded in real science and results.

3. Help reform the sport supplement industry.

The dishonest pill and powder pushers are the people I despise the most in this space. The scams are numerous: using fancy-sounding but worthless ingredients, cutting products with junk fillers like maltodextrin and even stuff like flour and sawdust (yes, this happens), using bogus science and ridiculous marketing claims to sell, under-dosing the important ingredients and covering it up with the label "proprietary blend," sponsoring steroid-fueled athletes so they pretend supplements are the secret to their gains, and more.

I wrote this book to help accomplish these goals, and I hope you enjoy it.

I'm positive that if you apply what you're about to learn, you too can dramatically transform your physique without ever having to feel like you're "on a diet" again.

So, are you ready? Great. Let's get to it.

WHAT MAKES
THE SHREDDED CHEF DIFFERENT?

"The only way to keep your health is to eat what you don't want,
drink what you don't like, and do what you'd rather not."
MARK TWAIN

As you've probably heard many times before, you *must* know how to eat to see good results from exercise.

You can lift all the weights you want, but your muscles can't grow unless they're fed the right types and amounts of nutrients needed for repair. Eat too little, and you will never grow noticeably bigger or stronger.

You can burn tons of calories on the treadmill every week and eat so "clean" that your diet could pass a white glove inspection, but if you don't know how to maintain a proper calorie deficit, you'll never get and stay lean. If you overeat by just a couple hundred calories every day, you can experience all the unpleasantness often associated with "being on a diet" (food restriction, hunger, and cravings) without really having much to show for it.

You've probably noticed that I'm more interested in the *quantitative* aspects of eating rather than the qualitative ones. I'm not talking about *types* of foods but *amounts*.

This is because, when it comes to body composition, *what* you eat isn't nearly as important as how much.

That said, this book is going to go far beyond "calorie counting," because in many ways calorie counting doesn't work.

You need to know a lot more than "eat this many calories" to make positive, sustainable, long-term changes in your body composition and health.

Once you get it right, though, everything falls into place and you gain complete control over your weight, musculature, body fat levels, and, to some degree at least, even energy levels and mood.

As you'll soon learn, a century of metabolic research has shown us exactly what it takes to lose fat and keep it off, and it has nothing to do with going low-carb or avoiding sugar or gluten or any other nutritional scapegoat.

The incredibly good news is that you can have the body you desire by eating a diverse diet of the foods you love. I promise you. And that's what *The Shredded Chef* is all about.

If you follow the advice in this book, you'll find it not only easy to "diet" for muscle growth or fat loss but also enjoyable. And you'll not only achieve short-term results but you'll also be able to comfortably maintain a lean, muscular physique for the long haul.

Once you start applying what you're going to learn in this book, it won't be long before people start taking notice. They'll tell you how "lucky" you are that you get to eat "whatever you want," including high-carb and even sugary indulgences. They'll be amazed when you don't fall off the wagon and prove that "healthy eating" isn't nearly as painful and boring as most people think.

So, as you can see, this is more than just a cookbook.

Sure, it's going to give you a large collection of balanced, nutritious meals that are easy to make and don't require gourmet cooking skills or exotic, expensive ingredients, but it's going to give you a lot more than that.

It's going to teach you how to build a diet in the Latin sense of the word—a "way of life"—and never again be tempted by people's collective obsession with the self-punishment masquerading as "dieting".

Table of Contents

Diet & Nutrition

THE GREAT "ONE TRUE DIET" HOAX

"You can have results or excuses. Not both."
ARNOLD SCHWARZENEGGER

If you give too much credence to mainstream diet trends, you're pretty much doomed.

Maybe you'll identify with the Paleo culture and become convinced that eating like a caveman is the way of the future. Or maybe you'll go for scapegoating the carbohydrate as the source of all your weight-loss woes and subject yourself to trial by ketogenic dieting. Or, heaven forbid, maybe you'll mire yourself in the swamps of outright quackery: "cleanses," "unclogging hormones," "biohacking," and the like.

You can fritter away months like this, jumping from one form of dietary dogma to another, with little to nothing to show for it in the gym and mirror. And, if you're like many people, you'll just suck it up and soldier on, continuing your quest to find the One True Diet that will give you the body you've always desired.

Here's the problem: there is no One True Diet. There is no "shortcut to shred." There are no "weight-loss foods" or "muscle-building hacks."

The "truth about dieting" is rather boring, actually. It doesn't have the sizzle to sell millions of books and millions in supplements. But it has this: it *works*. Efficiently. Unquestionably. Invariably.

What is this truth?

Well, it has several parts, or tiers, and can be envisioned as a pyramid of descending importance that looks like this:

Let's look at each of the layers in detail.

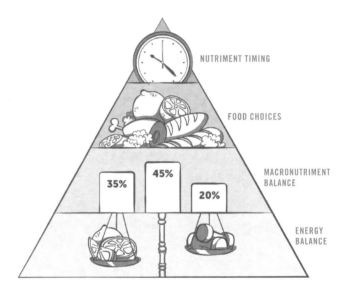

ENERGY BALANCE

Energy balance is at the bottom because it's the foundational principle of dieting. This is the one that dictates your weight gain and loss more than anything else.

What is energy balance, though?

Energy balance is the relationship between the energy you feed your body and the energy it expends. As you probably know, this is often measured in kilocalories.

The bottom-line, scientifically validated, unexciting reality—the one that makes book publishers and TV producers—is that meaningful weight loss requires you to expend more energy than you consume, and meaningful weight gain (both fat and muscle) requires the opposite: more consumption than expenditure.

If you're shaking your head, thinking I'm drinking decades-old Kool-Aid, answer me this:

Why has every single controlled weight loss study conducted in the last 100 years, including countless meta-analyses and systematic reviews, concluded that meaningful weight loss requires energy expenditure to exceed energy intake?

Why have bodybuilders dating back just as far, from Sandow to Reeves and all the way up the line, been using this knowledge to reduce and increase body fat levels systematically and routinely?

And why do new brands of "calorie denying" come and go every year, failing to gain acceptance in the weight loss literature?

The bottom line is that a century of metabolic research has proven, beyond the shadow of a doubt, that energy balance, operating according to the first law of thermodynamics, is the basic mechanism that regulates fat storage and reduction.[1]

MACRONUTRIENT BALANCE

Next on the diet pyramid is macronutrient balance.

In case you're not familiar with the term, the dictionary defines *macronutrient* as "any of the nutritional components of the diet that are required in relatively large amounts: protein, carbohydrate, fat, and minerals such as calcium, zinc, iron, magnesium, and phosphorous."

You've probably heard that "a calorie is a calorie," and while that's true for matters relating purely to energy balance and *weight* loss and gain, a calorie is *not* a calorie when we're talking *body composition*.

Don't believe me?

Well, Professor Mark Haub lost 27 pounds on a diet of protein shakes, Twinkies, Doritos, Oreos, and Little Debbie snacks, and you could do exactly the same if you wanted to (not that you should, though—more on this soon).[2]

We don't want just to gain and lose *weight*, though.

Our goal is more specific: we want to gain more muscle than fat, and we want to lose fat, not muscle. And with those goals, we have to watch more than just calories. We have to watch our macronutrient intake, too.

If you want to go beyond "weight loss" and learn to optimize your body composition, the macronutrient you have to watch most closely is *protein*.

HOW MUCH PROTEIN SHOULD YOU BE EATING?

Proteins are the primary building blocks of the body. They're used to build tissues like muscle, tendons, organs, and skin, as well as many other molecules vital to life, such as hormones, enzymes, and various brain chemicals.

Proteins are comprised of smaller molecules known as *amino acids,* which are linked together in a long chain that can be molded into different shapes.

Our bodies can produce twelve of the amino acids needed to form protein molecules, but we must get nine others from protein in the food we eat. The former are known as nonessential amino acids and the latter as essential amino acids.

How much protein you eat every day is the primary factor that determines whether your body is getting enough essential amino acids or not, but the quality of the protein you eat also matters.

Animal-based proteins like meat, fish, eggs, and dairy are particularly popular among athletes because they contain high but balanced amounts of essential amino acids, but certain plant-based proteins like rice and pea protein are high quality as well.

Generally speaking, your protein needs are going to be best met by animal sources, but with a bit of creative meal planning, vegetarians and vegans can get enough amino-acid-rich protein to build plenty of muscle and strength.

Now, your carbohydrate and dietary fat intakes can be all over the place without derailing you, but eating too little protein is the cardinal sin of dieting for us fitness folk.

The fact is that if you eat too little protein while restricting your calories for fat loss, you'll lose a significant amount of muscle as well.[3]

And on the flip side, if you eat too little protein while eating a surplus of calories to maximize muscle growth, you'll build less muscle.[4]

This is one of the reasons "bulking" has a bad rap. When done improperly, it packs on way more fat than muscle and is just counterproductive in the long run.

What is too little protein, you ask?

I could write an entire chapter on this alone, but here's what it boils down to for people that exercise regularly:

- If you're relatively lean and aren't dieting for fat loss, you should set your protein intake at 0.8 to 1 gram of protein per pound of body weight per day.
- If you're relatively lean and *are* dieting for fat loss, you should increase your intake slightly to 1 to 1.2 grams per pound of body weight per day. (Research shows the leaner you are, the more protein your body will need to preserve muscle while in a calorie deficit for fat loss.)[5]
- If you're obese (25% body fat and up in men and 35% and up in women), your protein intake should be set at 1 to 1.2 grams per pound of lean mass per day.

"But wait," you might be thinking, "aren't high-protein diets unhealthy?"

Well, the most common claim leveled against high-protein dieting is that it can cause damage to the kidneys and increase the risk of cancer and osteoporosis, but these claims simply aren't supported by sound scientific research.

Research shows that people with pre-existing kidney damage or dysfunction should restrict protein intake, but a high-protein diet has never been shown to cause kidney damage.[6]

Ironically, a high-protein diet has been shown both to lower blood pressure (especially in the case of plant-based protein) and to improve blood glucose control in diabetic patients.[7]

This would decrease their risk of kidney disease, not increase it.

Claims that a high-protein diet increases the risk of osteoporosis are even stranger, as studies show that it helps prevent the condition.[8]

And what about the rather disturbing claims that a high-protein diet increases the risk of cancer and that eating meat and cheese regularly is as unhealthy as smoking?

Well, while such sensationalism works wonders for website hits, it's misleading and scientifically bankrupt.

To quote Dr. Spencer Nadolsky from Examine. com:

"To even suggest that eating protein is as bad as smoking is pure sensationalism...

"A more accurate headline for this study would have been 'High protein for those between 50 years to 65 years old who have poor diet and lifestyle habits may be associated with increased cancer risk.'"

We're going to talk more about meat consumption and health later in the book, but the bottom line is this:

If you're physically active, a high-protein diet is, without question, going to help you improve your health, body composition, and performance.[9]

And while sedentary people don't need as much protein as those that exercise regularly, research shows that the current RDI (Recommended Daily Intake) of 0.8 grams per kg of body weight simply isn't enough to maintain lean mass and bone health, thereby avoiding muscle loss and osteoporosis, as they age.[10]

HOW MUCH CARBOHYDRATE
SHOULD YOU BE EATING?

Low-carbohydrate dieting has become all the weight loss rage these days, but, like most diet fads, it simply can't live up to its reputation.

There are about 20 studies that low-carb proponents bandy about as definitive proof of the superiority of low-carb dieting for weight loss.

If you read the abstracts of these studies, low-carb dieting definitely seems more effective, and this type of glib "research" is what most low-carbers base their beliefs on.

But there's a *big* problem with many of these studies, and it has to do with protein intake.

The problem is that the low-carb diets in these studies *invariably* contained more protein than the low-fat diets.

Yes, one for one ... without fail.

What we're actually looking at in these studies is a high-protein, low-carbohydrate diet vs. low-protein, high-fat diet, and the former wins every time.

But we can't ignore the high-protein part of the diet and then say it's more effective because of its low-carb element.

In fact, better designed and executed studies prove the opposite: when protein intake is high, low-carb dieting offers no special weight loss benefits.

Why is protein intake so important, exactly?

Because, as you know, if you don't eat enough protein when dieting to lose weight, you can lose quite a bit of muscle.[11]

This hampers your weight loss in several ways:

1. It slows down your metabolism.[12]
2. It reduces the amount of calories you burn in your workouts.[13]
3. It impairs the metabolism of glucose and lipids.[14]

This is why your number one goal when losing fat is *preserving lean mass.*

Now, let's turn our attention back to the "low-carb dieting is better for weight loss" studies mentioned earlier.

In many cases, the low-fat groups in these trials were given less protein than the recommended daily allowance, which any nutritionist or personal trainer will tell you is woefully inadequate for weight loss purposes.

In fact, research shows that even double and *triple* those levels of protein intake isn't enough to fully prevent muscle loss while restricting calories.[15]

So, what happens in terms of weight loss when you keep protein high and compare high and low levels of carbohydrates? Is there even any research available to show us?

Yup.

There are four studies I know of that meet these criteria, and gee whiz, look at that: when protein intake is high but carb intake varies, there is no significant difference in weight loss.[16]

The bottom line is that so long as you take in fewer calories than you burn and keep your protein intake high, you will maximize fat loss and minimize (if not completely avoid) muscle loss.

Going low-carb as well simply won't help you lose more fat.

HOW MUCH FAT
SHOULD YOU BE EATING?

Dietary fats play a vital role in the body because they're needed for a variety of physiological processes like cell maintenance, hormone production, insulin sensitivity, and more.

If dietary fat intake is too low, these functions can become compromised, which is why the Institute of Medicine recommends that adults should get 20 to 35% of their daily calories from dietary fat.[17]

That said, those percentages were calculated for the average sedentary person, who often eats less than someone that exercises regularly, especially if the person that exercises has a lot of muscle.

For example, a 190-pound sedentary male with a normal amount of lean mass would burn around 2,000 calories per day. Based on that, the IoM's research says he would need 45 to 80 grams of fat per day. That makes sense.

I'm 6'2 and 191 pounds, and I lift weights for about 4 to 6 hours per week. I have about 40 pounds more muscle than the average guy of my height and weight. Thus, my body burns a lot more calories than my "normal," sedentary counterpart–about 1,000 more calories per day to be exact.

Now, if I were to blindly apply the IoM's recommendation, my recommended fat intake would skyrocket to 65 to 115 grams per day. But does my body really need that much more dietary fat simply because I'm muscular and burn more energy through regular exercise?

No, it doesn't.

Based on the nutritional research I've reviewed, a dietary fat intake of about 0.3 grams per pound of fat-free mass (everything in your body that isn't fat) is all your body needs for its basic health needs.

This comes out to about 25 to 35% of your basal metabolic rate (which we'll talk more about soon), which is more in line with the IoM's research.

So, that's it for macronutrient balance. Let's move up another tier on the pyramid.

FOOD CHOICES

The cult of "clean eating" is more popular than ever these days.

While I'm all for eating nutritious ("clean") foods for the purpose of supplying our bodies with essential vitamins and minerals, eating nothing but these foods guarantees nothing in the way of building muscle or losing fat.

You can be the cleanest eater in the world and still be weak and "skinny-fat."

The reason for this comes back to the fact that, when we're talking body composition, how much you eat is more important than what.

Claiming that one food is "better" than another for losing or gaining weight is misleading because it misses the forest for the trees.

Foods don't have any special properties that make them better or worse for weight loss or gain.

What they do have, however, are varying amounts of potential energy—as measured in calories—and varying macronutrient profiles.

These two factors—the calories contained in foods and how those calories break down into protein, carbohydrate, and fat—are what make certain foods *more suitable* for losing or gaining weight than others.

As Professor Haub showed us earlier, and as the "If It Fits Your Macros" crowd simply won't shut up about, you can lose fat eating whatever you want so long as you regulate your caloric intake and maintain a state of negative energy balance.

Certain foods do make it easier or harder to lose and gain weight, though, due to their volume, calorie density, and macronutrient breakdown.

Generally speaking, foods that are "good" for weight loss are those that are relatively low in calories but high in volume (and thus satiating).[18]

Examples of such foods are lean meats, whole grains, many fruits and vegetables, and low-fat dairy. These types of foods also provide an abundance of micronutrients, which is especially important when your calories are restricted.

If you eat too much junk on a calorie-restricted diet, you can develop vitamin and mineral deficiencies.

Foods conducive to weight gain are the opposite: high in calories and low in volume and satiety.

These foods include the obvious like high-calorie beverages (soda, alcohol, fruit juice), candy, and other sugar-laden goodies. However, quite a few "healthy" foods fall into this category as well: oils, bacon, butter, low-fiber fruits, and whole-fat dairy products, for example. The more we fill our meal plans with calorie-dense, low-satiety foods, the more likely we are to get hungry and overeat.

Think of it this way: you can only "afford" so many calories every day, whether dieting to lose fat or gain muscle, and you have to watch how you "spend" them.

When dieting for fat loss, you want to spend the majority of your calories on foods that allow you to hit your daily macro- and micronutrient needs without "overdrafting" your energy balance "account." (I know, I'm getting carried away with this financial metaphor, but bear with me.)

When dieting for muscle growth, you have quite a few more calories to spend every day. This makes it easier to hit both your macronutrient and micronutrient targets with calories to spare, which you can then spend on, well, whatever you want.

Now, don't mistake this section as me railing against eating healthy foods. I'm *not* a fan of the people trying to prove that you can "eat junk and get shredded." Long-term health matters more than getting super lean while eating boxes of Pop Tarts every week.

Instead, here is my rule of thumb: take an 80-20 split.

If you get the majority (~80%) of your calories from relatively unprocessed, nutrient-dense foods, you can fill the remaining 20% with your favorite dietary sins and be healthy, muscular, and lean.

NUTRIENT TIMING

Last on the pyramid, and lowest in importance, is nutrient timing.

The CliffsNotes version here is that when and how often you eat doesn't really matter.

Increasing meal frequency doesn't speed up your metabolism.[19] Eating carbs at night doesn't make you fat.[20] The "post-workout anabolic window" is more fiction than fact.[21]

One of the many beauties of our bodies is they are incredibly good at adapting to meet the demands we place on them. So long as you get the other points of the pyramid right—proper energy balance, good macronutrient breakdown, and smart food choices—you have a lot of leeway here at the top.

You can eat three or thirteen meals per day. You can eat 80% of your carbohydrates at breakfast, dinner, or after your workout. You're not on the clock after a workout, slowly losing the fruits of your labor until you chug a shake.

THE BOTTOM LINE

If you've struggled to find a diet that actually works, that doesn't make you a slave to arbitrary rules and restrictions, that is enjoyable enough to be a lifestyle and not an ordeal, you now know the way.

Learn how to manipulate energy balance, keep protein intake high and adjust carbohydrate and fat to meet your needs and preferences, eat a wide variety of nutritious foods "supplemented" with some indulgences, and eat on a schedule you prefer, and you'll never look back.

CHAPTER SUMMARY

- A century of metabolic research has proven, beyond the shadow of a doubt, that energy balance, operating according to the first law of thermodynamics, is the basic mechanism that regulates fat storage and reduction.

- Eat too little protein while restricting your calories for fat loss and you'll lose a significant amount of muscle as well.

- Eat too little protein while eating a surplus of calories to maximize muscle growth and you'll build less muscle.

- If you're relatively lean and aren't dieting for fat loss, you should set your protein intake at 0.8 to 1 gram of protein per pound of body weight per day.

- If you're relatively lean and are dieting for fat loss, you should increase your intake slightly to 1 to 1.2 grams per pound of body weight per day.

- If you're overweight or obese, your first priority should be fat loss, and your protein intake should be set at 1 to 1.2 grams per pound of lean mass per day.

- So long as you maintain a proper calorie deficit and keep your protein intake high, you're going to maximize fat loss while preserving as much lean mass as possible. Going low-carb as well won't help you lose more fat.

- Foods don't have any special properties that make them better or worse for weight loss or gain.

- Generally speaking, foods that are "good" for weight loss are those that are relatively low in calories but high in volume (and thus satiating).

- Foods conducive to weight gain are the opposite: high in calories and low in volume and satiety. These foods include the obvious like caloric beverages, candy, and other sugar-laden goodies, but quite a few "healthy" foods fall into this category as well: oils, bacon, butter, low-fiber fruits, and whole-fat dairy products, for example.

- You can eat three or thirteen meals per day. You can eat 80% of your carbohydrates at breakfast, dinner, or after your workout. You're not on the clock after a workout, slowly losing gains until you chug a shake.

- There is evidence that eating protein in particular after a workout is better for long-term muscle growth.

HOW TO GET THE BODY YOU WANT WITH FLEXIBLE DIETING

"Little triumphs are the pennies of self-esteem."
FLORENCE KING

If you dread the idea of dieting, I understand. Most diets feel more like punishment than self-improvement.

Instead of educating you on how the metabolism truly works and giving you the tools you need to manage it effectively, most diet "gurus" resort to fear mongering and food restriction instead.

If you want to lose fat or build "lean muscle," they say, you can kiss just about everything you like eating goodbye.

Grains, anything containing gluten or sugar, high-glycemic carbs, red meat, processed foods, fruit, dairy, caloric beverages, granola, it's all gotta go.

All your toys. Throw them all into the fire.

Well, what if I told you that you could dramatically transform your body while eating foods you actually like, every day, seven days per week?

What if all you had to do to build muscle and lose fat was follow a handful of flexible dietary guidelines, not starve and deprive yourself?

And what if I promised you could forever break free of the restrictions and anxieties most people associate with dieting and learn to love it instead?

Too good to be true, you think? Downrightheresy?

I know. I used to think the same thing. I now know the truth, though, and in this chapter, I'm going to break it all down for you.

WHY FLEXIBLE DIETING ISN'T A "DIET"

What kind of "diet" worth a damn involves being *less* strict about the foods you eat? How can you possibly lose fat eating bucketfuls of carbs every day? Which self-respecting "dieter" would dare eat sugary treats with a clean conscience?

Such questions represent some of the common criticisms of flexible dieting. They also show why it's often considered the "anti-diet."

Much of the controversy stems from the fact that flexible dieting means different things to different people. And, like a superpower, it can be used for good or evil.

So, for the sake of thoroughness, let's start with something of an outline for flexible dieting. Here's how it shakes out:

1. How much you eat is more important than what you eat.
2. You should tailor your daily food choices to your preferences, goals, and lifestyle.
3. Forgive dietary lapses. "Keep calm and carry on."
4. Long-term compliance is the key to sustainable improvements.

Basically, flexible dieting is a way to take your body's basic energy and nutritional needs and turn them into an eating regimen that you actually enjoy.

Thou shalt not deprive yourself of foods you like.

Thou shalt eat on a schedule you like.

Thou shalt view dieting as a lifestyle, not a "quick fix."

Thou shalt accept dietary blunders and calmly get back in the saddle.

These are the commandments of flexible dieting. And they're getting more and more popular because they *work*.

Now, that all sounds good in theory, but you're probably wondering how the hell it plays out in practical terms. Let's find out.

HOW FLEXIBLE DIETING WORKS

Let's take a look at each of the points above to gain a better understanding of how to make flexible dieting work.

HOW MUCH YOU EAT IS MORE IMPORTANT THAN WHAT YOU EAT

As you know, "clean eaters" have their hearts in the right place, but their dieting philosophy isn't geared toward fat loss or muscle gain.

Sure, eating plenty of nutritious foods is important for overall health and longevity, but as you know, there are no foods that directly cause weight loss or weight gain.[1]

Sugar isn't your enemy and "healthy fats" aren't your savior.

The key to understanding these "shocking" statements is understanding the concept of "energy balance," which you learned about in the previous chapter.

A "negative energy balance" or "calorie deficit" results in weight loss, and a "positive energy balance" or "calorie surplus" results in weight gain.

Thus, in this sense, a calorie is a calorie.

Eat too much of the "cleanest" foods in the world—I'm looking at you, avocado toast—and you *will* gain weight.

Maintain a calorie deficit while following a "gas station diet" of the most nutritionally bankrupt crap you can find and you *will* lose weight.

TAILOR YOUR DAILY FOOD CHOICES TO YOUR PREFERENCES, GOALS, AND LIFESTYLE

You should eat foods you like. Every meal. Every day. For the rest of your life.

Yes, you read that right.

And no, I'm not talking about only getting to choose from foods generally recognized as "healthy," like fruits, vegetables, nuts, and seeds.

If you want to maximize your health, longevity, and overall well-being, you want to get the majority of your calories from these types of foods. That's true.

But once you're doing that, you "earn" the right to also eat foods often demonized as "unhealthy," like pizza, pasta, ice cream, cereal, bagels, and French fries.

My "daily indulgences" range from ice cream to chocolate to muffins to pancakes with syrup to cookies. It just depends on what I'm in the mood for and how many calories I can "afford."

This all applies regardless of your body goals as well.

You can be as lean, muscular, and as healthy as you want with flexible dieting, eating just as I outline above.

And this isn't theory—I'm speaking from experience. I maintain my physique by practicing what I preach:

◆ Flexible dieting exactly as laid out in this chapter.

◆ 4 to 6 hours of weightlifting per week.

◆ 1 hour of high intensity interval training per week.

◆ Smart use of supplements.

That's it.

Every day I eat several servings of fruits, vegetables, and high-quality proteins as well as foods that are "supposed" to make me fat and unhealthy, like grains, dairy, and sugar.

The key is balance. Eat more nutritious than non-nutritious foods and exercise regularly (with an emphasis on resistance training) and you've got it made.

FORGIVE DIETARY LAPSES "KEEP CALM AND CARRY ON"

Highly restrictive, very low-calorie diets lead to cravings. Cravings lead to "cheating." Cheating leads to bingeing. And bingeing leads to quitting.

Sound familiar? It should. It's the slippery slope of mainstream dieting, and millions of people tumble down it every year.

Flexible dieting is the most effective tool I know for breaking this cycle.

When you eat foods you like, balance your macronutrient intake properly, and only moderately restrict your calories, dietary "magic" happens. The psychological burden almost completely disappears, and you no longer have to battle the stomach demons that clamor for more food.

Losing weight becomes easy. Enjoyable, even.

That said, it doesn't mean you're never going to slip up. You might be hungrier than usual one day and roll with it. For instance, it's really easy to overeat at social events or when you've had a stressful week at work.

So you had a couple scoops of ice cream, effectively halving your calorie deficit for the day. Big deal.

So you took it further and overate for a few days, putting yourself in a slight calorie surplus, and gained a little fat as a result.

You've set yourself back what? A few days? A week, even?

Who cares? Keep calm and carry on.

Even a moderate weekend binge doesn't necessarily cause as much fat gain as you might think.

Again, you're looking at no more than a week or two of "damage" to undo.

And that's okay. There's no need for self-loathing or guilt bingeing.

Instead, I suggest that we should just plan for minor setbacks. Every so often you're going to eat more than you intended. You don't have to fear it.

LONG-TERM COMPLIANCE IS THE KEY TO SUSTAINABLE IMPROVEMENTS

"The best diet is the one you can stick to."

There's a lot of truth in that old saw. It captures the essence of successful dieting: sticking to the plan well enough and long enough to achieve and maintain the results you want.

Notice my emphasis on *sustainable* results that you can *maintain*.

That's the real goal. Not rapidly losing weight with a crash diet and then, when you can suffer it no longer, ballooning back to your previous self... or worse.

Flexible dieting makes reaching your body composition goals straightforward and pain-free. It's also, well, *flexible* enough to accommodate just about any lifestyle and become a long-term habit, not a "quick fix."

GETTING STARTED WITH FLEXIBLE DIETING

Okay, now that I've (hopefully) sold you on giving flexible dieting a try, let's put some rubber on the road.

First, a couple ground rules:

GET THE MAJORITY (80%+) OF YOUR DAILY CALORIES FROM RELATIVELY UNPROCESSED, NUTRITIOUS FOODS

I know I'm repeating myself here, but I'm doing it for your own good.

Just because you *can* eat a bunch of junk food and "fit your macros" doesn't mean you *should*. Remember that your body needs adequate fiber and a wide spectrum of vitamins and minerals to function optimally. I'm sorry to say that ice cream, Fruity Pebbles, and brownies won't get you there.

Here's a handy list of tasty, nutrient-dense foods that I eat regularly:

Dark, leafy greens (kale and spinach, mainly), bell pepper, Brussels sprout, mushroom, onion, tomato, white potato, sweet potato, berries, whole wheat, cheese and yogurt, egg, beans (black and pinto), pecan, almond, oats, rice (white and brown), lean beef, chicken, and turkey.

If I wanted even more variety, that list could go on and on. And your list may look totally different. But you get the idea.

EAT ON A SCHEDULE THAT FITS YOUR PREFERENCES AND LIFESTYLE

We recall that when you eat your food doesn't matter.

So long as you're managing your energy and macronutrient balances properly, meal timing and frequency aren't going to help or hinder your results.

That said, if you're serious about weightlifting and gaining lean muscle mass, you should know that eating protein and carbohydrate before and after resistance training can help you build muscle faster. [2]

So, if you're lifting weights regularly, I do recommend you consume 30 to 40 grams of protein both before and after your workouts.

Regarding carbohydrate intake, 30 to 50 grams of carbs before a workout can be great for boosting performance, and 1 gram per kilogram of body weight is sufficient for post-workout needs.

HOW TO CREATE YOUR FLEXIBLE DIETING PLAN

By now I'm sure you're beginning to see the real beauty of flexible dieting. This is going to be the easiest diet plan you've ever made.

Let's break this down into two goals: fat loss and muscle growth.

FLEXIBLE DIETING FOR LOSING FAT

As you know, the key to losing fat is maintaining a calorie deficit over time. So the first step is working out how many calories you should be eating.

Your body requires a certain amount of energy to stay alive. Every cell in your body needs a steady supply of fuel to do its job, and it must ultimately obtain this fuel from the food we eat.

The 24-hour measurement of how much energy your body uses to perform all basic functions related to staying alive (excluding any and all physical activity) is known as your *basal metabolic rate*, or *BMR*.

Basal means "forming a base, fundamental." *Metabolic* means related to the *metabolism*, which is "the physical and chemical processes in an organism by which it produces, maintains, and destroys material substances, and by which it makes energy available."

Basal metabolic rate can increase or decrease based on long-term dietary and exercise patterns (this is known as "metabolic adaptation" and is a fascinating subject unto itself) but a formula like the Katch McArdle will predict most people's BMR with a high degree of accuracy.

Here's how it works:

$$BMR = 370 + (21.6 \times LBM)$$

LBM refers to *lean body mass*, which refers to the nonfat components of the human body (and it's in kilograms for this calculation).

You calculate LBM by subtracting your body fat weight from your total body weight, giving you the weight of everything but your body fat.

Here's how it looks:

$$LBM = (1 - BF\%^*) \times total\ body\ weight$$
$$^*expressed\ as\ decimal\ numeral$$

For instance, I'm 191 pounds at about 8 percent body fat, so my LBM is calculated like this:

$$1 - 0.08 = 0.92$$
$$0.92 \times 191 = 176\ lbs.\ (LBM)$$

There are 2.2 pounds in a kilogram, so here is the formula to calculate my BMR:

$$176 / 2.2 = 80\ kg$$
$$370 + (21.6 \times 80) = 2,098\ calories\ per\ day$$

This BMR calculation doesn't give you a definitive answer to how much energy your body burns while at rest, but it's fairly accurate for most people.

Now, when you want to know the approximate amount of additional energy you burn through physical activity, you want to know your "total daily energy expenditure," or "TDEE."

This is the grand total of energy that your body burns in a 24-hour period, and it too changes from day to day (some days you move more and some days less).

Once you know your BMR, you can calculate your TDEE by multiplying it as follows:

◆ By 1.2 if you exercise 1 to 3 hours per week.
◆ By 1.35 if you exercise 4 to 6 hours per week.
◆ By 1.5 if you exercise vigorously for 6 or more hours per week.

The resulting number will be a fairly accurate measurement of the average total energy your body burns every day.

If you ate that amount of calories every day, your weight would remain more or less the same. Thus, to reduce your weight, you have to eat less... but how much less?

Calculate your calorie deficit.
When you want to lose fat, I recommend a moderate calorie deficit of 20 to 25%. Anything larger can cause unwanted side effects associated with "starvation dieting."

This means that you want to set your daily calorie intake at 75 to 80% of your calculated total daily energy expenditure (TDEE).

For example, my average daily TDEE is about 3,000 calories, so when I want to lose weight, I set my intake at about 2,300 calories.

Determine your macronutrient targets
Now that you have your calorie target worked out, it's time to turn it into protein, carbohydrate, and fat targets.

Here's how to do it:

◆ If you're in a normal body fat range (up to 20% in men and 30% in women), eat 1.2 grams of protein per pound of body weight.
◆ If you're obese (a man over 25% body fat or a woman over 35%), eat 1 gram of protein per pound of lean body mass.
◆ Eat 0.2 grams of fat per pound of body weight.
◆ Get the rest of your calories from carbohydrate.

Here's how it plays out for me:

Body Weight: 191 pounds

Calorie Intake: 2,300

230 grams of protein = 920 calories
(1 gram of protein is approximately 4 calories)
40 grams of fat = 360 calories
(1 gram of fat is approximately 9 calories)
255 grams of carbohydrate = 1020 calories
(1 gram of carbohydrate is also approximately 4 calories)

So, now that you have your numbers, it's time to turn them into a meal plan that you will enjoy.

First, make a list of foods you'd like to eat every day and head over to a resource like www.calorieking.com to learn their macronutrient profiles.

Many people like to use Excel for this, listing the foods and their protein, carbohydrate, fat, and calorie numbers in side-by-side columns.

Then, start piecing together meals using those foods until you're happy with the setup and your total daily intake is within 50 calories of your target.

Once you've made your plan, you now stick to it every day. If, along the way, you get tired of a certain food or meal, simply replace it with something else you'd like to eat that fits your numbers.

It's that simple!

FLEXIBLE DIETING FOR BUILDING MUSCLE

When you want to lose fat, you eat less than your TDEE. When you want to maximize muscle growth, you eat a bit more.

When you want to maximize muscle growth, you should eat about 10% more than your average TDEE. This slight calorie surplus allows your body to grow as efficiently as possible.

The macronutrient breakdown for "bulking" is different as well:

◆ Eat 1 gram of protein per pound of body weight.
◆ Eat 0.3 grams of fat per pound of body weight.
◆ Get the rest of your calories from carbohydrate.

So for me (and numbers are rounded for simplicity's sake):

190 grams of protein = 760 calories
60 grams of fat = 540 calories
500 grams of carbohydrate = 2,000 calories

WHY COUNTING CALORIES DOESN'T (SEEM TO) WORK FOR EVERYONE

I've helped thousands of people build muscle and lose fat, and here are the most common reasons why people struggle with counting calories or think it doesn't work.

They hate the idea of having to plan and track what they eat

Some people see meal planning or tracking intake with something like My Fitness Pal as a psychological burden.

Others have a lifestyle that involves a lot of unplanned meals prepared by others, which are basically impossible to measure in terms of calories.

Well, in my experience, when these people see how effortless weight loss is with calorie counting and flexible dieting, most never look back.

The changes may feel burdensome at first, but the payoff is immense: no hunger; no cravings; and no crossing your fingers, hoping that this is the diet that finally works.

They hate the idea of having to restrict their eating in any way

Some people have a strange relationship with food.

They want to eat what they want when they want, and they don't want to feel like a "slave" to the oppressive calorie count.

In my experience, these people find it harder to change. They will try *anything*—fad diets, cleanses, weight loss pills, etc.—before finally submitting to the master of energy balance and often choose to stay fat and wait for the next "metabolic miracle" over counting a calorie.

They overeat regularly

This is, of course, all too common.

A few extra bites at breakfast...a double portion of dressing at lunch...a little unplanned dessert at dinner.

All these "little" portions of extra calories add up and can easily negate the moderate calorie deficit you're trying to maintain on a daily basis.

The solution is simple: every single thing that goes into your mouth every day should be planned or tracked.

They don't measure and weigh food correctly

This is the accidental version of the above mistake. Instead of knowingly overeating, many people unknowingly do so through imprecise food measuring.

For example, according to the nutrition facts panel of my oatmeal, a dry cup contains 300 calories. I want to eat some, so I get my measuring cup out, fill it to the brim (a "slightly heaping" cup, if you will), and log 300 calories. But I'm wrong—it's actually just over 360 calories of oatmeal.

What tripped me up here is simple human error. "One cup" can be over- or under-shot.

What I should have done instead was weigh the oatmeal in grams. Eighty grams of dry oatmeal is eighty grams, no more and no less, and therefore is about 300 calories.

Anyway, I fail to do this and overeat by about 50 calories in that meal, and life goes on.

A few hours later, I want some peanut butter, so I decide to eat two tablespoons, which is 188 calories according to the label. Out comes the tablespoon, and I fill it with creamy nut butter, slightly above the rim, which I savor oh so sweetly.

The problem is 188 calories of peanut butter weighs 32 grams but my slightly overzealous scooping gave me 40 grams, which contains 235 calories.

I then repeat this same mistake a few more times—with my ketchup at dinner, my cream in my coffee, and my chocolate squares for dessert—and I've successfully erased my calorie deficit for the day without even realizing it.

They cheat like a competitive eater

I recommend having a moderate cheat meal every week when you're dieting.

It's a nice psychological boost and, depending on where you are in terms of body fat percentage, it can help keep the weight loss going.

Notice that I said one *moderate* cheat MEAL, though. Not a cheat DAY or an all-out binge meal, because either can undo some or all of a week's worth of fat loss. (Note that super-fatty meals with alcohol are the absolute worst.)

So, when you're cheating, you can end the day a few hundred calories above your normal daily intake, but don't go crazy.

If you need to, you can even reduce your carbohydrate and fat intake throughout the day to "save up" calories for the larger meal and thus keep your overall intake for the day in a reasonable range.

They calculate their total daily energy expenditure (TDEE) incorrectly

Unfortunately, this is really easy to do because the activity multipliers of scientific formulas commonly used to calculate TDEE are just too high. This is something most bodybuilders know but most "laymen" don't.

That's why the activity multipliers I've given in this book are slightly lower than what you typically find in calorie calculators.

Their metabolisms need to be "fixed"

When many people want to lose weight, they dramatically reduce calorie intake and dramatically increase energy output through many hours of exercise each week.

This approach will work for a time, but it will ultimately fail.

Why?

Because your body adapts to the amount of energy you feed it. Its general goal is to balance energy intake with output (to erase your calorie deficit).

You see, when you place your body in a calorie deficit, your metabolism naturally begins slowing down (burning less energy).[3] The more you restrict your calories, the faster and greater the down-regulation.[4]

Another adaptation that occurs is a reduction in the amount of spontaneous activity like walking around while on the phone, hopping to the bathroom, drumming your fingers when you read, or bobbing your legs when you think.[5]

The energy burned by these activities is known as non-exercise activity thermogenesis, or NEAT, and it plays a much larger role in total daily energy expenditure than most people realize.

Research shows that NEAT can vary by up to 2,000 calories per day among individuals.[6] The same research indicates that people could burn an additional 350 calories per day by taking simple actions to increase movement every day, like taking the stairs when possible, walking relatively short distances instead of driving, doing some chores instead of watching TV, etc.

Yet another factor is how much energy you burn while exercising.

It stands to reason that when you reduce your body weight, you also reduce the amount of energy expended during exercise (it costs more energy to move a heavier body). Research shows that this is the case.[7]

There's more to this than meets the eye, however, because studies have shown that when restricting calories for weight loss, energy expenditure is less than normal even when body weight is artificially increased with a weight vest.[8]

So, as you can see, the body has several ways to reduce energy expenditure and match intake with output. And when this happens, weight loss can stall despite a very low-calorie diet and large amount of exercise.

Most people in this rut don't understand what is happening physiologically and fight fire with fire: further calorie reduction or more exercise, which only results in more metabolic slowdown.

This can become a vicious cycle.

This process of dramatically and chronically slowing one's metabolic rate is often referred to as metabolic "adaptation" or even "damage," and fortunately, it can be resolved through a simple process known as "reverse dieting."

You can learn more about reverse dieting here: http://www.muscleforlife.com/reverse-diet/

They are impatient

Whenever someone writes me complaining about not losing weight, I always ask for the specifics.

Are they not losing *any* weight? For how long has this been going on? Are they looking leaner? Is their waist shrinking (which is a reliable sign of fat loss)?

The answers I receive are almost always along these lines:

"Well, I've lost about 1 pound per week, but shouldn't I be losing more?" or "I haven't lost weight in the last 4 days," or "I can't see my abs yet," and so on.

The point is that these people are usually making good progress with their weight loss goals but they have unrealistic, unachievable standards.

Standards that are often fueled by ridiculous, misleading 2- and 3-month transformations featured on big fitness websites or major network reality shows.

If you're losing about 1 pound per 7 to 10 days, you're doing great. Keep it up.

If your weight is more or less the same after 7 to 10 days, however, you simply need to move more or eat less.

They focus too much on the scale

While the scale moving down is clearly a good indicator, it's not the final word.

Especially not if you're weightlifting for the first time, because this alone will increase your body weight through muscle growth—yes, it's possible to build muscle and lose fat simultaneously—and additional glycogen (a form of carbohydrate that your body uses for energy) and water storage in the muscles you're training.

If people don't know this, however, they can be baffled as to why their pants are fitting looser and they're looking leaner yet their weight has remained exactly the same.

All that's happening is the additional muscle-related weight is "replacing" the weight of the fat lost.

Remember that *body composition* is the real key here, not just weight. We want to see your muscle mass going up and body fat percentage going down, which is more accurately assessed by the mirror and a waist measurement than a scale.

If, however, the scale, mirror, and waist measurements are all staying the same for 7 to 10 days, then it's time to change something.

These are the most common reasons people fail or feel like they're failing with counting calories. Avoid these pitfalls and follow the tips in this chapter and you'll have tremendous success with it and even find it *enjoyable*.

THE BOTTOM LINE

If you're skeptical about the workability of flexible dieting, I understand. I was pretty sure it was a complete waste of time when I first found it, but I quickly discovered otherwise.

You can eat the foods you like and have the body you want.

That's the big promise of flexible dieting and, as you'll soon see for yourself, it keeps its word.

Happy "dieting"!

CHAPTER SUMMARY

- If you get 80% of your daily calories from relatively unprocessed, nutrient-dense foods, you can fill the remaining 20% with foods most diet "gurus" frown upon.

- Every so often you're going to eat more than you intended. You don't have to fear it.

- If you want to lose weight, I recommend a moderate calorie deficit of 20 to 25%. Anything larger can cause unwanted side effects associated with "starvation dieting."

- When you want to maximize muscle growth, you should eat about 10% more than your average total daily energy expenditure.

- A lot of "little" portions of extra calories add up and can easily negate the moderate calorie deficit you're trying to maintain on a daily basis.

- When you're "cheating," you can end the day a few hundred calories above your normal daily intake, but don't go crazy.

- The body has several ways to reduce energy expenditure and match intake with output. And when this happens, weight loss can stall despite a very low-calorie diet and large amount of exercise.

- If you're losing about 1 pound per 7 to 10 days, you're doing great. Keep it up. If your weight is more or less the same after 7 to 10 days, however, you simply need to move more or eat less.

- We want to see your muscle mass going up and body fat percentage going down, which is more accurately assessed by the mirror and a waist measurement than a scale.

- If the scale, mirror, and waist measurements are all staying the same for 7 to 10 days, then it's time to change something.

HOW TO EAT RIGHT WITHOUT OBSESSING OVER EVERY CALORIE

"Sometimes magic is just someone spending more time on something than anyone else might reasonably expect."
CHRIS JONES

While calorie counting is the easiest way to lose weight reliably while eating foods you love, if you're not looking to lose weight, you can look and feel great without breaking out a calculator every time you eat.

This is because *maintaining* a certain body composition allows for a relatively laidback approach to dieting, which is guided by smart food choices and your natural appetite.

In this chapter, I'm going to share with you some simple dietary guidelines that will help you establish healthy dietary habits conducive to staying lean without planning or tracking everything you eat.

EAT A HIGH-PROTEIN DIET

Every few months some new fancy, faddish diet pops up on TV shows, in magazines, and on book bestseller lists that claims to be everything your hungry little heart can desire.

You know the pitch: easy weight loss, sky-high energy levels, perfect health, superhuman longevity, and on and on. Depending on whom you listen to, it all can get quite confusing.

Some regimens get more right than wrong and will be around for a while (Paleo and Mediterranean dieting, for example), while others just can't live up to the hype (the current low-carb craze), and others still are more harmful than helpful and, hopefully, will fade away into obscurity (the HCG diet and other forms of starvation dieting come to mind).

Well, the biggest common denominator among the better diets of the lot is that they entail eating plenty of protein.

Let's quickly discuss the major benefits of high-protein dieting.

YOU BUILD MORE MUSCLE AND GET STRONGER ON A HIGH-PROTEIN DIET

Muscle tissue is primarily composed of protein, so it shouldn't be a surprise that a high-protein diet helps you build it faster. And with more muscle comes more strength.

You see, when you train your muscles, you're simultaneously damaging and breaking down muscle tissue and beginning a process known as "protein synthesis" whereby the body creates (synthesizes) new muscle proteins to replace and add to the damaged tissues.

This is why exercise, and resistance training in particular, increases the protein needs of the body[1] and why a high-protein diet helps you build more muscle and strength.[1]

YOU LOSE MORE FAT AND LESS MUSCLE ON A HIGH-PROTEIN DIET

When you want to get leaner, the goal isn't just "weight loss"—it's *fat loss*.

That is, the goal is to lose fat and not muscle, and research clearly shows that a high-protein diet is better for both losing fat faster[2] and preserving muscle.[2] You simply lose more fat and less muscle on a high-protein diet than a low-protein one.

Furthermore, research shows that a high-protein diet is easier to stick to when in a calorie deficit because it results in less mood disturbance, stress, fatigue, and diet dissatisfaction than lower-protein diets, and improved dietary compliance means better fat loss results in the end.[3]

YOU FEEL FULLER ON A HIGH-PROTEIN DIET

One of the biggest dietary obstacles people run into is plain old hunger, especially when restricting calories for fat loss.

It can be incredibly hard to regulate food intake when your stomach feels like a grumbling pit all day, and a high-protein diet can help.

Specifically, research shows that increasing protein intake decreases appetite through several mechanisms, including favorably altering hormones related to hunger and fullness.[4]

This satiating effect not only applies to a high-protein diet in general but to individual meals as well: research shows that high-protein meals are more satiating than high-fat meals, which means you feel fuller longer, making you less likely to overeat.[5]

YOU PRESERVE MORE MUSCLE AS YOU AGE ON A HIGH-PROTEIN DIET

The degenerative loss of muscle associated with aging (known as *sarcopenia*) is debilitative and, ultimately, life threatening. Research shows that the more muscle you lose as you age, the more likely you are to die of various causes related to injury and disease.[6]

Elderly people can't use protein as efficiently as younger folk and thus need significantly more protein. This is why a high-protein diet is an effective way to help mitigate or even prevent the effects of sarcopenia, especially when combined with resistance training (yes, even the elderly can build muscle!).[7]

As an added bonus, a high-protein diet also reduces the risk of osteoporosis, another serious health risk associated with aging.[8]

WHAT CONSTITUTES A HIGH-PROTEIN DIET, EXACTLY?

As you know, the question of how much protein to eat is fairly complex, but when you review the large amount of literature available, a general consensus emerges:

- If you're relatively lean and not in a calorie deficit, 0.8 to 1 gram of protein per pound of body weight is enough to reap the many benefits of a high-protein diet.
- This also jives with the "gym lore" that bodybuilders have sworn by for decades: 1 gram of protein per pound of body weight.
- If you're relatively lean and in a calorie deficit, 1 to 1.2 grams of protein per pound of body weight is probably best.

Research shows that restricting calories increases the protein needs of resistance-trained athletes, especially as leanness increases (the leaner you are, the more protein your body will need to preserve muscle while in a calorie deficit).[9]

- If you're obese (over 25% body fat in men and over 35% in women), 1 gram of protein per pound of lean mass is adequate.

EAT PLENTY OF LOW-CALORIE, FIBROUS FOODS

Fiber is an indigestible type of carbohydrate found in many types of foods, including fruits, vegetables, legumes, and grains. It comes in two forms: soluble and insoluble fiber.

Soluble fiber dissolves in water and tends to slow the movement of food through the digestive system.

Research has shown that soluble fiber is metabolized by bacteria in the colon and hence has little effect on stool weight.[10] However, it can increase fecal output by stimulating the growth of healthy bacteria and fatty acids, and it is actually an important source of fuel for the colon.[11]

Some common sources of soluble fiber are beans, peas, oats, fruits like plums, bananas, and apples, vegetables like broccoli, sweet potatoes, and carrots, and nuts, with almonds being the highest in dietary fiber.

Insoluble fiber does not dissolve in water and contributes to stool weight.[12] It bangs against the walls of the intestines, causing damage, but research has shown that this damage and the resulting repair and cellular regeneration is a healthy process.[13]

Some common sources of insoluble fiber are whole-grain foods like brown rice, barley, and wheat bran, beans, vegetables like peas, green beans, and cauliflower, avocado, and the skins of some fruits like plums, grapes, kiwis, and tomatoes.

Fibrous foods with a high water content, like most vegetables and some fruits, are great for maintaining health and preventing weight gain.

They're extremely filling despite being low in calories, which helps regulate overall daily calorie intake, and are packed with vital micronutrients.

My favorite fibrous fruits and veggies include apples, bananas, Brussels sprouts, spinach, and oranges. The USDA recommends that adults eat 2 to 3 cups of both fruits and vegetables per day, and I've found this works extremely well for preserving both health and body composition.

LIMIT YOUR INTAKE OF LOW-QUALITY FATS

Fats help your body absorb the other nutrients that you give it; they nourish the nervous system, help maintain cell integrity, regulate hormone levels; and much more.

Not all fats are the same, though. Some types improve your health while others harm it.

Healthy fats are found in non-fried plant oils like olive oil, coconut oil, and peanut oil; nuts, seeds, and butters made from them; dairy products; and high-quality meat and seafood, like wild-caught fish and lean cuts of free-range animals fed natural diets.

There is abundant evidence in the literature of the health benefits conferred by these foods.

For example, research shows that regular nut consumption increases longevity, olive oil reduces systemic inflammation, certain fish abundant in omega-3 fatty acids protect your brain against the effects of aging, and that people that eat the most dairy are less likely to develop heart disease and diabetes than those that eat less.[14]

Unhealthy fats are found in fried foods like potato chips, donuts, and fried chicken; processed meats like low-quality sausage, cold cuts, beef jerky, cured meats, and hot dogs; and packaged foods like pastries, breakfast cereal, microwave popcorn, frozen pizza, and low-quality yogurt and peanut butter.

Again, the evidence is clear that these types of foods are inherently bad for the body.

Regular consumption of fried foods is associated with obesity and various types of chronic disease like hypertension, heart disease, and cancer. Processed meats contain various carcinogenic chemicals, and many packaged foods contain a processed form of fat called *trans fat*, which has been shown to increase the risk of heart disease, diabetes, infertility, and more.[15]

Trans fat is a scientifically modified form of saturated fat used to extend the shelf life of food and improve palatability. Meat and dairy products also contain miniscule amounts of trans fats, but these molecules are different than what we find in TV dinners.

The most common forms of trans fats added to foods are hydrogenated and partially hydrogenated oils (oils that have hydrogen atoms added to them). Any food that contains "hydrogenated oil" or "partially hydrogenated oil" contains trans fats.

The big problem with trans fats is how little it takes to affect our health adversely. One study conducted with over 120,000 female nurses found that replacing just 2% of daily calories with trans fats *doubled* the risk of heart disease.[16]

This is why the Institute of Medicine recommends that your trans fat intake be "as low as possible" and why the American Heart Association recommends you eat less than 2 grams of trans fat per day. Personally, I completely avoid foods with added trans fats, and I recommend that you do the same. (Sure, you can eat some now and then and be fine, but I wouldn't make it a regular part of my diet.)

Avoiding trans fats isn't as simple as finding foods with labels claiming them to be trans fat free, though. To meet the FDA's definition of "zero grams trans fat per serving," food doesn't have to contain no trans fats—it must simply contain less than one gram of trans fats per tablespoon, no more than 7% trans fats by weight, or less than 0.5 grams per serving. So if a bag of cookies contains 0.49 grams of trans fat per serving, the manufacturer can claim it's trans fat free on the packaging.

These "fake zero" products are a problem when we're supposed to eat less than 2 grams of trans fat per day, so keep that in mind when choosing which foods to eat daily.

You should also limit your intake of unhealthy fats because of the biopsychology of consuming such foods. Foods with high levels of unhealthy fats are often very tasty and calorie-dense as well, which can promote overeating.[17]

Notice that I'm advising you to *limit* your intake of unhealthy fats. I'm not forbidding them. And that's because if you have a generally healthy diet and exercise regularly, you can occasionally eat unhealthy foods without harming your health.

That is, you can use diet and exercise to get your body into such a good state of health that sporadic "lapses" have no long-term consequences.

GET THE MAJORITY OF YOUR DIETARY FAT FROM FISH, NUTS, AND OILS

These foods are high in unsaturated fat, which is a form of fat that's liquid at room temperature.

Research shows that unsaturated fats improve heart health, lower blood pressure levels, and decrease the risk of heart disease, stroke, and diabetes.[18]

This is why the American Heart Association recommends that you get the majority (i.e. over 50%) of your daily fat calories from unsaturated fats.

This is easy to do. A tablespoon of olive oil on a salad, for example, provides 12 grams of unsaturated fat, a handful of almonds about 9 grams, and a 4-ounce serving of salmon about 11 grams.

KEEP YOUR INTAKE OF SATURATED FATS RELATIVELY LOW (LESS THAN 10% OF YOUR TOTAL DAILY CALORIES)

Saturated fat is found in foods like meat, dairy products, eggs, coconut oil, bacon fat, and lard. If a fat is solid at room temperature, it's a saturated fat.

The long-held belief that saturated fat increases

the risk of heart disease has been challenged by recent research.[19]

This has been a boon to various diet "gurus" that promote high-fat eating, and as a result, we've seen a veritable renaissance of meat and dairy consumption.

The problem here is that the research used to promote this movement has also been severely criticized by prominent nutrition and cardiology researchers for various flaws and omissions.[20]

These scientists maintain that there is a strong association between high intake of saturated fatty acids and heart disease and that we should follow the generally accepted dietary guidelines for saturated fat intake (less than 10% of daily calories) until we know more.

Given the research currently available, I don't think we can safely say that we can eat all the saturated fats we want without any health consequences. And I'd rather "play it safe" and wait for further research before jumping into the bandwagon.

The CDC gives several simple ways to reduce your intake of saturated fat:

- Choose leaner cuts of meat that do not have a marbled appearance (i.e. where the fat appears embedded in the meat). Leaner cuts include round cuts and sirloin cuts. Trim all visible fat off meats before eating.
- Remove the skin from chicken, turkey, and other poultry before cooking.
- When reheating soups or stews, skim the solid fats from the top before heating.
- Drink low-fat (1%) or fat-free (skim) milk rather than whole or 2% milk.
- Buy low-fat or non-fat versions of your favorite cheeses and other milk or dairy products.
- When you want a sweet treat, reach for a low-fat or fat-free version of your favorite ice cream or frozen dessert. These versions usually contain less saturated fat.
- Choose baked goods, breads, and desserts that

are low in saturated fat. You can find this information on the Nutrition Facts label.
- Pay attention at snack time. Some convenience snacks such as sandwich crackers contain saturated fat. Choose instead to have non-fat or low-fat yogurt and a piece of fruit.

Don't think you have to do *all* of these things. You can simply pick what suits your diet and preferences best.

Personally, I eat around 3,000 calories per day, which means my saturated fat intake should be under 35 grams per day (which contains about 315 calories). I eat lean, skin-free meats and low-fat dairy products, but I do prefer butter over a low-fat spread and 2% milk over fat-free.

LIMIT YOUR INTAKE OF OVERLY PROCESSED FOODS

Health and diet gurus love to demonize "processed foods" as the root of all dietary evils, but just about every food you can eat has been processed in one way or another.

In fact, we've been processing foods for thousands of years, and not all modern methods are bad. For example, the process whereby vegetables are blanched and frozen is an effective way to preserve freshness and nutritional value. Seeds must be pressed into oil, and milk must be pasteurized to kill certain bacteria.

On the other hand, however, there are numerous food processing strategies that can be harmful to our health, like increasing shelf life by adding trans fats and other preservatives; improving taste by adding large amounts of salt, sugar, and fat; and preserving meat by smoking, curing, salting, or adding preservatives.

As you now know, you don't need to completely eliminate overly processed foods. You just need to limit them. Get the majority of your daily calories from relatively unprocessed foods and you'll be fine. Here are some practical ways to do this:

- Don't use store-bought salad dressings. Make your own from scratch. They taste better and are better for you.
- Throw out the salty, fatty, and highly processed snack foods like chips, pretzels, sugary cereals, and the like. Fruits, nuts, granola, and nut butters are much better choices.
- Cut out the nondairy creamers and go with products made with real dairy milk or soy- or nut-milks.
- Get rid of light butters and vegetable spreads. Use regular butter instead.
- Don't drink sodas or fruit juices. Drink water instead. If you have trouble with the taste of water, try adding some fruit like strawberry, lemon, lime, or watermelon for flavor.
- Keep your freezer full of frozen fruits and vegetables. Choose products marked with the USDA "U.S. Fancy" shield because these are higher quality than those graded "U.S. No. 1" or "U.S. No. 2."
- Choose whole grains over white. Switching from refined white bread, pasta, and rice to whole-grain counterparts is an easy way to increase the amount of fiber and other nutrients you get every day.

THE BOTTOM LINE

Counting or tracking calories and macronutrients is the surest way to guarantee results in your dieting, but I understand if you balk at the idea of doing this every meal for every day of the rest of your life.

Fortunately you don't have to.

Instead, you can do what I do: plan and track your food intake when you want to maximize fat loss or maintain a very low body fat percentage (below 10% for men and below 20% for women). This is when you need to be very precise with your calories, which I covered in the previous chapter.

Otherwise, use the strategies in this chapter to stay healthy and prevent weight gain.

CHAPTER SUMMARY

- Increasing protein intake decreases appetite through several mechanisms, including favorably altering hormones related to hunger and fullness.

- Fibrous foods with high water content, like most vegetables and some fruits, are great for maintaining health and preventing weight gain.

- Healthy fats are found in non-fried plant oils like olive, coconut, and peanut oil; nuts, seeds, and butters made from them; low-fat dairy products; and high-quality meat and seafood like wild-caught fish and lean cuts of free-range animals fed natural diets.

- Unhealthy fats are found in fried foods like potato chips, donuts, and fried chicken; processed meats like low-quality sausage, cold cuts, bacon, jerky, cured meats, and hot dogs; and packaged foods like pastries, breakfast cereal, microwave popcorn, frozen pizza, and low-quality yogurt and peanut butter.

- The Institute of Medicine recommends that your trans fat intake be "as low as possible," and the American Heart Association recommends you eat less than 2 grams of trans fat per day.

- The American Heart Association recommends that you get the majority (over 50%) of your daily fat calories from unsaturated fats.

- We should follow the generally accepted dietary guidelines for saturated fat intake (i.e. less than 10% of daily calories) until we know more about their effects on our bodies.

ORGANIC OR CONVENTIONAL FOOD? A SCIENCE-BASED REVIEW

---

*"When a man's stomach is full
it makes no difference whether he is rich or poor."*
EURIPEDES

A decade ago, the organic foods market was a piddling little niche that served a small share of consumers.

Today, it's one of the hottest trends in all of food, with many major producers rapidly expanding their organic divisions and the majority of Americans at least occasionally buying organic products.

Is this just another fad? Are organic foods worth the added expense? Are they *really* that much better than conventional fare?

Well, many people swear by the health benefits of eating organic like it's a religion, and some—the "non-believers"—claim it's nothing more than a brilliant marketing ploy to inflate bottom lines.

Who's right?

WHAT IS ORGANIC FOOD?

Before we dive into the advantages and disadvantages of organic foods, let's take a moment to clarify what they actually are.

Organic crops are grown without the use of synthetic pesticides, genetic engineering, petroleum- and sewer-sludge-based fertilizers, or irradiation.

Organic livestock are raised without the use of antibiotics, growth hormones, or animal byproducts, and must have access to the outdoors and eat organic feed.

You can see why organic foods are an easy sell: the definitions alone imply benefits. It's fair to assume that the fewer chemicals we ingest and the more natural a food is, the better. Like the multivitamin, many people buy organic foods on this "faith" alone.

In terms of labeling, it works like this …

LOOK FOR THE SEAL

For a food to be sold as organic, it must meet strict standards set by the U.S. Department of Agriculture (USDA) on how it's grown, handled, and processed. If a food meets these standards, it will feature the following seal:

Not all organic foods are the same, however.

100% Certified Organic

This label means that 100% of ingredients in a product, except salt and water, are organic.

Organic

This label means that 95% of the ingredients in a product, except salt and water, are organic.

Made with Organic Ingredients

This label means that 70% of the ingredients in a product, except salt and water, are organic.

WHAT ARE THE BENEFITS OF ORGANIC FOODS?

———

If I wanted to convince you that organic foods were a waste of money, I would parrot lines from a widely cited Stanford study that concluded, "The published literature lacks strong evidence that organic foods are significantly more nutritious than conventional foods."[1]

And many people do just that, treating the matter like an open-and-shut case on Judge Judy.

This is lazy and misleading, however, because there's a lot more to be considered in the scientific evaluation of organic foods.

First, the Stanford research has been lambasted by several authorities in the scientific community for cherry picking studies to support their conclusions and ignoring data that doesn't, using vague terminology, and stretching their findings to "answer" questions it simply can't (the most basic being "is organic food more nutritious or safer than conventional food?").[2]

Second, when you take the time to dive into the details and review the many papers covered in the analysis, you find several clear benefits in eating organic food.

ORGANIC CROPS ARE MORE NUTRITIOUS THAN CONVENTIONAL CROPS

One example is a well-designed and exhaustive study that shows that organic farming produces crops with 10 to 30% more nutrients, with vitamin C, antioxidants, and phenolic acids tending to be higher in organic foods and vitamin A and protein higher in conventional foods.[3]

Interestingly, the study, which was conducted by a large team of specialists and led by a scientist from Newcastle University, involved the review of essentially the same literature as the controversial Stanford study, but with more rigorous criteria to judge the quality of research analyzed and significance of their findings.

Apparently the Stanford scientists didn't feel a 10 to 30% increase in nutrient density was "significantly more nutritious" and thus dismissed it as unlikely to improve health.

This is an over-simplification, however, as relatively small increases in certain key nutrients *would* deliver health benefits to people eating an average Western diet.[4]

ORGANIC CROPS REDUCE YOUR EXPOSURE TO PESTICIDES

Research shows that organic crops are 85% less likely to contain pesticide residues than conventional foods, and at levels 10 to 100 times lower.[5] Multiple pesticide residues are rare in organic foods, and high-risk pesticides are particularly rare.

Crops aren't the only problem, either: conventional meats contain pesticides and other chemicals, which accumulate in adipose tissue.[6]

Furthermore, we should be concerned with the overall health risk posed by pesticide exposure, not just the number of residues we're exposed to.

Case in point: research shows that switching from conventional to organic foods reduces the pesticide health risk by 94%, thanks to the overall reduction of pesticide exposure and the elimination of high-risk chemicals in particular.[7]

This is especially important for pregnant women as studies show that pre-natal exposure to organophosphates used in growing conventional foods increases the risk of their children developing autism, ADHD, and asthma.[8]

In children, these chemicals have been shown to increase the risk of cognitive deficits, including reduced IQ.[9]

The American Academy of Pediatrics has also weighed in the matter, recognizing that an organic diet reduces a child's exposure to pesticides and may reduce the risk of diseases related to antibiotic resistance.[10]

ORGANIC MEATS CONTAIN LESS ANTIBIOTIC-RESISTANT BACTERIA

Antibiotic resistance in humans is a serious health problem, and research shows that ingesting meat from animals treated with antibiotics is a contributing factor.[11]

The reason for this is animals treated with antibiotics have become a fruitful source of antibiotic-resistant bacteria, which can then pass their resistance to other bacteria, and then from animal to man.[12]

Organic farmers aren't allowed to use antibiotics to treat animals producing organic food, which is why research shows that the incidence of bacteria resistant to ampicillin is 66% lower in organic meats than conventional.[13]

ORGANIC MEATS DON'T CONTAIN GROWTH HORMONES THAT MAY BE HARMFUL TO YOUR HEALTH

Research conducted by the EU Scientific Committee on Veterinary Measures relating to Public Health (quite a mouthful) back in 1999 confirmed that the use of hormones in cattle posed a potential health risk to consumers, and scientific concern over the use of these drugs has only grown since.[14]

While the debate as to the long-term effects on humans continues, the general question is becoming *how much* of an impact it has, rather than if it has any impact at all, and research shows that the consumption of animals treated with hormones may have wider-ranging effects than we once believed.[15]

WHAT ARE THE DISADVANTAGES OF ORGANIC FOOD?

"So what's the catch with organic foods?" you might be wondering. Well, there are a few notable disadvantages.

ORGANIC FOOD IS EXPENSIVE

If you want to go completely organic, you'd better be ready to open up your wallet.

If you have the money to spare, then you can't go wrong by trading all your conventional foods in for the organic varieties.

If that would strain your budget, though, you can get the most bang for your organic buck by choosing organic for some foods and conventional for others (and we'll talk more about this in a minute).

ORGANIC FOODS DON'T LAST AS LONG

It's a minor point, but the lack of preservatives in organic foods means they spoil quicker, which can mean more frequent shopping trips and wasted food.

This in turn contributes to the expense of eating organic.

IT CAN BE HARD TO FIND A GOOD VARIETY OF ORGANIC FOODS

If you don't have a Whole Foods in your neighborhood, it can be tough to find a store with a large selection of organic foods.

That said, farmer's markets are becoming more prevalent, you can find quite a few organic foods online, or you can even grow your own if you've got a DIY streak in you.

WHICH FOODS ARE WORTH BUYING ORGANIC?

In a perfect world, we'd get all our food from local organic farmers and enjoy delicious farm-to-table eating every day. But who has the time and money to actually do this?

Fortunately, you don't have to go "all in" with organic to make it worthwhile. Some foods absorb chemicals more thoroughly than others and simply washing or removing the skin isn't enough to rid them of pesticide residues.

Because of this, choose organic over conventional for the following foods and you can dramatically reduce your exposure to pesticides:

Apples, strawberries, grapes, celery, peaches, spinach, sweet bell peppers, nectarines (imported), cucumbers, cherry tomatoes, snap peas (imported), potatoes, hot peppers, and blueberries

On the other side of the coin is the "Clean Fifteen," which are fifteen conventional foods that rank lowest in pesticide residues and thus the least important when considering what to buy organic:

Avocados, sweet corn, pineapples, cabbage, sweet peas (frozen), onions, asparagus, mangoes, papaya, kiwis, eggplant, cantaloupe, cauliflower, and sweet potatoes.

Organic dairy is also a worthwhile "investment" because the chemicals in the pesticide-laden feed that conventional livestock eat usually find their way into the dairy fat. Conventional butter often has pesticide residues, for example, whereas organic butters don't.[16]

By the same token, if you eat fatty meats regularly, going organic is also a good idea.

6 WAYS TO GET ORGANIC FOOD ON THE CHEAP

By now you'd probably like at least to integrate some organic foods into your diet, but you're also probably (and understandably) worried about the price.

While organic foods *are* going to cost more than their conventional counterparts, there are quite a few strategies you can use to make the switch quite affordable.

EAT WITH THE SEASON

Locally grown foods are almost always cheaper than imported ones, so if you let what's in season guide your meal planning, you won't be eating organic strawberries in winter, but you'll save quite a bit of money.

BUY IN BULK

Local organic co-ops and health food stores have bulk sections, which can save you serious money on foods like legumes, grains, and spices.

In fact, you may even save money by switching from conventional store-bought foods to organic co-ops by buying large quantities of what's in season and storing, drying, canning, and freezing the foods for use throughout the year.

The Coop Directory Service (http://www.coop-directory.org/) is a great online resource for finding co-ops in your area.

LOOK FOR DEALS ON RIPE FOODS

Most health food stores have sections for food that doesn't look "pretty" anymore, like dotted bananas, and food that will expire in a day or two.

These foods are often heavily discounted, and you can sort through them to "cherry pick" the best candidates, so it's a win-win.

BUY FROZEN WHEN POSSIBLE

Not only are frozen foods generally cheaper than their fresh counterparts, but research shows that, nutritionally speaking, frozen foods are equal to, and in some cases better than, fresh foods.[17]

This is also nice to know when you're buying seasonal food in bulk. Use what you need, then blanch and freeze the rest!

AVOID PRE-PACKAGED FOODS

As convenient as they are and as pretty as the packaging is, remember that you're paying a large premium for these organic "luxuries."

Stick to whole food products that you have to cook and prepare yourself and you'll save money.

CHOOSE STORE BRANDS WHEN POSSIBLE
Many supermarkets and boutique stores carry their own generic lines of organic foods, including produce, pasta, grains, condiments, and more.

These generic products are quite a bit cheaper than the big brands, and while they don't look as nice as name brands, don't be fooled: they're held to the same farming and processing standards.

Eating organic foods may not be the secret to good health, but the benefits of organic foods are real and, in some cases, fairly significant.

Research shows that by minimizing your exposure to harmful pesticides and other chemicals, including organic foods in your diet will likely reduce your risk for disease and improve longevity, and that's well worth the added expense! [18]

CHAPTER SUMMARY

- Organic crops are grown without the use of synthetic pesticides, genetic engineering, petroleum- and sewer-sludge-based fertilizers, or irradiation.

- Organic livestock are raised without the use of antibiotics, growth hormones, or animal byproducts, and must have access to the outdoors and eat organic feed.

- Organic crops are more nutritious than conventional crops.

- Organic crops reduce your exposure to pesticides.

- Organic meats contain less antibiotic-resistant bacteria.

- Organic meats don't contain growth hormones that may be harmful to your health.

- You don't have to go "all in" with organic to make it worthwhile. Certain foods ("The Dirty Dozen") contain higher amounts of pesticide residues than others ("The Clean Fifteen").

- Organic full-fat dairy is also a worthwhile "investment" because the chemicals in the pesticide-laden feed that conventional livestock eat find their way into the dairy fat.

- While organic foods *are* going to cost more than conventional foods, there are quite a few strategies you can use to make the switch quite affordable.

Cooking

THE MINIMALIST'S GUIDE TO COOKING GREAT FOOD

"Cooking is at once child's play and adult joy.
And cooking done with care is an act of love."
CRAIG CLAIBORNE

Many people think that cooking good food is far more complex than it really is.

Ever walk into a grocery store and see the row of rotisserie chickens lined up for busy shoppers? It looks so convenient, but did you know that roasting your own chicken is literally as simple as tossing some spices on a bird and sticking it in the oven for an hour or two?

Or let's take microwave dinners, "ready-to-bake" meals, and the like. One look at the ingredients list shows that they barely qualify as food, and, ironically, the fifteen minutes it takes to cook a frozen pizza could have been used putting together and cooking your own healthier, whole-food pie.

The point is that cooking real food, and *good* food, is surprisingly simple, affordable, and fast … once you learn a handful of basics on cooking and storing food.

So, let's get to it.

THE 12 MOST COMMON COOKING MISTAKES

It's kind of a shame that most of us make it through our formal education without any actual training on cooking. We spend hour after hour drilling math equations and sentence structures, yet we spend almost zero time on the skills needed to feed ourselves well.

Thus, it's no surprise that many of us have fallen victim to common cooking mistakes that make our meals harder to make and less enjoyable to eat.

Let's go over the twelve most common mistakes here.

TASTING ONLY AFTER YOU'RE DONE COOKING

How many times have you tried a new recipe only to be disappointed by the flavor of the final result?

Remember, recipes are based on one person's preferences, so your desired spice levels or flavors may differ from what's printed. Tasting throughout the cooking process will prevent culinary letdowns.

Plus, cooking is an ongoing, sensuous affair that needs your attention to go from okay to great.

FAILING TO PREPARE IN ADVANCE

Beginning cooks wing recipes on the fly while more experienced chefs plan ahead to make a meal as enjoyable as possible.

Here's how:

Get inspired to eat good food

Read food magazines, browse the web, look at pictures, and reminisce on dishes from your childhood. Your ideas will flow. Keep brainstorming and write them down.

Draft a menu

Draft a simple menu with some hot and cold items with a variety of ingredients, tastes, and textures.

And remember to keep it *simple*. You still have your training wheels on—no Tour de France just yet!

Make grocery and prep lists

Once you're happy with your menu, I highly recommend you take the time to create a grocery list for everything you'll need to buy.

Then make a prep list that lays out what you're going to cook and when, starting with the foods that take the longest to cook and finishing with the shortest (such as preparing a garnish).

You should also plan to consolidate your prep work by "batching" it—wash all vegetables at the same time, peel all the onions, mince all the garlic, and so forth.

BOILING WHEN YOU SHOULD SIMMER

It's tempting to pump up the heat to put a dish on the table faster, but the result is going to be a cloudy, tough, or dry mess.

When a recipe calls for a simmer, aim for a heat level that produces a bubble breaking the surface every second or two.

Any more than that and you're courting disaster.

ASSUMING YOUR OVEN IS OPERATING PERFECTLY

Most beginning cooks aren't even aware that individual ovens can have hot spots, cool spots, and other uneven idiosyncrasies.

To find yours, conduct a "bread test" by placing a single layer of bread on a cookie sheet and baking for a few minutes at 350 degrees. The toasting will reveal your oven's hot spots, allowing you to adjust the way you bake future recipes accordingly.

For instance, if the bread in the back left corner of your oven comes out browner than pieces on the right or in the front, either rotate your dishes as you bake them for even cooking or position the dishes so that they sit in a more evenly heated area of the oven. Doing so will prevent hot spots from affecting your dishes' cooking.

Even better, though, is convection baking, which uses hot air to cook instead of heating elements. The major benefits of convection baking are very even heat distribution (eliminating cold spots) and 10 to 20% faster cooking times.

Although convection baking generally isn't recommended for things that can shift or splatter easily (like quick breads or other bakery items), it's fantastic for meats, fish, vegetables, and anything else that's firm.

NOT HEATING YOUR PAN BEFORE ADDING FOOD

If you're searing or sautéing, a well-heated pan will prevent food from sticking and ensure you get the sear or crust you're looking for.

What you're after is called "thermal shock," which has that lovely "pssshhhhh" sound.

If you aren't sure your pan is hot enough, try flicking a drop of water onto it. If there's no sizzle, it isn't ready.

OVERCROWDING YOUR PAN

The easiest way to lose the succulent sizzle is to overcrowd your pan. Remember, no searing means no crust!

So, cook your food in batches instead, ensuring that each gets that lovely golden-brown patina!

MEASURING INGREDIENTS IMPROPERLY

You don't need to measure down to the microgram to be a successful cook, but you do need to invest in proper measuring cups and spoons for both dry and wet ingredients.

Pay attention, also, to the way you fill your utensils. Packing sugar or flour into a 1-cup scoop will result in significantly more ingredient than the recipe called for. Instead, lightly spoon the ingredient into the cup and level it off with a knife.

TURNING YOUR FOOD TOO OFTEN

Lazy cooks rejoice!

If you turn meat that's cooking on the stove or grill too often, you will interfere with its ability to form a nice sear or breading coat. Instead, let meat cook undisturbed for the length of time indicated in the recipe. Turn it once and once only.

FAILING TO USE A MEAT THERMOMETER

The meat thermometer is the beginning chef's best friend.

Don't gauge doneness by appearance alone. Invest in a good digital thermometer and use it to cook your meat to a degree that's both safe and desirable.

We'll talk more about how to use a thermometer later in this chapter.

LEAVING ALL YOUR SALT IN THE MARINADE OR BREADING

Use salt in any marinade or breading, but then season your meat directly before cooking to ensure adequate coverage.

Despite the fact that a high-sodium diet is prevalent here in the West, most people don't salt their food enough (their sodium comes mainly from packaged foods).

If there's a magic spice, it's salt. Once a rare and valuable commodity, it enhances every flavor and food. So, as a general rule, salt your dishes liberally and enjoy.

NOT LETTING YOUR MEAT ACCLIMATE TO ROOM TEMPERATURE

When you cook a steak that's come straight from the refrigerator, you'll wind up with a seared outside and a still-cold inside.

For better results, let your meats sit on the counter for 15 to 30 minutes before cooking so that they can come up to room temperature for more even cooking. (And be sure to wipe the counter down thoroughly before using the same surface to chop vegetables.)

USING LOW-QUALITY INGREDIENTS

Cooking with a cheap tube of ground meat just isn't the same as high-quality beef. The same goes for frozen and canned versus fresh fruit and vegetables. If you're used to the former, you might be surprised how much better the latter taste.

Remember that simple cooking techniques applied to first-rate ingredients will beat fancy techniques and inferior ingredients every time.

The bottom line is great ingredients make great food, so buy the highest quality you can afford.

A food's quality is largely influenced by how it was raised and harvested, but how you store food before cooking it plays a key role in the overall quality of the end result.

Read on to learn how to buy, store, and cook several different types of animal protein.

HOW TO BUY, STORE, AND COOK FISH

You've probably heard many times about how healthy fish is, but let's do a quick review.

Fish is well known as a "brain food" because it's low in calories, high in protein, and, most importantly, packed full of omega-3 fatty acids, which are essential fats that your body needs but can't produce on its own.

One of the major benefits of getting enough omega-3s in your diet is a healthier heart.

Heart attacks are one of the two most common causes of early death around the world, and omega-3s are believed to play a positive role in preventing them.[1] In fact, one study of more than 40,000 men in the U.S. found that those who ate one or more servings of fish each week were 15% less likely to have heart disease.[2]

Observational studies have also demonstrated that fish-eaters have a slower rate of cognitive decline, potentially protecting against devastating diseases like Alzheimer's. The consumption of omega-3s is also linked to a lower risk of type 1 diabetes in children, a protective agent against vitamin D deficiency, and a 42% lower risk of macular degeneration in women.[3]

If you're an athlete, fish deserve even more of your attention, as the consumption of good-quality fish oil supplements has been shown to increase muscle protein synthesis, reduce muscle soreness, help prevent weight gain, and more.[4]

The bottom line? You need omega-3 fatty acids in your diet, and fish is a great way to get them.

THE SMART WAY TO BUY FISH

When purchasing fish, your first consideration should be mercury content.

The Natural Resources Defense Council offers the following guidelines for minimizing the potential impact of fish-based mercury on your diet.[5]

LOWEST MERCURY CONTENT
EAT THESE FISH AS FREQUENTLY AS YOU'D LIKE

ANCHOVIES, BUTTERFISH, CATFISH, CRAWFISH/CRAYFISH, CROAKER (ATLANTIC), FLOUNDER, HADDOCK (ATLANTIC), HAKE, HERRING, MACKEREL (N. ATLANTIC, CHUB), MULLET, PERCH (OCEAN), PLAICE, POLLOCK, SALMON (CANNED OR FRESH), SARDINE, SHAD (AMERICAN), SOLE (PACIFIC), TILAPIA, TROUT (FRESHWATER), WHITEFISH, WHITING

MODERATE MERCURY CONTENT
EAT SIX OR FEWER SERVINGS OF THESE FISH PER MONTH

BASS (STRIPED, BLACK), CARP, COD (ALASKAN), CROAKER (WHITE PACIFIC), HALIBUT (ATLANTIC, PACIFIC), JACKSMELT (SILVERSIDE), LOBSTER, MAHI MAHI, MONKFISH, PERCH (FRESHWATER), SABLEFISH, SKATE, SNAPPER, TUNA (CANNED CHUNK LIGHT), TUNA (SKIPJACK), WEAKFISH (SEA TROUT)

HIGH MERCURY CONTENT
EAT THREE OR FEWER SERVINGS OF THESE FISH PER MONTH

BLUEFISH, GROUPER, MACKEREL (SPANISH, GULF), SEA BASS (CHILEAN), TUNA (CANNED ALBACORE), TUNA (YELLOWFIN)

HIGHEST MERCURY CONTENT
AVOID EATING THESE FISH ALTOGETHER

MACKEREL (KING), MARLIN, ORANGE ROUGHY, SHARK, SWORDFISH, TILEFISH, TUNA (BIGEYE, AHI)

In addition to choosing your fish based on mercury content, you'll see different fish being advertised as "wild caught" or "farm raised."

Though "wild caught" sounds like the healthier alternative, the science is ambiguous.

In terms of nutritional profiles, few significant differences exist between wild-caught and farm-raised fish. Wild-caught trout, for example, have more calcium and iron than their farm-raised counterparts, which offer more vitamin A and selenium. Farmed and wild-caught rainbow trout, however, are nearly identical in terms of nutrients.

In many cases, farm-raised fish offer significantly more of those all-important omega-3 fatty acids mentioned earlier. Farmed Atlantic salmon, for instance, provide more omega-3s than wild-caught Atlantic salmon.

The presence of contaminants in wild-caught versus farm-raised fish is also less of a concern than many have made it out to be.

A 2004 study made waves when it reported that levels of potentially carcinogenic chemicals in farmed fish were ten times higher than in their wild-caught brethren.[12] What the headlines didn't say, though, is the amount of chemicals present was still less than 2% of the amount considered dangerous.

Further studies have found similar levels of contaminants in farm-raised and wild-caught fish.[13]

The issue of environmental impact of farmed and wild-caught fish is also murky, as both involve unsustainable practices. The Seafood Watch program sponsored by the Monterey Bay Aquarium (www.seafoodwatch.org) is one of the best sources of information on the specific concerns impacting different types of fish.

Regardless of the type of fish you purchase and whether you opt for wild caught or farm raised, keep the following guidelines in mind:

- Purchase from a reputable supplier. A highly regarded local fish market is likely to have better-quality product than a large-chain grocery store.
- Give fish the smell test. Fresh, unfrozen fish should smell of seawater or cucumber. Avoid fish that gives off a strong, unpleasant odor.
- Look for fish with elastic flesh. If possible, press a finger into the fish. The flesh of fresh fish will bounce back. If the indentation remains, the fish is past its prime.
- Look for liquid on the meat. Milky liquid present on a fresh fish fillet is a sign of rot.
- Examine the quality of the skin. When purchasing fillets with the skin intact, scales should be smooth and shiny. Ruffled scales or a dull appearance are indications of age.

If purchasing fresh fish isn't an option for you, frozen fish, whether purchased locally or from an online retailer, may be a viable alternative.

- Look for "frozen-at-sea" (fas) designations. These fish are flash-frozen as soon as three seconds after being brought onboard the ship, giving them a superior flavor and quality over longer-processed alternatives.
- Watch out for freezer-burned areas. White, dehydrated areas or visible ice crystals indicate moisture loss in the fish, usually as a result of thawing and refreezing.
- Look for moisture-proof, vapor-proof packaging. Fish packaged in this way fare better than those in over-wrapped packaging.

THE SMART WAY TO STORE FISH

You want to cook fresh fish within 24 hours of purchase and freeze whatever you don't cook in this time. Once prepared, cooked fish can be stored in the refrigerator for up to 2 to 3 days.

To temporarily store fresh fish, wrap whole fish or fish fillets loosely and store them in packed ice to minimize moisture loss.

Frozen fish can be stored from three months to a year, depending on the fat content.

Fatty fish like mackerel and trout should be kept frozen for no more than 3 months. Lean fish like cod and flounder can be stored frozen for up to 6 months, while lean crustaceans like lobster, shrimp, and scallops can be kept frozen for up to a year.

To thaw frozen fish for cooking, place fish in the refrigerator and allow 18 to 24 hours per pound to thaw. If necessary, thaw frozen fish faster by placing the fish under cold running water.

THE SMART WAY TO COOK FISH

The wide variety of fish available gives minimalist chefs a number of options for preparing them to bring out their texture and flavor.

Here are simple guidelines for cooking delicious fish:

Baking

Season fish as desired and place on an oiled baking sheet. Bake uncovered in the oven at 450° F for 10 minutes per every inch of thickness.

Pan frying

Heat a small amount of oil or butter over medium to medium-high heat. Cook fish 4 to 5 minutes per side.

Grilling

Brush grill grate with oil and place over charcoal or gas grill with lid closed. Place seasoned fish directly on grill rack and cook 4 to 5 minutes per side (per inch of thickness) over direct heat, or 15 minutes when using indirect heat. For best results, use thicker cuts of fatty fish, or grill smaller fish in a fish grill basket.

Poaching

Place seasoned fish in pan and add just enough wine, water, fish stock, or milk to cover. Cook fillets 8 to 10 minutes covered and just below boiling. Use the remaining poaching liquid as the base for a sauce.

Microwaving

In a pinch, nearly any boneless fish fillet can be microwaved. Cut fish in half and place in microwave-safe dish with thick portions on the outside of the dish. Add a small amount of liquid, cover with plastic wrap, and pierce the wrap a few times to vent the fish. Cook three minutes per pound on high power and salt after cooking.

And if you don't have the time or inclination to make a full-blown recipe, mix the following together for a delicious fish seasoning:

> 1 tbsp. dried basil
> 1 tbsp. dried crushed rosemary
> 1 tbsp. dried parsley
> 2 tsp. sea salt
> 2 tsp. ground black pepper
> 1 tsp. dried oregano leaves
> 1 tsp. garlic powder

HOW TO BUY, STORE, AND COOK MEAT

Meat is high in protein, iron, zinc, B-vitamins (including B12), and other nutrients such as carnosine and creatine, which improve physical performance.

While research shows that it's reasonable to assume that eating too many processed meat products can cause health issues, this simply doesn't apply to fresh, high-quality meat that you cook yourself.

This section is going to help you get the best for your money.

THE SMART WAY TO BUY MEAT

When purchasing meat, the biggest rule is commonsensical: if it smells bad, don't buy it.

It's also pretty obvious to see which meat is fresh and which isn't.

The freshest cuts of red meat should appear bright red, for example. Red meat that has begun to brown has been exposed to air for some time and should be avoided. Pass on meat that has been vacuum sealed and is beginning to show bloated pockets of air.

Fresh chicken should be similarly free of bad odors and obvious signs of aging like bruises or greenish spots. It should also feel soft and not slimy or powdery.

The "cleanest," most chemical-free meats are found at local butcher shops, farmers markets, co-ops, or directly from local farmers (who often sell affordable "shares" of cows, pigs, and other animals).

THE SMART WAY TO STORE MEAT

The U.S. Department of Agriculture offers the following guidelines for safe meat storage:

- Store raw ground meats and poultry in the refrigerator at 40° F or less for no more than 1 to 2 days. If the meat cannot be used in this period, freeze it.
- Store raw roasts, steaks, and chops (beef, veal, lamb, and pork) in the refrigerator for up to 3 to 5 days. Freeze what can't be used.
- Store cooked meats and poultry in the refrigerator for no more than 3 to 4 days after preparation.

If you'll be storing red meat or poultry in the freezer, your goal should be to minimize exposure of the meat to the air, as this leads to freezer burn.

Either vacuum seal the meat or wrap it tightly in a combination of plastic wrap or freezer paper, covered in aluminum foil and sealed inside a zippered bag. Meat can be stored in this way for at least three months.

To thaw frozen red meat or poultry, place the package in the refrigerator for 24 to 48 hours (longer if needed for larger cuts or roasts). Thawing meat on the counter can cause outer layers of the meat, which will thaw first, to attract bacteria while the inner layers of the meat remain frozen.

THE SMART WAY TO COOK MEAT

Many of the same preparation methods described for fish can be used for poultry and red meat, though cooking times and temperatures must be altered.

Red Meat

Two alternatives exist for preparing red meat: dry-heat cooking and wet-heat cooking.

Dry-heat cooking methods include grilling, broiling, sauteing, roasting, and stir-frying.

Wet-heat methods include steaming, poaching, stewing, slow cooking, pot roasting, and braising.

As a general rule, cook steaks, which are naturally tender, with dry heat methods and shorter cooking times.

Roasts, which have more collagen and elastin than steaks, need longer, slower cooking periods using wet heat methods to melt these connective tissues and create a more tender dish.

Poultry

Poultry can be cooked using all of these techniques, as dictated by the specific cut being prepared.

Whole chickens, for instance, are a cost-effective alternative to purchasing individual chicken breasts, though their substantial nature requires longer cook times.

Thin chicken breast fillets, on the other hand, must be monitored carefully to avoid becoming dried out.

Remember Your Meat Thermometer

Remember earlier in this chapter when we talked about the importance of using a good meat thermometer?

Well, this tip is important enough to warrant its own section.

Where should you place your meat thermometer?

Imagine you've got a steak with one thick end and one thin end. If you put the steak on the grill for

20 minutes and then insert your meat thermometer, you'll probably find that the thin end of the steak has cooked faster than the thick end.

Since the temperature to which you cook your food is so important, getting your meat thermometer placement right is just as critical.

Poultry

If you're cooking a whole chicken or turkey, measure temperature at the inner thigh, near the breast but not touching the bone. If your bird is stuffed, measure the stuffing temperature to ensure it reaches 165 degrees. If you're cooking individual chicken breasts, measure at the thickest part of the breast.

Beef, pork, and lamb

Insert the thermometer into the center of the thickest part of the meat, keeping away from bone, fat, and gristle

Ground meat

If ground meat or poultry is being used in a dish, like meatloaf or casserole, insert into the thickest part of the meal without touching the serving dish. You may also insert the meat thermometer sideways into ground meat patties.

What temperatures are you looking for?

Once your meat thermometer is inserted (or once your dish has finished cooking, if you're using an oven-proof thermometer that can heat up with your recipe), aim for the following temperatures:

Rest Your Meat

If you rush your meat from the stove, oven, or grill to your plate and mouth, you'll miss out on some of the moist, tender experience you're after.

The reason is that the cooking process pushes the natural juices to the innermost portions of the meat, leaving everything else rather dry and tough. When you give the meat a few minutes to rest, however,

USDA RECOMMENDED SAFE MINIMUM INTERNAL TEMPERATURES	
BEEF, PORK, VEAL, LAMB, STEAKS, ROASTS & CHOPS	145 °F
FISH	145 °F
BEEF, VEAL, LAMB GROUND	160 °F
EGG DISHES	160 °F
TURKEY, CHICKEN & DUCK WHOLE, PIECES & GROUND	165 °F

STEAK DONENESS	REMOVE AT	COOKED TEMPERATURE
RARE	125 °F	130 °F
MEDIUM RARE	135 °F	140 °F
MEDIUM	145 °F	150 °F
WELL DONE	155 °F	160 °F

the juices trapped in the middle will seep out to the edges and "rehydrate" the cut.

THE MINIMALIST'S GUIDE TO SEASONING YOUR FOOD

———

If you've ever taken a bite of plain, bland chicken breast, you know that unseasoned meat isn't much to write home about.

Even a simple dash of salt and ground black **pepper can turn a good cut** of red meat from uninspired to outstanding.

There's a lot more you can do, though, to make **meat simply outstand**ing.

SALT

For years, we've been hearing that we need to eat **less salt.**

In fact, our collective salt anxiety began in the **early 1900s, whe**n French doctors suggested that **six of their high b**lood pressure patients also con**sumed a high-sa**lt diet.

These fears were compounded in the 1970s, **when Lewis Dahl** of the Brookhaven National Lab**oratory induced** high blood pressure in rats by **feeding them a di**et of 500 grams of sodium daily **(for comparison,** the average U.S. adult consumes **3.4 grams of sodi**um daily).

Dahl also suggested the fact that countries with **high-sodium diets,** like Japan, had higher rates of **high blood pressure** and strokes.

His findings, and the foundation for fearing sodium in general, **have** begun to unravel, though. **New research** indicates that this elemental compound may not be as harmful as previously believed.

It started with an extensive review of the sodium literature published in 2003, which concluded, "There is little evidence for long-term benefit from reducing salt intake."[14]

Eight years later, a meta-analysis of seven studies encompassing more than 6,250 subjects bolstered these findings, concluding that there's no evidence supporting cutting salt as an effective means of reducing the risk for heart attack, stroke, or death in those with either normal or high blood pressure.[15]

Further research published in 2015 found that a *lower* consumption of sodium may actually be associated with a greater risk of dying from heart disease.[16]

So should you be watching your salt? Is it necessary to cut back on sodium to reduce your risk of high blood pressure, stroke, and cardiovascular disease?

Although the science isn't yet completely clear, what we do know for sure is that sodium is necessary for our bodies to function. It is sodium that binds water throughout the body and transports it wherever it's needed to maintain the appropriate balance of intracellular and extracellular fluids.

We also know that genetics and cultural factors come into play. That is, some people are more sensitive to sodium than others.

The bottom line is this:

As long as you're not eating a large amount of pre-packaged and/or highly processed foods and you don't have a strange obsession with over-salting every meal you eat, it's unlikely that you'll run into any sodium-related problems.

Now that we have that out of the way, let's talk salt and cooking.

As you now know, the most important seasoning in your kitchen is salt. A dash of salt enhances the flavor of meat and fish. It also elevates any other seasonings it's paired with.

You should experiment with different types of salts.

Kosher salt, sea salt, and table salt all have slightly different flavor profiles and can be applied in a number of different ways, including brining, rubbing, and seasoning.

As you add salt, think small and gradual. Keep a bowl of salt on the counter and season at every stage of the cooking process in small increments.

If you're making a hearty soup, for instance, add

salt every time you add something new to the pot (unless you're adding salty ingredients like bacon and capers).

And if you happen to overdo it?

No problem. Adding a bit of cream or unsalted butter will help mellow the flavors. Some chefs swear by Julia Child's tip of grating raw potatoes into a dish, letting them simmer and absorb the salty broth for 7 to 8 minutes, and then straining them out.

The saltiness of your food will also change as it sits or as its temperature changes. Take ham, for instance. When it's served cold, ham is perceived as being saltier than when it's served warm, where its taste becomes more savory in nature. Salting a ham dish, therefore, requires a different approach based on the recipe and its final serving style.

Similarly, you may find that you pull leftovers out of the fridge and notice a different flavor profile on the day after it's been cooked. A previously salty food may have mellowed, while other combinations of seasonings could cause the sensation of saltiness to increase. In either case, it's a good idea to taste your leftovers and add salt, if needed, before serving.

There's even a reason why professional chefs toss salt from a height of 10 to 12 inches above the pot or pan: it's a great way to visualize how much salt you're adding and to distribute the salt more evenly throughout the dish.

ACIDS

If you remember your high school chemistry class, you know that acids and bases sit on opposite ends of the pH scale. Acids are simply molecules that can easily lose a hydrogen ion, and in the practice of cooking, that gives them a sour, tangy, bright, or sharp taste.

Professional chefs use acids like vinegar, lemon juice, and lime juice to enhance savory or sweet foods.

A beef stew, for instance, may benefit from a splash of red wine vinegar, while a bit of lemon juice added to a fruit salad will make its sweet flavors pop.

In some instances, acids may even be used to "cook" foods through their ability to alter the structure of proteins. Traditional ceviche uses fresh lime juice to cook the seafood included, while pickled eggs can be considered "cooked" by the acid of the vinegar, even though heat has never been applied.

The most practical application of acids is using them when you're plating your food. When you're done cooking your meal, drizzle a bit of lemon or lime juice over your dish and it will bring out the best in what you've made!

Marinades also benefit greatly from acids.

If you just slap your seasonings onto a tough cut of meat, your flavor isn't going to penetrate very far. Turn them into a marinade by incorporating an acid like vinegar, tomato juice, or citrus juice, however, and their protein-altering effects will help your seasonings to be absorbed beyond the meat's outer layers.

Acids are also great when used in vinaigrette dressings. Instead of buying salad dressing, make your own by mixing one part acid with three parts oil, and then add spices or seasonings as desired. Adjust the ratio slightly and change up your additions, and the possibilities really are endless.

Adding acids to recipes requires a careful hand, but don't worry. If you go too far, you can rebalance the meal by adding sugar or oil, as appropriate to the recipe you're preparing.

SPICES AND SEASONINGS

There are as many spice and seasoning options available to you as there are different cuisines in the world. Every spice pairing represents the opportunity to take the same set of ingredients in a completely different direction.

Take a stir-fry of chicken breast and bell peppers, for example. With different spice and seasoning combinations, the flavor profile of the dish could be colored Asian, jerk, or even Italian.

Make it a point to experiment with as many

flavors as possible, incorporating fresh, ground, and whole spices as you go:

- "Warm" flavors: cardamom, cinnamon, nutmeg, curry, turmeric
- "Hot" flavors: black pepper, red pepper flakes, cayenne pepper, Sriracha, Tabasco
- "Green" flavors: basil, parsley, sage, rosemary, tarragon, mint, thyme
- "Pungent" flavors: garlic, garlic powder, onion powder, scallion, mustard, horseradish
- "Zesty" flavors: ginger, orange zest, lemon zest
- "Smoky" flavors: chipotle, chili powder, smoked salt, diced bacon
- "Nutty" flavors: walnuts, sesame, soy, pecans, pistachios
- "Sweet" flavors: sugar, molasses, maple syrup, honey

Watch out for "dead" herbs and spices, too. To do this, check your "use by" dates regularly and replace those that have expired. You can also know if a spice or herb is still good by giving it a quick smell. No smell equals no flavor, which equals no taste in your food. The rule of thumb is when in doubt, throw them out.

If you want the highest quality spices and herbs, grown your own.

For example, basil, thyme, rosemary, and mint can all be easily grown in kitchen-window pots and, once harvested, stored in the refrigerator as you would fresh flowers: cut their stems, place them upright in a jar of water, and cover them with a plastic bag.

When you add your spices and herbs in the cooking process matters as well.

Fresh herbs like basil, tarragon, parsley, and oregano are delicate and subtle and should be added once cooking is complete, just before serving. Dried herbs, on the other hand, are potent and diffuse well during the cooking process. Add them in the beginning.

THE BOTTOM LINE

This chapter may seem a bit large for something called a "minimalist's guide," but you've just learned the 20% of cooking tips that produce 80% of cooking results.

Put just some of them into practice and you might be surprised how much better your food tastes.

Refer back to this chapter regularly until it all becomes second nature, and you'll be a whole new chef.

THE RIGHT KITCHEN EQUIPMENT FOR THE JOB

---

*"I like the Japanese knives,
I like French knives. Whatever's sharp."*
WOLFGANG PUCK

You don't need much equipment to have a well-stocked kitchen. A good set of knives and pans is essential. Fancy blenders, pasta machines, juicers, and the like are not.

You don't need a food processor or garlic press if you have a knife. A pan doubles as a meat mallet and baking dish.

Buy the best quality knives and pans you can afford, and they will serve you well. Not only will they perform better, but they will last longer too, likely saving you money in the long run.

KNIVES

You can head over to your local big-box retailer and pick up a basic set of knives. Not even professional chefs need ten or more knives to run their kitchens.

This shopping list is a good place to start:

- A 2- to 3-inch paring knife for peeling fruit and cutting smaller vegetables.
- A 5-inch boning knife for cutting around bones in meat.
- An 8-inch chef's knife for all types of chopping.
- A 10-inch serrated or bread knife.

In terms of material, most knives are stainless steel.

French knives tend to be softer, which makes them easier to sharpen but also more vulnerable to damage. German companies use harder steel, making them trickier to sharpen but also more resistant to wear and tear. Japanese knives are also made from very hard steel. They tend to be lighter and are usually the prettiest.

In terms of brands, I like Wusthof, Shun, and Global. They're not cheap, but their craftsmanship is outstanding.

Part of caring for your knives and extending their lifespan is proper honing and sharpening.

Sharpen a knife too frequently and you'll wear it down. Sharpen it too infrequently and you'll have a dull knife that requires more force to cut, which is dangerous.

Also, never wash your knives (or anything sharp) in the dishwasher because it dulls them. Hand-wash them.

You can test a knife's sharpness by, with one hand, holding up a sheet of paper by a corner with two fingers. With the other hand, bring the knife to an edge of the paper and try to run it through. If it cuts into the paper, it's sharp enough. If it doesn't, it isn't.

If you use a proper cutting board (more on that soon) and you hone your knives after each use, you shouldn't have to sharpen your knives more than once every 3 to 6 months.

HOW TO HONE A KNIFE

The edges of knives are very thin and can become bent and warped with use.

These blemishes dull the blades, so you should use a honing steel to straighten the edges out, bringing them back into proper alignment and thus sharpness.

To hone your knives, you first need a honing steel. Buy one from the brand of knives that you choose.

Here's a simple visual of what you're going to do:

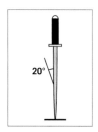  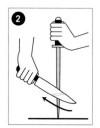

The motion is simple:

1. Hold the honing steel in your non-dominant hand with the tip pointing down, like you would a skiing pole.
2. Place the heel of the blade (the part where the sharpened edge meets the handle) on top of the steel near its base at a 20-degree angle.
3. Draw the knife down the steel in a sweeping motion, stroking the entire blade against the steel, maintaining the 20-degree angle.
4. Hone the other side of the knife by placing it under the steel and repeating the sweeping motion.
5. Hone each side 2 to 3 times.

SHARPENING A KNIFE

Knife sharpening is different from honing.

Over time, cutting and steeling your knives will wear metal away from the edges. Moreover, some folds and blemishes can become increasingly permanent.

You must sharpen your knives every 3 to 6 months to correct these issues.

You can sharpen your knives manually or electrically. Manual sharpening requires a whetstone and quite a bit of practice. Instead, I recommend you go electric.

CUTTING BOARDS

While we're talking knives, we should talk about cutting boards because they matter quite a bit.

A proper cutting board keeps your blades sharp and resists deep gouges and moisture. It also needs to be large enough to accommodate all cutting and chopping needs and heavy enough to stay in place.

The two types of cutting boards I like most are wood and polypropylene.

Nice wood boards are beautiful, easy on your knives, and very resistant to gouges. Polypropylene boards are cheaper and a bit more prone to gouging but are also easy on your knives.

If you buy a wood board, you're going to want to oil it every 3 to 4 weeks to keep moisture out and prevent warps and cracks. I recommend a product called Howard's Butcher Block Oil, which is a food-grade mineral oil stabilized with vitamin E.

PANS

Like knives, you don't need a cupboard stuffed full of pots and pans.

Instead, you should own a few well-chosen pieces that allow you to cook whatever you want and that give you the performance needed to cook better.

I judge cookware based on the following criteria:

Temperature control. How responsive are they to changes in heat?

Heat retention and distribution. How well do they hold heat, and how evenly does the heat distribute across the cooking surfaces?

Handle insulation. How hot do the handles get? If they aren't insulated, be sure to use towels or a potholder when transferring the contents to another container.

Cover fit. How snugly do the covers fit? Do they seal in juices?

Price. How affordable are they?

Generally speaking, here's how you identify good cookware:

Thick, solid, and sits perfectly flat on the stove.

Conducts and holds heat well and responds quickly to changes in temperature.

Sturdy, heatproof, and secure handles.

Lids that are comfortable in your hand.

These high-quality pans usually have an aluminum or copper base and a stainless steel lining. Many chefs prefer copper because it heats and cools quicker.

When it comes to brands, I'm partial to All-Clad.

Here are the four types of cooking pots you should invest in.

SKILLET

Every kitchen needs a good skillet. It's perfect for pan-searing and pan-roasting meats, as well as reducing sauces.

A traditional skillet (i.e. not non-stick) is particularly good at searing and making pan sauces, thanks to the brown, crusty bits that food elements leave behind on its plain surface.

You'll also want a non-stick skillet for cooking delicate items that tend to fall to pieces like stir-fries, pancakes, fish, and egg dishes.

My favorite non-stick is a good, pre-seasoned cast-iron piece, like those offered by Le Creuset (expensive) or Lodge (not).

You might think that cast-iron is clunky junk, but there's a reason why every restaurant and professional chef worth a lick uses iron cookware. Several reasons, actually:

Cast-iron is rugged, to the point of being virtually indestructible.

It's non-stick without the toxic chemicals found in standard non-stick cookware, which release into the food and air when heated.

It heats up evenly and retains its temperature well.

It can be moved from stove to oven for recipes that require both.

Cast-iron pieces are great for stewing, sautéing, and roasting because the entire surface heats up evenly, including the sides.

They're also ideal for searing meat or fish and finishing it in the oven.

SAUCEPAN

Saucepans are the perfect size and shape for all kinds of kitchen tasks.

They don't take up much space and are good for making rice, sauces, vegetables, gravies, creams, puddings, and many other foods.

I recommend that you buy two sizes: a 2-quart, which is good for cooking foods that stick easily, and a 3- to 4-quart for sauces and vegetables.

STOCKPOT

This is the pot you turn to for your bigger jobs like steaming lobsters, cooking large batches of pasta and bushels of corn, and creating homemade sauces and stocks.

Something to keep in mind with stockpots is that heavier pots perform better. They hold heat better and are less likely to stick and scorch.

In terms of size, I think 12 quarts is best. It's the "smallest" big pot that you can use for pretty much all stockpot needs while still being small enough to store with your other cookware.

BAKING PAN

Trimming your baking cupboard of excess items can be a challenge because different types of baking require different types of pans.

(You can't bake a cake in a muffin tin!)

That said, you can whittle down your collection by avoiding items you will hardly use and purchasing items that can serve double duty.

I keep my baking cupboard stocked with the following basics:

- A 9"x13" baking pan. This can be either glass, ceramic, or metal and you'll be able to use it for sweet treats like cakes and bars, as well as savory casseroles, pasta dishes, and meats.
- A square baking pan. Go with either 8"x 8" or 9"x 9".
- Sheet pans. Buy two and invest in commercial-quality aluminum or steel. Non-stick pans deteriorate faster, and dark coated pans will cook baked goods too quickly.

You can also pick up the following if you plan on making the foods they were designed for:

- A muffin pan. If you don't bake muffins or cupcakes often, choose paper soufflé cups instead to reduce storage requirements.
- A pie pan. I recommend a glass or ceramic pan with a 9" or 10" diameter. Extra-deep pie dishes will accommodate more filling, if desired.
- A round cake pan. Again, either 9" or 10" will work. If you bake layer cakes regularly, invest in a set of cake pans.
- A 9" x 5" loaf pan. Look for a heavy-duty pan that can stand up to the wear of cakes, breads, meatloaf, and more.

You may have noticed that I don't recommend silicone baking pans, which are a fairly popular non-stick option.

The problem is that they're poor conductors of heat (which is why baked goods rarely brown in them) and are prone to scratches. Stick with metal, glass, or ceramic baking pans for the best results.

MISCELLANEOUS

Now that we have the essentials out of the way, let's look at some additional equipment that you might find worthwhile if it fits your lifestyle and budget.

DIGITAL SCALE

A food scale not only allows you to be precise in your cooking, it also helps you avoid one of the most common diet mistakes that people make —underestimating how much you're actually eating.

As I mentioned earlier, if you're eyeballing foods and portions, you can count on eating more calories than you estimate.

A food scale makes it easy to follow recipes exactly and stick to your macronutritional and calorie targets. I like a digital scale because you can weigh everything in the same bowl, zeroing out after each ingredient is added.

MEASURING CUPS AND SPOONS

Opt for metal or glass. Plastic warps over time, making the measuring cups less precise.

FOOD PROCESSOR

Anything that needs to be chopped, mixed, or shredded can be prepared in a food processor.

You can turn sirloin into ground meat, oats into flour, cream into butter, almonds into nut butter, and frozen bananas into delicious copycat ice cream. You can even use a food processor to make pasta and pastry dough.

VEGETABLE PEELER
Go with a swivel type. It makes peeling so much easier.

MEAT THERMOMETER
Under- or over-cooked meat is enough to ruin an entire dish.

This is why I highly recommend you use a meat thermometer. It's the easiest and most reliable way to make sure your meats always come out right.

In choosing a meat thermometer, you've got two primary options:

- Instant-read digital meat thermometers. Insert this type of thermometer into your meat, and within 20 to 30 seconds, you'll get a digital readout of its temperature. Analog alternatives also exist that feature a needle moving up and down a temperature scale, but they are less precise.
- Leave-in meat thermometers. Both digital and analog varieties of this type of thermometer exist. They are oven safe and designed to remain in your food throughout the cooking process. There are even technologically advanced types that include features like audible alerts, programmable timers, and wireless readings that can be accessed via a smartphone.

I don't really see the need for a fancy Bluetooth thermometer, so I use a simple instant-read digital one instead.

MICROPLANE
Although "Microplane" is technically the brand name of the Microplane Company, the word "microplane" has come to refer to any long, thin rasp-like grater with a handle.

And whatever brand you purchase, you can use this kitchen implement to grate cheese, citrus, spices and more.

When purchasing a microplane, look first for a sturdy handle that's well-connected to the plane itself. If you'll grate primarily spices, look for one with small teeth; if cheeses are more your style, look for a larger variety. If you'll be grating several different foods, a box-style microplane with multiple faces will probably best suit your needs.

SLOW COOKER
The humble slow cooker is many a chef's best friend because nothing is easier than mixing up a smorgasbord of ingredients in the morning and returning home to delicious dinner.

Not all slow cookers are made equal, though. Here's what you need to know:

Crockpot size
Slow cooker capacity is measured in quarts and models range from roughly 2 to 8. Choose based on how much food you plan on making. While a 2 to 3 quart model works well for 1 to 2 servings, you'll need 4 to 6 quarts to make 3 to 5 servings and 6 to 8 (or more) quarts to prepare 5+ servings.

Temperature controls
Manual models have a simple dial for setting the cooking temperature (usually low, high, and warm) and little else. Digital models, on the other hand, often allow you to set exact cooking temperatures and program cook times and even cook times at different temperatures.

Removable crock
A slow cooker with a removable crock is much easier to clean and serve than a single-piece unit.

Breakfast

"BLT" EGGS BENEDICT 68

CRISPY POLENTA SQUARES
WITH WARM BLUEBERRY SAUCE 69

SALMON AND ASPARAGUS
OMELET 70

AVOCADO AND EGG
BREAKFAST SANDWICHES 73

EGGS AND TOMATO
BREAKFAST MELTS 74

IRRESISTIBLE
HAM AND CHEESE BAKE 75

HUEVOS RANCHEROS 76

SPICED CARIBBEAN OATMEAL
WITH YOGURT SWIRL 78

HIGH PROTEIN BANANA OATCAKES 79

CREAMY BLUEBERRY-BANANA
SMOOTHIE 80

CINNAMON-SPICED
SWEET POTATO PANCAKES 83

COCONUT AND MACADEMIA
FRENCH TOAST 84

ALMOND BUTTER
BANANA SMOOTHIE 85

Breakfast is a controversial meal these days.

Some "experts" say breakfast is vital for preserving health and preventing weight gain, while others claim skipping it entirely is the trick to staying lean and healthy.

Scientific research cuts both ways as well.

For example, one study conducted by scientists from Harvard School of Public Health found that men who regularly skipped breakfast had a 27% higher risk of heart attack or death from heart disease.[1] Another found that skipping breakfast was associated with a higher risk of weight gain.[2]

On the other hand, a study conducted by scientists at the University of Alabama involved an extensive review of the literature and concluded that missing breakfast has either little or no effect on weight gain.[3] In fact, the data showed that breakfast eaters tend to consume more calories than those who skip it.

What's the deal, then? Does skipping breakfast make it easier or harder to lose weight? Does it have no effect whatsoever?

And then there's the context of bodybuilding, which gives rise to new concerns related to body composition.

When we enter this realm, we hear talk of "starvation mode," muscle loss, and metabolic damage, but how reasonable are such fears? Does skipping breakfast really impair muscle growth and metabolic health?

Well, let's find out.

THE TRUTH ABOUT SKIPPING BREAKFAST AND WEIGHT LOSS

Let's start this section with a review of the Harvard studies cited above.

The first thing that jumps out is the major difference between the people that did and didn't eat breakfast is that non-breakfast eaters were generally hungrier later in the day and ate more at night.

Eating food at night isn't a problem per se, but research shows that meal skipping can lead to overeating and an increase in total overall energy intake.[4] That is, some people that skip meals tend to eat more calories than non-skippers.

Overeating, in turn, leads to fat gain, and overweight people are at an increased risk of heart disease. Thus, there can be an association between skipping breakfast and an increased incidence of cardiac events and heart disease, but that doesn't mean there's a causal relationship.

The lead author of the study, Leah Cahill, summarized this simply:

"Skipping breakfast may lead to one or more risk factors, including obesity, high blood pressure, high cholesterol, and diabetes, which may in turn lead to a heart attack over time."[5]

With that in mind, let's now look at the University of Alabama study.

What researchers found is that only a handful of rigorous, well-executed studies have tested the effects of eating and not eating breakfast.

Moreover, you have to go all the way back to 1992 to find the only long-term, carefully controlled trial that randomly assigned people to eat or skip breakfast routinely and then measured the effect on their body weight.

The 1992 study was carried out by scientists at Vanderbilt University and showed that eating or skipping breakfast had no significant effect on weight loss.[6] What mattered weren't breakfast habits but overall eating habits and diet compliance, which merely confirms what metabolic researchers have been saying for decades.

We can find an abundance of support for these findings in the research available on the intermittent fasting style of dieting.

In case you're not familiar with it, intermittent fasting is a style of dieting that has you eat and not eat on a regular schedule, with particular emphasis placed on not eating, or fasting.

You see, with a normal type of diet, you eat food every few hours from, let's say, 8 AM until 9 PM. That is, every day you eat food intermittently for approximately 13 hours and eat nothing for about 11 hours.

With intermittent fasting, you flip this equation on its head.

You eat food intermittently for, let's say, ~8 hours and eat nothing for ~16 hours. For example, you might start eating at 1 PM, stop at 9 PM, and not eat again until 1 PM the next day.

Now, as you can imagine, many intermittent fasting protocols involve skipping breakfast. And research shows they are just as workable and healthy as traditional forms of dieting.[7]

But what about claims that skipping breakfast can cause your metabolism to slow down?

Nonsense.

In a well-designed trial published in 2014, scientists from the University of Bath found that in healthy adults with normal body fat percentages, eating or skipping breakfast had no effect on resting metabolic rate.[8]

In fact, one study found that metabolic rate didn't decline until 60 hours without food, and the reduction was a mere 8%.[9] Contrary to popular myth, research shows that the metabolism actually speeds up after 36 to 48 hours of not eating.[10]

So, the bottom line is this: if you enjoy breakfast, you should eat it; if you enjoy skipping it, you should skip it.

Many people I've worked with like eating breakfast because they enjoy breakfast food. Others find that a hearty breakfast helps curb their hunger throughout the day, which in turn helps prevent overeating. Still others may find it energizing.

On the other hand, many others prefer to skip breakfast because they just don't like standard morning fare or they prefer fasting until lunch. Some like to "save" those calories and eat a larger lunch, dinner, or both.

Both groups do equally well in the end.

CAN SKIPPING BREAKFAST WORK FOR BODYBUILDING, TOO?

Many bodybuilders, and people in general looking to build muscle and strength, are afraid that skipping breakfast will slow down their progress. This fear is rooted in the simple belief that going for too long without food causes muscle loss.

Well, there's truth here. If you go too long without food, your body will break down muscle tissue for energy.[11]

That said, what many people don't know is just how long you have to go without food for that to occur.

Well, one study found that amino acids obtained from the breakdown of muscle tissue were responsible for about 50% of glucose maintenance at the 16-hour mark of fasting and 100% at the 28-hour mark.[12]

This is why many intermittent fasting protocols designed for athletes and bodybuilders don't have you going for more than 16 hours without food.

Furthermore, this is why well-designed protocols also recommend that your last meal before the fast be high in a slow-burning form of protein like casein or egg.

The purpose of this is to provide the body with a large infusion of amino acids so it doesn't have to break down muscle tissue. Instead, it can use the amino acids provided by the protein, which will remain available for several hours after eating it.

Here's what it boils down to:

Many methods of intermittent fasting involve skipping breakfast, and research shows bodybuilders can do just as well on these diets as traditional ones that include breakfast.[13]

Again, it simply boils down to personal eating preferences.

THE BOTTOM LINE

There's a lot of truth in the old saying that the best diet and training programs are the ones you're going to stick to.

No matter how perfectly designed a diet or workout routine is, if it doesn't fit your lifestyle, you're better off finding an alternative that does.

For example, planning and tracking calorie intake is the most effective and reliable way to lose fat, but some people really chafe at it for one reason or another.

These people shouldn't completely ignore the realities of energy balance but should focus instead on establishing good eating habits that are conducive to weight loss.

The same goes for eating or skipping breakfast.

If skipping breakfast helps you better stick to your diet, you should do it. If it doesn't, don't.

So long as your diet is set up properly as a whole, you can't go wrong either way.

"BLT" EGGS BENEDICT

SERVES **1** | PREP TIME **15 MINUTES** | COOKING TIME **15 MINUTES**
575 CALORIES | **33** GRAMS PROTEIN | **62** GRAMS CARBOHYDRATES | **24** GRAMS FAT

YOU'VE PROBABLY heard that eggs raise "bad cholesterol" levels or otherwise increase the risk of heart disease, but more recent research has completely debunked these long-standing claims.[14]

EGGS are one of the cheapest ways to incorporate protein into your diet, along with being both healthy and delicious.

HOLLANDAISE-MUSTARD SAUCE

1 *tablespoon light mayonnaise*
½ *tablespoon water*
1 *teaspoon whole-grain mustard*
½ *teaspoon lemon juice*
   Pinch of ground cayenne pepper

EGGS BENEDICT

1 *tablespoon white vinegar*
½ *tablespoon extra-virgin olive oil*
1 *ounce Canadian bacon, diced*
½ *small onion, thinly sliced*
4 *cups chopped kale (stems removed)*
   Ground black pepper, to taste
1 *whole-grain English muffin, split*
2 *tomato slices*
2 *large eggs*

1 To make the sauce, into a blender or food processor, add mayonnaise, water, mustard, lemon juice, and cayenne. Process until smooth. Transfer the sauce to a small bowl and reserve.

2 To prepare eggs, add about 3 inches of water into a large skillet. Pour in vinegar and bring to a low simmer over medium heat.

3 Meanwhile, warm oil in medium nonstick skillet over medium-high heat. Sauté the Canadian bacon and onion, stirring constantly, until golden brown, about 4 minutes. Remove the pan from heat and toss in kale. Stir until the greens wilt, about 2 minutes, and season with pepper.

4 Toast English muffin halves until lightly golden. Place onto a plate, layering a tomato slice and kale mixture onto each half. Place the pan in the oven to stay warm (keep the oven turned off).

5 Crack eggs into a mug one by one and slip them into the simmering water. Cook approximately 3 to 5 minutes, carefully removing the eggs with a slotted spoon once they reach desired doneness. Top poached eggs onto the prepared English muffins and drizzle with Hollandaise-style sauce. Serve.

CRISPY POLENTA SQUARES WITH WARM BLUEBERRY SAUCE

SERVES **4** | PREP TIME **15 MINUTES**, PLUS **45 MINUTES** FOR POLENTA TO SET | COOKING TIME **20 MINUTES**

467 CALORIES | **27** GRAMS PROTEIN | **72** GRAMS CARBOHYDRATES | **8** GRAMS FAT

3   *cups water*

3   *cups 2% milk*

2   *teaspoons salt*

1¾ *cups yellow cornmeal*

3   *scoops vanilla protein powder*

2   *cups fresh or frozen blueberries*

1   *tablespoon honey*

2   *teaspoons extra-virgin olive oil*

1   *banana, peeled and sliced*

1 In a large, heavy-duty pot over medium-high heat, bring water and milk to a boil. Add salt and gradually whisk in cornmeal.

2 Reduce the heat to low and cook until the mixture thickens and cornmeal is tender, stirring often, about 10 to 15 minutes. Remove from the heat. Add the protein powder and stir until no lumps are visible. Pour the polenta into an 8-inch by 8-inch casserole dish and place in the fridge to set, about 30 to 45 minutes. After the mixture solidifies, cut it into 2-inch by 2-inch squares.

3 To prepare blueberry sauce, add blueberries and honey into a blender. Process until smooth, about 1 minute.

4 Warm oil in a large skillet over medium-high heat. Working in batches, brown polenta squares, cooking about 2 minutes per side. Transfer polenta squares to a dish.

5 Add blueberry sauce to the skillet. Stirring constantly, let the blueberry sauce warm over medium-high heat. Pour hot blueberry sauce over polenta and top with banana slices.

SALMON AND ASPARAGUS OMELET

SERVES **1** | PREP TIME **10 MINUTES** | COOKING TIME **10 MINUTES**

560 CALORIES | **64** GRAMS PROTEIN | **13** GRAMS CARBOHYDRATES | **28** GRAMS FAT

2 teaspoons extra-virgin olive oil

½ small onion, diced

2 asparagus spears,
cut into 1-inch pieces

1 (6-ounce) wild Pacific salmon fillet,
cut into 1-inch cubes

1 clove garlic, minced

3 pitted Kalamata olives, sliced

1 teaspoon capers

1 Roma tomato, diced

Salt and ground black pepper,
to taste

2 whole eggs, lightly beaten

4 egg whites, lightly beaten,
or ¾ cup liquid egg white
substitute

1 Add oil to a medium nonstick skillet and warm over medium-high heat. Add onion and asparagus, sautéing for 2 to 3 minutes. Stir in salmon pieces, lightly browning salmon pieces on all sides. Add garlic, olives, capers, and tomato; cook for another minute.

2 Add salt, pepper, whole eggs, and egg whites into the pan. Continually stir for about 1 minute, keeping the edges of the omelet from browning. Using a spatula, carefully flip omelet and cook for about 30 seconds. Serve immediately.

AVOCADO AND EGG BREAKFAST SANDWICHES

SERVES **4** | PREP TIME **15 MINUTES** | COOKING TIME **15 MINUTES**

289 CALORIES | **16** GRAMS PROTEIN | **29** GRAMS CARBOHYDRATES | **13** GRAMS FAT

AVOCADOS MAY HELP YOU LOSE WEIGHT. Not only are avocados a source of healthy fats, they're packed with fiber too. This is why one study found participants who ate avocado with their lunch felt "23% more satisfied and had a 28% lower desire to eat over the next 5 hours," compared to participants whose lunch didn't contain avocado.[15]

AVOCADOS CONTAIN MORE POTASSIUM THAN BANANAS. Inadequate potassium intake is extremely common and associated with high blood pressure, heart attacks, strokes, and kidney failure.[16] Just half of an avocado (about 100 grams) contains 14% of the daily recommended intake of potassium, compared to the 10% found in a medium-sized banana.

AVOCADOS CAN REDUCE THE RISK OF HEART DISEASE. Research shows that eating avocados can significantly improve your cholesterol profile, thereby reducing your risk of heart disease.[17]

---

8 *egg whites*
or 1½ cups liquid egg white substitute

Salt and ground black pepper, to taste

Ground cayenne pepper, to taste

1 *tablespoon extra-virgin olive oil*

¼ *cup diced red bell pepper*

¼ *cup chopped scallions*

¼ *cup seeded and diced tomatoes*

8 *slices whole-grain bread, toasted*

1 *medium avocado, peeled, pitted, and sliced*

1 In a medium bowl, add egg whites and use a fork or whisk to beat together. Stir in the salt, pepper, and cayenne.

2 Add the olive oil to a small nonstick skillet and warm over medium-high heat. Add 1 tablespoon each of bell peppers, scallions, and tomatoes. Stirring constantly, sauté for 1 minute; mix in ¼ of the egg whites. Cover with a lid, reduce heat to low, and cook until eggs have set, about 1 to 2 minutes. Use a spatula to fold eggs over themselves (in half) and then fold in half again. Remove eggs from pan and reserve. Repeat process 3 more times until all the egg whites and vegetables have been used.

3 Lay eggs onto 4 pieces of toasted bread and layer avocado slices on top. Close with top half of bread, cut each sandwich in half, and serve.

EGGS AND TOMATO BREAKFAST MELTS

SERVES **1** | PREP TIME **15 MINUTES** | COOKING TIME **10 MINUTES**
335 CALORIES | **27** GRAMS PROTEIN | **31** GRAMS CARBOHYDRATES | **13** GRAMS FAT

1 whole-grain English muffin, split

½ teaspoon extra-virgin olive oil

2 scallions, finely chopped and divided

4 egg whites, whisked, or ¾ cup liquid egg white substitute

Salt and ground black pepper, to taste

¼ cup halved cherry tomatoes

¼ cup shredded Mexican cheese blend

1 Preheat the broiler.

2 Add English muffin halves into a toaster and toast until golden brown. Place onto a baking sheet.

3 Warm oil in a small nonstick skillet over medium heat. Add half the scallions and sauté for about 2 to 3 minutes. Add egg whites into the pan, along with salt and pepper. Stir with a spatula until eggs are fully cooked; remove from heat.

4 Layer the muffin halves with scrambled egg whites, tomatoes, and cheese. Broil until cheese melts, about 1 to 1½ minutes. Use a spatula to transfer breakfast melts to a plate, garnish with remaining scallions, and serve.

IRRESISTIBLE HAM AND CHEESE BAKE

SERVES **6** | PREP TIME **20 MINUTES** | COOKING TIME **35 MINUTES**, PLUS **10 MINUTES** TO COOL

273 CALORIES | **26** GRAMS PROTEIN | **6** GRAMS CARBOHYDRATES | **17** GRAMS FAT

2 *cups shredded low-fat sharp cheddar cheese, divided*

1 *tablespoon extra-virgin olive oil*

2 *scallions, sliced*

1 *cup sliced shiitake mushrooms*

½ *cup chopped red bell pepper*

¾ *cup seeded and diced tomatoes*

1 *cup finely diced lean ham steak*

1 *cup finely chopped broccoli florets*

7 *large whole eggs*

5 *egg whites*
 or 1 cup liquid egg white substitute

¼ *cup 2% milk*

 Salt and ground black pepper, to taste

1 Preheat the oven to 375°F. Coat an 8-inch by 8-inch casserole dish with cooking spray, and layer 1 cup cheese on the bottom of the dish.

2 In a large skillet, warm oil over medium heat. Sauté scallions, mushrooms, and red pepper until tender, about 5 to 6 minutes. Add tomatoes and cook 2 to 3 minutes before stirring in ham and broccoli. Remove from heat. Using a spatula, spread mixture evenly in the baking dish over the cheese.

3 In a large bowl, whisk together whole eggs, egg whites, milk, salt, and pepper. Slowly pour over vegetable mixture in the baking dish and top with the remaining 1 cup cheese.

4 Bake until eggs are set and a knife inserted near the center comes out clean, about 30 to 35 minutes. Let the casserole cool for 8 to 10 minutes before cutting and serving.

HUEVOS RANCHEROS

SERVES **1** | PREP TIME **15 MINUTES** | COOKING TIME **10 MINUTES**
438 CALORIES | **24** GRAMS PROTEIN | **26** GRAMS CARBOHYDRATES | **26** GRAMS FAT

2 teaspoons extra-virgin olive oil, divided

½ small onion, finely chopped

1 tomato, diced

1 jalapeño pepper, seeded and finely chopped

Salt and ground black pepper, to taste

2 (6-inch) corn tortillas

2 large eggs

1 ounce queso fresco (fresh Mexican cheese), crumbled

2 tablespoons chopped fresh cilantro

1 In a small nonstick skillet, warm 1 teaspoon oil over medium-high heat and add onion. Cook for 1 minute and then stir in tomato, jalapeño, salt, and pepper. Sauté a few more minutes until most of the tomato's liquid has evaporated. Remove from heat and reserve.

2 Using a separate small nonstick skillet, warm tortillas over high heat until crispy, about 1 minute each. Transfer tortillas to 2 plates.

3 Next, make the sunny-side-up eggs. Warm remaining 1 teaspoon oil in the skillet over medium-high heat. Gently crack eggs into the pan and season with salt and pepper. Cover with a lid and cook for 3 to 4 minutes until whites are set.

4 Top each tortilla with an egg. Spoon reserved tomato mixture over each egg. Garnish with cheese and a sprinkle of cilantro before serving.

SPICED CARIBBEAN OATMEAL WITH YOGURT SWIRL

SERVES **4** | PREP TIME **10 MINUTES** | COOKING TIME **5 MINUTES**
292 CALORIES | **17** GRAMS PROTEIN | **31** GRAMS CARBOHYDRATES | **12** GRAMS FAT

OATMEAL IS A GREAT SOURCE OF SOLUBLE FIBER. Soluble fiber is a non-digestible carbohydrate that grows in plants. When eaten, it reaches the colon intact and is then fermented, promoting the growth and activity of "good" gut bacteria or probiotics. Research shows that starting the day with oatmeal can help prevent overeating thanks to this super-filling soluble fiber.[18]

OATMEAL CAN DECREASE THE RISK OF HIGH BLOOD PRESSURE. All of that fiber isn't just great for your waistline, it's heart-healthy as well. Soluble fiber has been shown to decrease low-density lipoprotein (LDL) cholesterol—the "bad" kind—by 5% to 10%, thereby reducing the risk of high blood pressure and cardiovascular disease.[19]

OATMEAL MAY REDUCE THE RISK OF TYPE 2 DIABETES. Research shows that eating oatmeal can improve insulin sensitivity. One study found that feeding oatmeal to patients with type 2 diabetes resulted in a whopping 40% reduction in insulin dosage.[20]

---

3 cups 2% milk

1 cup quick-cooking oats

1 tablespoon brown sugar, unpacked

½ teaspoon ground cinnamon

    Pinch of ground nutmeg

¼ cup chopped pistachios

    Pinch of salt

1 (6-ounce) container 2% Greek yogurt

1 Combine milk, oats, sugar, cinnamon, nutmeg, pistachios, and salt in a medium pot and warm over medium-high heat. Bring mixture to a boil, stirring constantly until oatmeal is cooked, about 2 minutes.

2 Remove from heat and swirl in the yogurt. Serve.

HIGH PROTEIN BANANA OATCAKES

SERVES **2 (2 OATCAKES PER SERVING)** | PREP TIME **5 MINUTES** | COOKING TIME **10 MINUTES**

357 CALORIES | **30** GRAMS PROTEIN | **47** GRAMS CARBOHYDRATES | **6** GRAMS FAT

1 cup old-fashioned oats

6 egg whites or 1 cup plus
 2 tablespoons liquid egg white
 substitute

1 ripe banana, peeled and sliced

1 cup 2% cottage cheese

½ teaspoon ground cinnamon

1 tablespoon granulated sugar

1 In a medium bowl, add oats, egg whites, banana, cottage cheese, cinnamon, and sugar. Mix with a spatula until the batter is smooth.

2 Coat a medium pan with cooking spray and warm over medium heat. Spoon about one quarter of the batter into the pan, cooking until golden brown, about 1 to 2 minutes. Flip the oatcake with a spatula and cook another 30 to 60 seconds. When done, it will be golden brown and firm. Transfer to a plate and reserve.

3 Reapply cooking spray and repeat with remaining batter until all 4 oatcakes are cooked. Serve.

CREAMY BLUEBERRY-BANANA SMOOTHIE

SERVES **2** | PREP TIME **10 MINUTES**

228 CALORIES | **12** GRAMS PROTEIN | **31** GRAMS CARBOHYDRATES | **7** GRAMS FAT

GREEK YOGURT IS ALL THE RAGE these days for a few good reasons: it has twice the protein of regular, non-strained yogurt, it's creamy and delicious, and it comes in 0%, 2%, and full-fat varieties (2% is my favorite).

AS A SNACK, IT'LL HELP YOU STAY FULL LONGER, and if you have some at night, it can help with muscle recovery while you're resting due to the casein content.[21]

TO PACK THIS SMOOTHIE WITH EVEN MORE PROTEIN, just add a scoop of a favorite vanilla protein powder.

---

1 banana, preferably frozen, peeled and sliced

½ cup frozen blueberries

1 teaspoon honey

½ cup 2% Greek yogurt

1 tablespoon whole flaxseed

1 cup 2% milk

1 Into a blender, add banana, blueberries, honey, yogurt, flaxseed, and milk. Process until smooth, about 1 minute. Pour into 2 glasses and serve

CINNAMON-SPICED SWEET POTATO PANCAKES

SERVES **1 (2 PANCAKES PER SERVING)** | PREP TIME **10 MINUTES** | COOKING TIME **5 MINUTES**
506 CALORIES | **39** GRAMS PROTEIN | **63** GRAMS CARBOHYDRATES | **11** GRAMS FAT

SWEET POTATOES ARE ONE OF THE WORLD'S BEST SOURCES OF VITAMIN A. One large sweet potato contains more than 100% of the recommended daily intake of vitamin A, which plays a role in bone growth and immune system health.[22]

SWEET POTATOES MAY HELP PROTECT AGAINST CANCER. In addition to vitamin A's anti-cancer properties, several studies suggest the beta-carotene found in sweet potatoes may decrease the risk of breast and ovarian cancer in women.[23]

1 medium (5-ounce) sweet potato
½ cup old-fashioned oats
1 large egg
4 egg whites or ¾ cup liquid egg white substitute
½ teaspoon vanilla extract
½ teaspoon ground cinnamon
¼ cup 2% plain yogurt

1 Prick sweet potato several times with a fork. Wrap potato in a wet paper towel and microwave for 5 minutes on high power. Carefully run potato under cool water and then remove its skin with a knife.

2 Add oats into a blender or a food processor and process until oats are powder-like. Transfer to a medium bowl and reserve.

3 Add the sweet potato into the blender or food processor, puréeing until smooth. Place into the bowl with oats. Stir in whole egg, egg whites, vanilla, cinnamon, and yogurt. Mix well until the batter is smooth.

4 Coat a medium nonstick pan with cooking spray and warm over medium-low heat.

5 Spoon half the batter into the pan and cook until golden brown, about 1 to 2 minutes. Use a spatula to flip the pancake and cook again until golden brown and firm, about another 30 to 60 seconds. Transfer the pancake to a plate.

6 Reapply cooking spray to the pan and repeat with remaining batter. Serve.

COCONUT AND MACADEMIA FRENCH TOAST

SERVES 2 (2 PIECES PER SERVING) | PREP TIME **5 MINUTES** | COOKING TIME **10 TMINUTES**
510 CALORIES | **43** GRAMS PROTEIN | **46** GRAMS CARBOHYDRATES | **18** GRAMS FAT

FRENCH TOAST

- ½ cup 2% milk
- 2 large eggs
- 2 egg whites or 6 tablespoons liquid egg white substitute
- 2 scoops vanilla protein powder
- ½ teaspoon ground cinnamon
- 4 slices whole-grain bread

TOPPING

- 1 banana, peeled and sliced
- 2 tablespoons chopped macadamia nuts
- 2 tablespoons unsweetened coconut flakes

1 In a shallow dish, add milk, eggs, and egg whites, whisking together with a fork. Add protein powder and cinnamon, whisking again until completely mixed.

2 Soak a slice of bread in the mixture until soggy—letting it sit at least 30 seconds or so is ideal.

3 Coat a medium nonstick pan with cooking spray and warm on medium-high heat. Add 1 or 2 bread slices into the pan (no crowding the pan!) and cook until golden brown, about 2 minutes. Use a spatula to flip the slices, cooking again until firm, another 1 to 2 minutes. Transfer to a plate and repeat with remaining bread.

4 Meanwhile, in a small bowl, mix banana, nuts, and coconut flakes. Garnish each French toast piece with the topping. Serve.

ALMOND BUTTER-BANANA SMOOTHIE

SERVES **1** | PREP TIME **5 MINUTES**

505 CALORIES | **33** GRAMS PROTEIN | **46** GRAMS CARBOHYDRATES | **25** GRAMS FAT

ALMONDS ARE PACKED WITH MACRO- AND MICRONUTRIENTS. According to the USDA's National Nutrient Database, a single ounce of almonds contains 3.5 grams of fiber, 6 grams of protein, and 14 grams of fat, including 9 grams of healthy monounsaturated fat. It also satisfies 37% of your daily vitamin E requirement, 32% of your daily manganese needs, as well as 20% of your magnesium, copper, vitamin B2 (as riboflavin), and phosphorus RDA needs.[24]

ALMONDS MAY HELP CONTROL CHOLESTEROL LEVELS. A 4-month study of pre-diabetic patients found that subjects who got 20% of their daily calories from almonds lowered their LDL ("bad") cholesterol by an average of about 10%.[25]

ALMONDS KEEP YOU FULLER, LONGER. Research published in the European Journal of Clinical Nutrition found that feeding 137 participants a 1.5-ounce snack of almonds every day over a 4-week period significantly reduced their perceived levels of hunger and their interest in eating.[26]

---

1 *banana, preferably frozen, peeled and sliced*

2 *tablespoons almond butter*

1 *cup unsweetened almond milk*

1 *teaspoon honey*

1 *tablespoon ground or whole flaxseed*

1 *scoop vanilla protein powder*

1 In a blender, add banana, almond butter, almond milk, honey, flaxseed, and protein powder. Process until smooth, about 1 minute. Pour into a glass and serve.

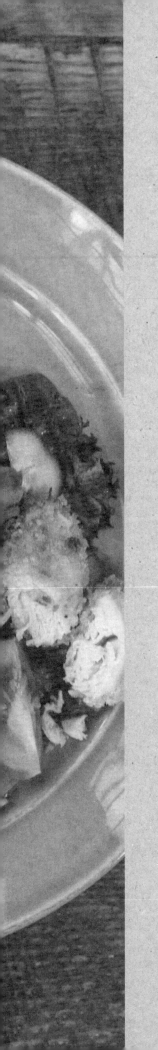

=Salads=

CLASSIC COBB SALAD

SERVES **2** | PREP TIME **20 MINUTES**

446 CALORIES | **40** GRAMS PROTEIN | **23** GRAMS CARBOHYDRATES | **23** GRAMS FAT

1 *small head iceberg lettuce, cored and chopped*

8 *ounces boneless, skinless chicken breast, cooked and cut into ¼-inch cubes*

2 *hard-boiled eggs, peeled, and chopped*

2 *tomatoes, chopped*

1 *avocado, peeled, pitted, and sliced*

1 *cup grated carrots*

¼ *cup shredded low-fat mild cheddar cheese*

Salad dressing, like Red Wine Vinaigrette or Cucumber Ranch Dressing

1 Combine everything in a large bowl and toss. Divide into separate bowls and serve with a dressing of your choice.

COCONUT-CRUSTED CHICKEN SALAD

SERVES **2** | PREP TIME **15 MINUTES** | COOKING TIME **30 MINUTES**
454 CALORIES | **31** GRAMS PROTEIN | **36** GRAMS CARBOHYDRATES | **21** GRAMS FAT

POPULATIONS THAT CONSUME LARGE AMOUNTS OF COCONUT ARE SOME OF THE HEALTHIEST IN THE WORLD. The Tokelauans are a community living in the South Pacific that consumes nearly 60% of their calories from coconuts, and research shows they're in excellent health and show virtually no evidence of heart disease.[1]

COCONUT CAN HELP YOU CONTROL YOUR HUNGER. Obesity tends to be higher among high-fat dieters than those that eat low-fat diets, mainly due to the caloric density of the foods consumed.[2] Evidence suggests, however, that a type of fat found in coconut called a medium-chain triglyceride (MCT) can help curb hunger.[3]

COCONUT CAN IMPROVE YOUR CHOLESTEROL PROFILE. A study conducted by researchers at the Federal University of Alagoas in Brazil found that supplementation with coconut oil for 12 weeks improved the ratio of LDL ("bad") to HDL ("good)" cholesterol levels.[4]

VINAIGRETTE

- 1 tablespoon extra-virgin olive oil
- 1 tablespoon honey
- 1 tablespoon white vinegar
- 2 teaspoons Dijon mustard

CHICKEN SALAD

- 6 tablespoons shredded unsweetened coconut
- ¼ cup panko breadcrumbs
- 2 tablespoons crushed cornflakes
- Salt and ground black pepper, to taste
- 3 egg whites, lightly beaten, or ½ cup liquid egg white substitute
- 1 (6-ounce) boneless, skinless chicken breast, trimmed of fat
- 6 cups mixed baby greens
- ¾ cup shredded carrots
- 1 cucumber, sliced
- 1 tomato, sliced

1 Preheat the oven to 375°F. Line a baking sheet with parchment paper.

2 In a small bowl, whisk together oil, honey, vinegar, and mustard. Reserve.

3 In a small, shallow dish, mix coconut, panko, cornflakes, salt, and pepper. In another bowl large enough to fit the chicken, add egg whites and lightly beat them with a fork.

4 Season chicken with salt and pepper. Dip chicken in egg whites followed by the coconut-panko mixture, using your fingers to press coconut mixture onto the chicken if needed. Place chicken onto the prepared baking sheet, lightly coat with cooking spray, and bake for 15 minutes. Flip chicken and bake until cooked through, about 10 to 15 more minutes.

5 To serve, add 3 cups baby greens to each plate. Top with carrots, cucumber, and tomato. Slice chicken diagonally and divide evenly between each salad. Drizzle with dressing.

SPICY SANTA FE TACO SALAD

SERVES **4** | PREP TIME **25 MINUTES** | COOKING TIME **20 MINUTES**

347 CALORIES | **22** GRAMS PROTEIN | **28** GRAMS CARBOHYDRATES | **18** GRAMS FAT

TOPPING

½   *pound 93% lean ground turkey*

½   *cup canned black beans, rinsed and drained*

1   *tablespoon minced jalapeño pepper*

2   *beefsteak tomatoes, chopped*

1   *clove garlic, peeled and minced*

3   *tablespoons chopped scallions*

2   *tablespoons chopped fresh cilantro, plus more for garnish*

¾   *cup frozen corn kernels*

    Salt and ground black pepper, to taste

1¼   *teaspoons ground sweet paprika*

AVOCADO DIP

¼   *cup 2% Greek yogurt*

¼   *cup water*

1   *medium avocado, peeled, pitted, and chopped, divided*

1½   *tablespoons chopped fresh cilantro*

½   *teaspoon cayenne pepper*

    Salt and ground black pepper, to taste

SALAD

5   *cups shredded iceberg lettuce*

½   *cup shredded Mexican cheese blend*

1   *beefsteak tomato, chopped*

2   *tablespoons chopped fresh cilantro*

2   *tablespoons crushed tortilla chips*

1 Warm a large nonstick skillet over medium-high heat. Add ground turkey to the skillet, using a wooden spoon to break the meat into small pieces. Cook for 4 to 5 minutes, stirring frequently, until the meat is no longer pink.

2 Stir in beans, jalapeño, tomatoes, garlic, scallions, cilantro, corn, salt, pepper, and paprika. Cover, reduce heat to low, and cook for 15 minutes. Remove the lid from the skillet and simmer until the liquid reduces, about 5 more minutes.

3 Meanwhile, make the avocado dip: into a blender, add yogurt, water, half the avocado, cilantro, cayenne, salt, and pepper. Process until smooth; reserve.

4 Divide the lettuce between 4 plates. Top with turkey mixture, cheese, tomatoes, cilantro, and remaining chopped avocado. Spoon the avocado dip over the top and garnish with crushed tortilla chips.

PERFECT PROTEIN SALAD WITH BUTTERMILK DRESSING

SERVES 1 | PREP TIME 20 MINUTES

349 CALORIES | **30** GRAMS PROTEIN | **29** GRAMS CARBOHYDRATES | **15** GRAMS FAT

2 cups baby spring mix

2 scallions, chopped

1 small cucumber, halved and sliced

4 white button mushrooms, halved and sliced

¼ medium avocado, peeled and chopped

½ cup 2% cottage cheese

1 hard-boiled egg, peeled and chopped

3 tablespoons low-fat buttermilk

Juice of 1 lemon

1 clove garlic, minced

Salt and ground black pepper, to taste

1 Into a medium bowl, add spring mix, scallions, cucumber, mushrooms, avocado, cottage cheese, and egg.

2 In a small bowl, add buttermilk, lemon juice, garlic, salt, and pepper. Use a fork to combine.

3 Drizzle the dressing over the salad, toss, and serve.

TROPICAL CHICKEN SALAD WITH PINEAPPLE AND PECANS

SERVES **1** | PREP TIME **25 MINUTES**

323 CALORIES | **42** GRAMS PROTEIN | **22** GRAMS CARBOHYDRATES | **9** GRAMS FAT

1 (6-ounce) boneless, skinless chicken breast, cooked and cubed

2 tablespoons chopped celery

¼ cup chopped pineapple

¼ cup peeled orange segments

1 tablespoon chopped pecans

¼ cup halved seedless grapes

Salt and ground black pepper, to taste

2 cups torn romaine lettuce

1 In a medium bowl, add chicken, celery, pineapple, oranges, pecans, and grapes. Gently mix together with a spoon until combined and season with salt and pepper.

2 On a plate, make a bed of lettuce. Top with the chicken mixture and serve.

GRILLED MEDITERRANEAN SALAD WITH SUN-DRIED TOMATO VINAIGRETTE

SERVES **4** | PREP TIME **10 MINUTES** | COOKING TIME **15 MINUTES**

171 CALORIES | **10** GRAMS PROTEIN | **11** GRAMS CARBOHYDRATES | **9** GRAMS FAT

¼ *cup balsamic vinegar*

½ *teaspoon capers*

½ *teaspoon minced garlic*

2 *tablespoons roughly chopped dry-packed sun-dried tomatoes*

2 *red bell peppers, seeded and cut into large strips*

8 *asparagus spears*

1 *zucchini, sliced*

½ *red onion, sliced*

2 *teaspoons extra-virgin olive oil*

Salt and ground black pepper, to taste

4 *hard-boiled eggs, peeled and quartered*

2 *tablespoons roughly chopped Kalamata olives*

¼ *cup crumbled reduced-fat feta cheese*

Chopped fresh basil, to taste

1 Into the bowl of a food processor, add vinegar, capers, garlic, and sun-dried tomatoes. Process until well-combined. Reserve.

2 In a large mixing bowl, combine the red peppers, asparagus, zucchini, and red onion. Add the olive oil, salt, and pepper. Toss to combine.

3 Prepare a grill to medium-high heat. Lightly coat the grill grates with cooking spray. Once the grill is hot, grill vegetables, turning occasionally, until lightly charred.

4 In a bowl, add grilled veggies and vinaigrette, tossing to combine. Divide vegetables between 4 plates. Top with eggs, olives, feta, and basil.

SUPERGREEN SALAD

SERVES **4** | PREP TIME **10 MINUTES**

420 CALORIES | **17** GRAMS PROTEIN | **18** GRAMS CARBOHYDRATES | **33** GRAMS FAT

DARK LEAFY GREENS REDUCE THE RISK OF VARIOUS DISEASES. Research shows that vegetables like spinach, kale, romaine lettuce, leaf lettuce, mustard greens, collard greens, chicory, and Swiss chard are rich sources of various micronutrients that help reduce the risk of a wide variety of diseases, including heart disease, high blood pressure, cataracts, stroke, and cancer.[5]

DARK LEAFY GREENS ARE A GREAT SOURCE OF VITAMIN K. Vitamin K, one of the four fat-soluble vitamins, helps support healthy blood coagulation, leads to a reduction in the calcification and stiffening of arteries (which can increase the risk of cardiovascular disease), and may ultimately play a role in anti-aging treatments and cancer therapy.

DARK LEAFY GREENS HELP PRESERVE VISION AND EYE HEALTH. Kale, dandelion greens, mustard greens, and Swiss chard are great sources of lutein and zeaxanthin, two molecules that have been associated with lower rates of age-related eye degeneration.[6]

---

4 *cups chopped kale (stems removed)*

4 *cups fresh spinach leaves*

3 *tablespoons extra-virgin olive oil*

1 *tablespoon lemon juice*

Salt and ground black pepper, to taste

6 *hard-boiled eggs, peeled and quartered*

2 *medium avocados, peeled, pitted, and sliced*

½ *small red onion, sliced*

4 *tablespoons grated Parmesan cheese*

1 In a large bowl, add kale, spinach, olive oil, lemon juice, salt, and pepper. Toss to combine, coating the greens with dressing. Divide the salad between 4 plates.

2 Top each bed of greens with eggs, avocados, and red onion. Sprinkle each salad with cheese and serve immediately.

LOW-FAT TZATZIKI

SERVES **16** (2 TABLESPOONS PER SERVING) | PREP TIME **5 MINUTES**
12 CALORIES | **1** GRAM PROTEIN | **1** GRAM CARBOHYDRATES | **0** GRAMS FAT

1 *small cucumber*

¾ *cup 2% Greek yogurt*

¾ *teaspoon Worcestershire sauce*

2 *tablespoons finely chopped fresh mint*

Salt, to taste

1 Peel the cucumber, cut it lengthwise, and use a spoon to remove and discard the seeds. Into a blender or food processor, add half of the cucumber. Purée until smooth and transfer to a small bowl.

2 Add yogurt, Worcestershire sauce, mint, and salt to the cucumber purée in the bowl, and mix well. Finely chop remaining cucumber half and stir it into the tzatziki sauce. Use within 2 days.

CREAMY JALAPEÑO-CILANTRO DRESSING

SERVES **7** | PREP TIME **5 MINUTES**

38 CALORIES | **2** GRAMS PROTEIN | **3** GRAMS CARBOHYDRATES | **2** GRAMS FAT

½ cup low-fat buttermilk

¼ cup light mayonnaise

¼ cup 2% Greek yogurt

1 small jalapeño pepper, seeded

¼ cup chopped fresh cilantro

1 tomatillo, husked, rinsed, and chopped

1 clove garlic

1 scallion, sliced

Juice of ½ lime

⅛ teaspoon cumin

Salt and ground black pepper, to taste

1 Add all the ingredients into a blender. Pulse until smooth. Use immediately or refrigerate until needed.

RED WINE VINAIGRETTE

SERVES **2** | PREP TIME **5 MINUTES**

123 CALORIES | **0** GRAMS PROTEIN | **0** GRAMS CARBOHYDRATES | **14** GRAMS FAT

1 tablespoon red wine vinegar

½ teaspoon Dijon mustard

¼ teaspoon dried thyme

¼ teaspoon minced garlic

　　Pinch of ground black pepper

2 tablespoons extra-virgin olive oil

1 Into a small bowl, add all the ingredients. Using a fork, whisk ingredients together until combined.

CUCUMBER RANCH DRESSING

SERVES **7** | PREP TIME **5 MINUTES**

42 CALORIES | **2** GRAMS PROTEIN | **4** GRAMS CARBOHYDRATES | **2** GRAMS FAT

1 *small cucumber, peeled*

½ *cup low-fat buttermilk*

¼ *cup light mayonnaise*

¼ *cup 2% Greek yogurt*

3 *tablespoons fresh parsley leaves*

1 *clove garlic, peeled*

¼ *cup sliced scallions*

Juice of ½ lemon

Salt and ground black pepper, to taste

1 Slice the cucumber lengthwise. Use a spoon to remove and discard the seeds. Roughly chop the cucumber and add to the blender, along with remaining ingredients. Pulse until smooth. Use immediately or refrigerate until needed.

Sandwiches
&
Soups

COCONUT CARROT-GINGER SOUP

SERVES **4** | PREP TIME **15 MINUTES** | COOKING TIME **35 MINUTES**

170 CALORIES | **6** GRAMS PROTEIN | **21** GRAMS CARBOHYDRATES | **7** GRAMS FAT

1 *teaspoon extra-virgin olive oil*

1 *medium onion, chopped*

10 *carrots, unpeeled and sliced*

3 *cloves garlic, minced*

2 *teaspoons peeled and grated fresh ginger*

4 *cups low-sodium chicken broth*

1 *(14-ounce) can lite coconut milk*

Chopped fresh cilantro, to taste

Salt and ground black pepper, to taste

1 In a medium pot, warm olive oil over medium-high heat. Add the onion and sauté for about 3 minutes. Add carrots, garlic, and ginger; stirring frequently, cook for about 5 minutes.

2 Stir in broth and coconut milk. Bring soup to a boil over high heat; reduce heat to low and simmer until carrots until tender, about 30 minutes.

3 Remove soup from the heat and stir in cilantro. Carefully use an immersion blender to purée soup until very smooth; or, transfer the soup in batches into a blender or food processor to purée. Season with salt and pepper. Serve immediately.

ITALIAN LENTIL SOUP WITH CHICKEN

SERVES **4** | PREP TIME **20 MINUTES** | COOKING TIME **55 MINUTES**

318 CALORIES | **35** GRAMS PROTEIN | **39** GRAMS CARBOHYDRATES | **2** GRAMS FAT

½ pound dried lentils, rinsed and picked over

2 (6-ounce) boneless, skinless chicken breasts, trimmed of fat

1 tablespoon (3 cubes) chicken bouillon

4 cups water

1 small onion, finely chopped

1 ripe tomato, chopped

2 cloves garlic, minced

1 teaspoon garlic powder

1 teaspoon ground cumin

¼ teaspoon sweet paprika

¼ teaspoon dried oregano

Salt, to taste

1 scallion, thinly sliced

¼ cup chopped fresh cilantro

1 Into a medium, heavy-duty pot over medium-high heat, add lentils, chicken, chicken bouillon, and water. Cover with a lid and bring to a boil. Let mixture simmer until the chicken is cooked, about 20 minutes.

2 Use tongs to transfer cooked chicken from the pot to a plate. Let cool for a few minutes and then use 2 forks to shred the meat. Return shredded chicken to the pot, along with onion, tomato, garlic, garlic powder, cumin, paprika, and oregano.

3 Cover the pot with a lid and bring to a simmer. Cook until the lentils are soft, about 25 minutes, adding more water if the soup gets too thick.

4 Remove from heat. Season with salt and garnish with scallions and cilantro. Serve.

SUPREMELY SPICY CHILI

SERVES **12** | PREP TIME **30 MINUTES** | COOKING TIME **2 ½ HOURS**

460 CALORIES | **37** GRAMS PROTEIN | **36** GRAMS CARBOHYDRATES | **18** GRAMS FAT

2 tablespoons canola oil

2 red bell peppers, seeded and chopped

2 jalapeño peppers, finely chopped

3 Anaheim chiles, roasted, peeled, seeded, and chopped

3 poblano chiles, roasted, peeled, seeded, and chopped

2 yellow onions, chopped

1 pound boneless chuck steak, trimmed of fat and cut into ¼-inch cubes

2 pounds 92% lean ground beef

1 pound lean Italian sausage,

¼ cup minced garlic

2 teaspoons granulated onion

2 teaspoons garlic powder

3 tablespoons chili powder

2 teaspoons ground hot paprika

2 teaspoons ground cumin

2 teaspoons ground cayenne pepper

2 teaspoons ground coriander

2 teaspoons salt

2 teaspoons ground black pepper

1 cup tomato paste

2 cups tomato sauce

12 ounces lager beer

1 cup low-sodium chicken broth

2 (15.5-ounce) cans pinto beans, undrained

2 (15.5-ounce) cans kidney beans, undrained

½ cup thinly sliced scallions

1 Warm a large stockpot or Dutch oven over high heat and add oil. Cook bell peppers, jalapeños, Anaheim chiles, poblano chiles, and onions until tender, about 5 minutes.

2 Add cubed beef chuck and brown on all sides. Mix in ground beef, sausage, and garlic. Gently stir, trying not to break meat up too much. Cook until meat is browned and cooked through, about 7 to 10 minutes.

3 Stir in granulated onion, garlic powder, chili powder, paprika, cumin, cayenne, coriander, salt, and pepper. Cook for 1 minute and then stir in the tomato paste and tomato sauce. Cook for 2 minutes.

4 Pour in beer, chicken broth, pinto beans, and kidney beans. Thoroughly mix and reduce the heat to medium-low. Simmer for 2 hours, stirring occasionally. Top with scallions and serve.

CUMIN-SPIKED BLACK BEAN SOUP

SERVES **2** | PREP TIME **15 MINUTES** | COOKING TIME **55 MINUTES**

309 CALORIES | **20** GRAMS PROTEIN | **47** GRAMS CARBOHYDRATES | **5** GRAMS FAT

BEANS ARE A PLENTIFUL SOURCE OF POTASSIUM. Potassium is by far one of the most common nutrient deficiencies, and it's not one that can be easily solved with supplements. One cup of cooked white beans, however, contains nearly 30% the potassium your body needs each day. Adzuki, soy, lima, kidney, Great Northern, and pinto beans are other great choices.

BEANS ARE INCREDIBLY HIGH IN FIBER. The average American consumes just 15 grams of fiber daily, despite the Institute of Medicine's recommendations of 21 to 25 grams daily for adult women and 30 to 39 grams daily for adult men. One cup of cooked beans contains around 12 grams of fiber, which makes it easier to meet your fiber requirement.

BEANS CAN HELP PREVENT OVEREATING. Beans are naturally low in sugar, they can help prevent insulin spikes that can increase hunger.[1] They're also high in protein and carbohydrates, which is why research conducted by scientists at the University of Sydney found that beans are among the most filling foods you can eat.[2]

---

2 teaspoons extra-virgin olive oil

1 small onion, finely chopped

1 carrot, peeled and chopped

2 celery stalks, chopped

½ jalapeño pepper, seeded and chopped

2 cloves garlic, minced

1 teaspoon ground cumin

1 bay leaf

4 cups low-sodium chicken broth

1 (14.5-ounce) can black beans, drained and rinsed

2 teaspoons red wine vinegar

Chopped fresh cilantro, to taste

Salt and ground black pepper, to taste

1 In a medium pot, warm olive oil over medium-high heat. Add the onion and sauté for about 3 minutes.

2 Add carrot, celery, and jalapeño; sauté for about 5 minutes. Stir in garlic, cumin, and bay leaf, and sauté for about 30 seconds. Add chicken broth and black beans. Bring soup to a simmer and reduce heat to low; cook until flavors have melded together, about 30 to 45 minutes.

3 To serve, remove bay leaf. Stir in red wine vinegar and cilantro; season with salt and pepper. Serve immediately.

SLOW COOKER CHICKEN ENCHILADA SOUP

SERVES **4** | PREP TIME **20 MINUTES** | COOKING TIME **4 HOURS 10 MINUTES**
429 CALORIES | **42** GRAMS PROTEIN | **41** GRAMS CARBOHYDRATES | **10** GRAMS FAT

2 teaspoons extra-virgin olive oil

½ cup chopped onion

3 cloves garlic, minced

1 (8-ounce) can tomato sauce-

3 cups low-sodium chicken broth

1 to 2 teaspoons chopped canned chipotle chiles in adobo sauce

1 (15-ounce) can black beans, rinsed and drained

1 (14.5-ounce) can diced tomatoes

2 cups frozen corn

1 teaspoon ground cumin, plus more to taste

½ teaspoon dried oregano

2 (8-ounce) boneless, skinless chicken breasts, trimmed of fat

Salt, to taste

¼ cup chopped scallions

¾ cup shredded reduced-fat cheddar cheese

¼ cup chopped fresh cilantro

1 Place a medium pot over medium-low heat and add oil. Sauté onion and garlic until soft, about 3 to 4 minutes. Slowly stir in tomato sauce, chicken broth, and chipotles. Once soup comes to a boil, carefully transfer it to the bowl of a slow cooker.

2 Into the slow cooker bowl, add beans, tomatoes, corn, cumin, and oregano; stir to combine. Add chicken breasts to the slow cooker. Cover with a lid and cook on low heat for 4 hours.

3 Transfer chicken from the slow cooker to a small bowl. Let cool for a few minutes and then use forks to shred the meat. Return to the soup, along with salt and cumin to taste.

4 To serve, ladle the soup into the bowls and top with scallions, cheese, and cilantro.

CHICKEN POT PIE SOUP

SERVES **4** | PREP TIME **20 MINUTES** | COOKING TIME **20 MINUTES**
385 CALORIES | **37** GRAMS PROTEIN | **43** GRAMS CARBOHYDRATES | **7** GRAMS FAT

CELERY MAY HELP PREVENT INFLAMMATION IN THE DIGESTIVE TRACT. No, celery isn't a "zero calorie food" (in fact, there is no such thing), but it can still do amazing things for your digestion. In animal studies, the fibrous carbohydrate found in celery has been shown to fortify the lining of the stomach and reduce the risk of stomach ulcers.[3]

CELERY IS RICH IN ANTIOXIDANTS. To date, scientists have identified dozens of antioxidants in celery, from the well-known—like vitamin C and flavonoids—to the wmore obscure, such as *lunularin*, *bergapten*, and *psolaren*. Together, these nutrients can help protect against undesirable oxidative damage to organs and blood vessels.

CELERY MAY HELP PROTECT AGAINST PANCREATIC CANCER. According to recent research conducted by University of Illinois scientists, two specific antioxidants, *apigenin* and *luteolin*, found in celery have the potential to kill human pancreatic cancer cells.[4] While these results have been seen in lab studies only, they still show interesting promise in supporting the health benefits of celery.

---

2 cups low-sodium chicken broth

2 tablespoons cornstarch

4 cups 2% milk

2 (6-ounce) boneless, skinless chicken breasts, cooked and chopped

1 large celery stalk, chopped

½ medium onion, chopped

8 ounces baby portobello mushrooms, sliced

2 chicken bouillon cubes

Pinch of dried thyme

Salt and ground black pepper, to taste

1 (10-ounce) bag frozen classic mixed vegetables (peas, carrots, green beans, and corn)

2 medium red potatoes (7.5 ounces each), cut into ¾-inch cubes

1 In a large, heavy-duty pot over medium-low heat, add the chicken broth, cornstarch, and milk. Bring to a simmer, letting the liquid thicken.

2 Into the pot, add chicken, celery, onion, mushrooms, bouillon, thyme, salt, pepper, and frozen vegetables. Let mixture return to a low simmer. Partially cover the pot with a lid and cook until vegetables soften, about 10 minutes.

3 Uncover the pot and add potatoes. Cook until potatoes are tender, about 5 minutes. Taste and season with salt and pepper before serving.

WHITE BEAN SOUP WITH TURKEY SAUSAGE AND KALE

SERVES **4** | PREP TIME **20 MINUTES** | COOKING TIME **30 MINUTES**

351 CALORIES | **34** GRAMS PROTEIN | **20** GRAMS CARBOHYDRATES | **16** GRAMS FAT

2 teaspoons extra-virgin olive oil

1 onion, chopped

1 clove garlic, minced

1¼ pounds lean turkey sausage, casings removed

6 cups low-sodium chicken broth

1 cup canned white beans, drained and rinsed

1 cup roughly chopped kale (stems removed)

Salt and ground black pepper, to taste

1 In a medium heavy-duty pot, warm oil over medium-high heat. Add onion and garlic, sautéing for 2 to 3 minutes. Add sausage, using a wooden spoon to break the meat into small pieces. Sauté for 5 to 6 minutes, stirring frequently, until the meat is cooked through.

2 Stir in chicken broth and beans. Cover with a lid and simmer on low heat for 10 minutes.

3 Add the kale and continue simmering with the pot covered for another 10 minutes.

4 Season with salt and pepper, and divide soup into 4 bowls to serve.

CHICKEN SALAD SANDWICHES

SERVES **2** | PREP TIME **5 MINUTES**

283 CALORIES | **28** GRAMS PROTEIN | **27** GRAMS CARBOHYDRATES | **7** GRAMS FAT

1 celery stalk, finely chopped

1 tablespoon finely chopped onion

1 tablespoon pine nuts

1 heaping teaspoon spicy brown mustard

1 heaping teaspoon fat-free sour cream

1 heaping teaspoon fat-free plain yogurt

Pinch of salt and ground black pepper

2 (3-ounce) cans chunk chicken, rinsed and drained twice

4 slices whole-grain bread

2 lettuce leaves

1 In a bowl, add celery, onion, pine nuts, mustard, sour cream, yogurt, salt, and pepper; stir to combine. Add chicken and use a fork to mix well.

2 Make the sandwiches by dividing the chicken salad onto 2 bread slices. Top each one with 1 lettuce leaf and remaining slice of bread. Serve.

SLOW COOKER ITALIAN SLOPPY JOE

SERVES **4** | PREP TIME **10 MINUTES** | COOKING TIME **4 HOURS 10 MINUTES**

373 CALORIES | **32** GRAMS PROTEIN | **31** GRAMS CARBOHYDRATES | **15** GRAMS FAT

1   *pound lean Italian turkey sausage, casings removed*

½   *cup chopped onion*

3   *cloves garlic, minced*

1   *red bell pepper, seeded and chopped in ½-inch pieces*

1   *green bell pepper, seeded and chopped in ½-inch pieces*

1⅓ *cups canned crushed tomatoes*

½   *teaspoon dried rosemary*

    Salt and ground black pepper, to taste

4   *whole-wheat 100-calorie potato rolls*

4   *slices reduced-fat provolone cheese*

1   *cup baby spinach*

1 Warm a large nonstick skillet over medium-high heat. Add sausage, using a wooden spoon to break the meat into small pieces. Sauté for 5 to 6 minutes, stirring frequently, until the meat is cooked through.

2 Stir in onion and garlic. After cooking about 2 minutes, transfer sausage mixture to the slow cooker bowl. Add peppers, tomatoes, rosemary, salt, and pepper. Stir to combine.

3 Cover the slow cooker with a lid and set the heat to low. Cook for 4 hours.

4 To serve, fill a roll with a heaping ½ cup of meat. Top with cheese and baby spinach.

SLOW-COOKER FRENCH DIP SANDWICHES

SERVES **8** | PREP TIME **30 MINUTES** | COOKING TIME **9 TO 12 HOURS**

324 CALORIES | **35** GRAMS PROTEIN | **24** GRAMS CARBOHYDRATES | **10** GRAMS FAT

1 tablespoon minced garlic

1 tablespoon chopped fresh rosemary

1 tablespoon chopped fresh thyme leaves

Salt and ground black pepper, to taste

2 pounds lean beef round roast, trimmed of fat

1 teaspoon Worcestershire sauce

2 (14.5-ounce) cans low-sodium beef broth, plus more if needed

3 large onions, sliced

1 large red bell pepper, seeded and sliced into strips

1 large green bell pepper, seeded and sliced into strips

2 (8-ounce) baguettes

8 slices reduced-fat mozzarella

1 In a small bowl, mix together garlic, rosemary, thyme, salt, and pepper. Rub roast entirely with the spice mix and place it in the slow cooker.

2 Add Worcestershire sauce and enough broth to cover the meat. Cover with the lid and cook on low until the meat is fork-tender, 9 to 12 hours, depending on roast thickness.

3 An hour before the meat is done, add onions and bell peppers into the slow cooker. When roast is tender, transfer the meat to a cutting board and shred with a fork or slice with a knife.

4 Using a slotted spoon, remove the onions and peppers from the broth. Use a gravy separator to remove any fat from broth or leave it in the fridge overnight to skim off the solidified fat.

5 To serve, preheat the broiler. Slice baguette and top with 2 ounces beef, plus onions, peppers, and cheese. Place under the broiler until cheese melts and serve with ramekins of broth for dipping.

TURKEY TACO LETTUCE WRAPS

SERVES **4** | PREP TIME **20 MINUTES** | COOKING TIME **25 MINUTES**

196 CALORIES | **22** GRAMS PROTEIN | **4** GRAMS CARBOHYDRATES | **8** GRAMS FAT

1 pound 93% lean ground turkey

1 teaspoon garlic powder

1 teaspoon ground cumin

1 teaspoon chili powder

1 teaspoon ground sweet paprika

½ teaspoon dried oregano

Salt and ground black pepper, to taste

½ small onion, chopped

¼ red bell pepper, seeded and chopped

½ cup canned tomato sauce

8 large iceberg lettuce leaves, washed and dried

½ cup chopped fresh cilantro

1 Warm a large nonstick skillet over medium-high heat. Add ground turkey to the skillet, using a wooden spoon to break the meat into small pieces. Cook for 4 to 5 minutes, stirring frequently, until the meat is no longer pink.

2 Stir in garlic powder, cumin, chili powder, paprika, oregano, salt, and pepper. Add onion, bell pepper, and tomato sauce. Cover the skillet with a lid, reduce the heat to low, and simmer for 20 minutes.

3 To serve, place 2 lettuce leaves on each plate. Divide filling between lettuce leaves, placing in the center of each leaf. Garnish with cilantro and serve.

HEALTHY AVOCADO-EGG SALAD SANDWICH

SERVES **2** | PREP TIME **5 MINUTES**

303 CALORIES | **15** GRAMS PROTEIN | **29** GRAMS CARBOHYDRATES | **15** GRAMS FAT

2 large hard-boiled eggs, peeled

½ medium avocado, peeled, pitted, and cut into ½-inch dice

1 tablespoon 2% Greek yogurt

½ teaspoon Dijon mustard

½ tablespoon finely chopped fresh chives

Salt and ground black pepper, to taste

12 thin cucumber slices

4 slices whole-grain bread, toasted

1 Separate the egg yolks from the egg whites. In a small bowl, add yolks, avocado, yogurt, mustard, chives, salt, and pepper. Mash together with a fork.

2 Chop egg whites and stir into yolk mixture.

3 Divide cucumber between 2 bread slices. Spoon egg salad onto the bread and close with top half of bread. Slice sandwiches in half and serve.

CUBAN SANDWICH QUESADILLA

SERVES **1** | PREP TIME **5 MINUTES** | COOKING TIME **5 MINUTES**
280 CALORIES | **22** GRAMS PROTEIN | **22** GRAMS CARBOHYDRATES | **12** GRAMS FAT

1 (6-inch) whole-wheat tortilla

1 slice reduced-fat Swiss cheese

2 ounces deli ham

1 dill pickle, thinly sliced

Dijon mustard, to taste

1 Coat a medium nonstick pan with cooking spray and warm over low heat. Add tortilla to the pan.

2 Layer ingredients on half of the tortilla in the following order: cheese, ham, pickle, and mustard. When cheese has melted, use a spatula to fold quesadilla in half and flip it to warm the other side.

3 Transfer quesadilla to a plate, slice into quarters, and serve.

BAGUETTE WITH ROAST BEEF, ARUGULA, AND SHAVED PARMESAN

SERVES **1** | PREP TIME **5 MINUTES**

292 CALORIES | **21** GRAMS PROTEIN | **30** GRAMS CARBOHYDRATES | **9** GRAMS FAT

1 (2-ounce) baguette (about 2 inches long)

2 ounces lean roast beef

½ cup baby arugula

1 tablespoon shaved Parmesan cheese

Salt and ground black pepper, to taste

1 teaspoon extra-virgin olive oil

1 teaspoon balsamic vinegar

1 Slice baguette lengthwise. Place bottom half onto a plate and layer with roast beef, arugula, and cheese.

2 Season with salt and pepper, and drizzle evenly with olive oil and balsamic vinegar. Close with top half of bread and serve.

Shakes & Snacks

GREEN 'N' MEAN SALSA

SERVES **4** (1 CUP PER SERVING) | PREP TIME **10 MINUTES**

128 CALORIES | **2** GRAMS PROTEIN | **15** GRAMS CARBOHYDRATES | **7** GRAMS FAT

2 poblano peppers, halved
   and seeded

2 serrano peppers, halved
   and seeded

1 avocado, peeled, pitted,
   and diced

1 clove garlic, peeled

1 cup chopped fresh cilantro

½ green bell pepper, seeded and
   chopped

½ medium sweet onion, chopped

¼ head iceberg lettuce, chopped

½ cup water

   Juice of 2 limes

1 (15-ounce) can diced tomatoes,
   drained

1 Into a blender or food processor, add all the ingredients except canned tomatoes. Blend until mostly smooth with a slight chunky consistency. (Do this in batches, if needed, depending on the size of blender or food processor.)

2 Transfer the mixture into a large bowl. Stir in drained canned tomatoes and mix well. Serve.

PERFECT SPICY GUACAMOLE

SERVES **2** | PREP TIME **10 MINUTES**

337 CALORIES | **4** GRAMS PROTEIN | **20** GRAMS CARBOHYDRATES | **29** GRAMS FAT

2 avocados

½ small red onion, finely chopped

¼ cup chopped fresh cilantro

1 tablespoon lime juice, plus more if needed

½ teaspoon salt, plus more if needed

Pinch of ground black pepper

2 serrano peppers, seeded and finely chopped, plus more if needed

1 Halve both avocados, removing and discarding the pits. Use a spoon to scoop the avocado's flesh into a medium bowl.

2 Add remaining ingredients into the bowl. Using a fork, mash the ingredients together into desired smooth or chunky consistency.

3 Taste the guacamole, adding additional lime juice, salt, and serrano pepper, depending on taste. Serve.

CREAMY GARLIC DIP

SERVES **9 (2 TABLESPOONS PER SERVING)** | PREP TIME **2 TO 3 MINUTES**

29 CALORIES | **1** GRAM PROTEIN | **5** GRAMS CARBOHYDRATES | **1** GRAM FAT

1 cup low-fat sour cream

2 tablespoons light mayonnaise

Juice of 1 lime

1 teaspoon garlic powder

Pinch of ground black pepper

1 Add all the ingredients into a small bowl. Use a spatula to mix well and serve immediately.

AVOCADO-MINT PROTEIN SMOOTHIE

SERVES **1** | PREP TIME **5 MINUTES**

664 CALORIES | **29** GRAMS PROTEIN | **103** GRAMS CARBOHYDRATES | **22** GRAMS FAT

1 cup unsweetened almond milk

4 fresh mint leaves

1 banana, peeled and sliced

½ medium avocado, peeled and pitted

3 whole dates (2.5 ounces), pitted

1 tablespoon dark chocolate chips

1 scoop vanilla protein powder

1 Into a blender, add almond milk, mint, banana, avocado, dates, chocolate chips, and protein powder.

2 Blend ingredients until smooth. Pour smoothie into a glass and serve.

ORANGE BEET PROTEIN SHAKE

SERVES **2** | PREP TIME **5 MINUTES**

192 CALORIES | **25** GRAMS PROTEIN | **25** GRAMS CARBOHYDRATES | **0** GRAM FAT

2 cups water

2 cups beet greens

2 beets, peeled and diced

2 oranges, peeled

2 scoops vanilla protein powder

Juice of ½ lemon

1 Into a blender, add water, greens, beets, oranges, protein powder, and lemon juice.

2 Blend the ingredients until smooth. Pour shake into 2 glasses and serve.

BLUEBERRY-COCONUT PANCAKE BATTER SMOOTHIE

SERVES **1** | PREP TIME **5 MINUTES**

431 CALORIES | **24** GRAMS PROTEIN | **67** GRAMS CARBOHYDRATES | **9** GRAMS FAT

½ cup coconut water

1 cup low-fat buttermilk

¼ cup 2% cottage cheese

¼ cup 2% Greek yogurt

1 tablespoon coconut flour

2 tablespoons honey or date paste

1 tablespoon shredded
  unsweetened coconut

½ teaspoon baking soda

¼ cup fresh blueberries,
  plus more for garnish

1 Into a blender, add coconut water, buttermilk, cottage cheese, yogurt, coconut flour, honey, coconut, and baking soda. Blend until smooth.

2 Add blueberries and pulse a few times just until slightly broken up.

3 Pour the pancake smoothie into a glass and garnish with a small handful of blueberries. Serve.

ICED PUMPKIN-PECAN PROTEIN BARS

SERVES **9** | PREP TIME **20 MINUTES** | COOKING TIME **25 MINUTES**, PLUS **TIME TO COOL**
143 CALORIES | **12** GRAMS PROTEIN | **12** GRAMS CARBOHYDRATES | **6** GRAMS FAT

BARS

- 4 *large eggs*
- 1 *cup pumpkin purée*
- ¼ *cup pure maple syrup*
- 2 *tablespoons unsweetened almond milk*
- 1 *teaspoon vanilla extract*
- ⅓ *cup coconut flour*
- 2 *scoops vanilla whey protein powder*
- 2 *tablespoons ground flaxseed*
- 2 *teaspoons ground cinnamon*
- ¼ *teaspoon baking soda*
- ½ *teaspoon ground nutmeg*
- ¼ *teaspoon sea salt*
- ⅛ *teaspoon ground cloves*

TOPPING

- 1 *scoop vanilla protein powder*
- *Room temperature water, as needed*
- ¼ *cup chopped pecans*

1 Preheat the oven to 375°F. Prepare a baking sheet by lining with parchment paper or a silicone mat.

2 In a large bowl, add eggs, pumpkin, maple syrup, almond milk, and vanilla. Use a fork to whisk together until combined.

3 In a medium bowl, add coconut flour, protein powder, flaxseed, cinnamon, baking soda, nutmeg, salt, and cloves, stirring together to combine.

4 Slowly stir dry ingredients into the pumpkin mixture until well combined; let sit for 2 to 3 minutes.

5 Separate batter into 9 parts, about ⅓ cup each. Form batter into rectangular bars by hand (like Clif bars) and place onto the prepared baking sheet.

6 Bake bars until golden brown on the bottom with a top just beginning to crack, about 22 to 25 minutes. Let bars cool for 5 minutes and then transfer to a wire rack.

7 Once bars have fully cooled, prepare the icing. Add protein powder to a small bowl, slowly stirring in water until mixture is thick and smooth.

8 Transfer icing into a small Ziploc bag and use scissors to cut off a small piece of the corner. Squeeze icing out of the cut corner, drizzling evenly over the top of the bars. Sprinkle chopped pecans over the bars.

9 For best results, let icing set for 1 hour or more. Store bars in an airtight container.

MANGO GREEN SMOOTHIE

SERVES **4** | PREP TIME **5 MINUTES**

271 CALORIES | **13** GRAMS PROTEIN | **37** GRAMS CARBOHYDRATES | **9** GRAMS FAT

WHILE IT'S TRUE YOUR BODY IS REGULARLY EXPOSED TO A WIDE VARIETY OF TOXIC SUBSTANCES, and while some of them are particularly nasty and can accumulate in body fat, there's no evidence that trendy "cleanses" and "detox diets" help mitigate the damage or rid the body of toxins.

THAT IS, YES, YOUR BODY HAS A CERTAIN AMOUNT OF HARMFUL CHEMICALS DEPOSITED INTO ITS FAT STORES, but no, drinking a bunch of lemonade for a week isn't going to do anything about it.

SO, ENJOY GREEN SMOOTHIES BECAUSE THEY'RE TASTY AND NUTRITIOUS—not because they're "detoxing" your body.

---

2 *bananas, preferably frozen, peeled and sliced*

3 *cups fresh baby spinach*

1½ *cups diced fresh mango (about 2 mangos)*

¼ *cup shelled raw hemp seeds*

3¼ *cups 2% milk*

2 *cups ice cubes*

1 Into a blender, add banana slices, spinach, mango, hemp seeds, milk, and ice.

2 Blend until smooth, pour into 4 glasses, and serve.

CHAI-BANANA PROTEIN SHAKE

SERVES **1** | PREP TIME **10 MINUTES**, PLUS **TIME TO STEEP AND CHILL TEA**

243 CALORIES | **24** GRAMS PROTEIN | **30** GRAMS CARBOHYDRATES | **3** GRAMS FAT

1 cup water

2 chai tea bags

⅓ cup 2% milk

⅓ cup 2% Greek yogurt

½ banana, preferably frozen, peeled and sliced

½ scoop vanilla protein powder

2 teaspoons maca powder (optional)

6 ice cubes

Ground cinnamon, to taste

1 In a small pot, add water and bring to a boil over high heat. Remove from heat, add tea bags, and let tea steep for 30 minutes to fully infuse with chai flavor. Place tea in the fridge or freezer to fully chill.

2 Once tea is cool, add milk, yogurt, banana, protein powder, and (optional) maca powder into a blender. Process until smooth.

3 Pour in cold tea and blend until smooth. Add ice and continue puréeing until ice is crushed.

4 Pour shake into a glass, garnish with cinnamon, and enjoy.

LOW-CARB CHOCOLATE-ESPRESSO PROTEIN SHAKE

SERVES 1 | PREP TIME **5 MINUTES**

335 CALORIES | **24** GRAMS PROTEIN | **11** GRAMS CARBOHYDRATES | **23** GRAMS FAT

¾ cup unsweetened almond milk

¼ cup heavy cream

2 cups ice cubes

1 scoop chocolate protein powder

1 tablespoon unsweetened cocoa powder

1 teaspoon instant espresso powder dissolved into 2 tablespoons hot water

1 tablespoon granulated sugar

1 Into a blender, add almond milk, cream, ice, protein powder, cocoa powder, hot water with espresso powder, and sugar.

2 Blend ingredients until smooth. Pour smoothie into a glass to drink immediately or freeze for later enjoyment.

MAPLE-WALNUT PROTEIN MUFFINS

SERVES **12** | PREP TIME **10 MINUTES** | COOKING TIME **25 MINUTES**, PLUS **TIME TO COOL**
176 CALORIES | **15** GRAMS PROTEIN | **15** GRAMS CARBOHYDRATES | **7** GRAMS FAT

3 egg whites or ½ cup liquid egg white substitute

3 tablespoons unsalted butter, softened

¼ cup maple syrup

½ cup 2% milk

½ cup whole-wheat flour

¼ cup wheat germ

¼ cup oat bran

6 scoops chocolate protein powder

2 teaspoons baking powder

1 teaspoon baking soda

½ cup chopped walnuts

1 Preheat the oven to 350°F. Line a standard 12-cup muffin pan with paper liners or lightly coat cups with cooking spray.

2 In a medium bowl, add egg whites, butter, maple syrup, and milk. Use a fork to mix well.

3 In a large bowl, add flour, wheat germ, oat bran, protein powder, baking powder, and baking soda. Combine with a spatula.

4 Using the spatula, add wet ingredients to the dry ingredients, stirring only until the dry ingredients are moistened. When there's just a trace of visible flour, gently fold in the nuts.

5 Divide batter among 12 prepared muffin cups, filling each cup three-fourths of the way full.

6 Bake until toasty brown on top and a toothpick inserted into the middle of a muffin comes out clean, about 20 to 25 minutes.

7 Let muffins cool for a few minutes before removing from the pan. Allow to fully cool before serving. Store remaining muffins in an airtight container.

NO-BAKE MATCHA GREEN TEA FUDGE BARS

SERVES **10** | PREP TIME **10 MINUTES**, **OVERNIGHT** REFRIGERATION
194 CALORIES | **21** GRAMS PROTEIN | **12** GRAMS CARBOHYDRATES | **7** GRAMS FAT

MATCHA CONTAINS HIGH AMOUNTS OF DISEASE-FIGHTING ANTIOXIDANTS. Matcha, which is just powdered green tea leaves, contains high amounts of molecules that are most responsible for tea's many proven health benefits, including a reduced risk of heart disease, cancer, and various neurodegenerative conditions.[1]

THE EGCG IN MATCHA MAY HELP YOU LOSE WEIGHT. Matcha is particularly rich in one molecule in particular—epigallocatechin gallate, or EGCG—that is most associated with green tea's weight loss benefits.[2]

MATCHA CAN ENHANCE YOUR MENTAL CLARITY. Matcha contains an amino acid known as theanine, which has been shown to improve alertness, focus, attention, memory, and mood.[3]

---

8 *scoops vanilla brown rice protein powder*

4 *teaspoons matcha green tea powder*

½ *cup oat flour*

⅓ *cup almond butter*

1 *cup plus 2 tablespoons unsweetened almond milk*

2 *tablespoons Truvia*

Zest of 1 lemon

2 *ounces dark chocolate, finely chopped*

1 Prepare an 8-inch by 8-inch baking pan by lining it with parchment paper, using 2 sheets placed in opposite directions.

2 In a small bowl, add protein powder, matcha, and oat flour. Use a fork to thoroughly combine; reserve.

3 In the bowl of a stand mixer, add almond butter, almond milk, Truvia, and lemon zest. Mix on low to combine (or alternatively mix by hand with a spatula). Slowly add the protein powder mixture, stirring to combine.

4 Transfer matcha fudge to the prepared pan, using a spatula to evenly spread the mixture. Cover with plastic wrap and place in the fridge overnight.

5 Lift the parchment paper from the pan and place onto a cutting board. Slice fudge into 10 pieces.

6 Using either a microwave or double boiler on the stove, gently stir the chocolate until melted. Drizzle melted chocolate over the bars.

7 Store bars in an airtight container.

NO-BAKE CHOCOLATE PROTEIN BARS WITH QUINOA

SERVES **8** | PREP TIME **25 MINUTES**, PLUS **TIME** TO CHILL

331 CALORIES | **11** GRAMS PROTEIN | **49** GRAMS CARBOHYDRATES | **13** GRAMS FAT

QUINOA IS EXTREMELY NUTRIENT DENSE. A single cup of cooked quinoa contains 8 grams of protein, 5 grams of fiber, and anywhere from 10 to 60% of your daily requirements for various vitamins and minerals including manganese, magnesium, phosphorus, folate, copper, iron, zinc, potassium, and vitamins B1, B2, and B6. It even contains small amounts of calcium, niacin, vitamin E, and omega-3 fatty acids, too.

QUINOA IS HIGHER IN FIBER THAN MOST GRAINS. Depending on the variety, one cup of uncooked quinoa contains anywhere from 17 to 27 grams of fiber.[4] That's more than double of what's found in most grains!

QUINOA IS A GREAT ALTERNATIVE TO GLUTEN-CONTAINING GRAINS. Most people think quinoa is a grain, but it's actually a seed. Seeds are naturally free of gluten, making quinoa a good choice for those with celiac disease or gluten intolerance.

⅓ cup dry quinoa, rinsed

⅔ cup water

16 whole dates, pitted

½ cup raw almonds

½ cup almond butter, preferably crunchy

½ cup chocolate protein powder

1 tablespoon honey (optional)

1 Add quinoa and water to a medium pot; bring to a boil over medium heat. Cover with a lid, reducing heat to low so mixture is at a simmer. Let cook for 15 minutes before removing from the heat. Cool quinoa and refrigerate it a minimum of 2 hours or even overnight.

2 Add dates into the bowl of a food processor, pulsing to turn it into a paste. Transfer the date paste to a small bowl.

3 Next, add raw almonds into the food processor, pulsing until they break into small pieces but before they turn into flour. Return dates to the food processor bowl, along with reserved quinoa, almond butter, protein powder, and (optional) honey. Blend until ingredients are well combined.

4 Divide mixture into 8 parts and form each one into a bar shape. Refrigerate for 1 to 2 hours until hardened and store in an airtight container.

PEANUT BUTTER PROTEIN SWIRL BROWNIES

SERVES **10** | PREP TIME **15 MINUTES** | COOKING TIME **25 MINUTES**
234 CALORIES | **12** GRAMS PROTEIN | **25** GRAMS CARBOHYDRATES | **11** GRAMS FAT

BATTER

- 1 *(15-ounce) can garbanzo beans, drained and rinsed*
- 2 *large eggs*
- 2 *tablespoons unsweetened cocoa powder*
- ¼ *cup coconut sugar*
- ½ *teaspoon salt*
- 2 *tablespoons peanut butter*
- 2 *teaspoons vanilla extract*
- 1 *scoop unflavored whey protein*
- 6 *ounces dark chocolate, chopped, or 1 cup dark chocolate chips*

TOPPING

- ½ *cup 2% Greek yogurt*
- 2 *tablespoons egg whites or liquid egg white substitute*
- 1 *teaspoon vanilla extract*
- 2 *tablespoons peanut butter*
- 1 *scoop unflavored whey protein*
- 1 *teaspoon honey*

1 Preheat the oven to 350°F. Prepare an 8-inch by 8-inch baking pan by coating with cooking spray.

2 Into a blender or food processor, add garbanzo beans, eggs, cocoa powder, coconut sugar, salt, peanut butter, vanilla, and whey protein. Blend the ingredients until smooth. Transfer brownie batter to a medium bowl.

3 Using either a microwave or double boiler on the stove, gently stir the chocolate until melted. Stirring constantly, slowly pour the melted chocolate into the brownie batter. Use a spatula to evenly spread into the prepared pan. Set aside.

4 In a small bowl, add the topping ingredients and mix to combine. Pour topping over the brownie batter. Gently drag the tip of a knife through the mixture to create brownie swirls.

5 Bake brownies until topping is set and edges are golden brown, about 20 to 25 minutes. Let cool slightly and cut into 10 pieces. Store in an airtight container.

Lean Meat

Scientists are on quite the "meat will kill you" kick these days.

Every few months, some new scientific study is published blaming red meat intake for everything from heart disease to cancer to flat-out death-by-anything.

Then, mainstream newspapers and magazines catch on and the sensationalism begins. Bold headlines splash onto newsstands like "All red meat is bad for you," "Red meat is blamed for one in 10 early deaths," and "Scientists warn red meat can be lethal."

Millions of people take these warnings at face value and eliminate red meat from their diets out of fear, but are the sound bites true? Is red meat actually as dangerous as we're being led to believe?

Well, the first thing you need to know is that the media are woefully skilled at misinterpreting scientific research.

Another thing you need to know is the difference between observational research and experimental trials.

Observations are the first step of the scientific method and are meant to point the way for further research or generate hypotheses. They can point to correlations but cannot be used to establish causation. Ever.

For example, there's a statistical correlation between the number of people who drowned by falling into a pool and the number of films Nicolas Cage appeared in.

Cage's movies may be bad, but deadly? I don't think so.

Jokes aside, the point is that observational research can never provide enough evidence for establishing what's really going on behind the data. Only clinical trials allow scientists to create a rigorous, controlled environment where they can test and validate or invalidate theories.

Do the media care about this, though? Absolutely not. All they need is a whiff of a correlation to break a story proclaiming causation.

This is what is happening with the red meat scare. The media is taking observational research and reporting correlations as definitive facts.

For example, scientists from Harvard published a study in 2012 that followed over 120,000 women and men and found that a single daily serving of unprocessed red meat was associated with a 13% increased risk of death from all causes.[1] A single daily serving of processed red meat was associated with a 20% increased risk.

That whipped health writers into a frenzy almost overnight. The spark turned into chain lightning, and eating red meat became the new smoking.

There were serious problems with this study and its findings, though.

For example, in analyzing subjects' diets, hamburger was included in the category of "unprocessed red meat," and was likely a major contributor to the category. No, not homemade ground beef patties made from pasture-raised, hormone- and antibiotic-free cows, just hamburgers. The morsels that fast food dreams are made of.

Another flaw is the study tracked whole grain intake but didn't track refined grain intake, which means we're left to wonder about how many of those hamburgers were mashed between fluffy, white flour McDonald's buns.

Yet another pothole, and this one is pretty large, is how the data on food intake was gathered. Subjects filled out "food frequency questionnaires," which are limited checklists of foods and beverages with a section to report how often each was consumed over a period of time.

One of the major and well-documented problems with food frequency questionnaires is people often report what they think they should be eating rather than what they actually ate.[2] And let's face it—most of us struggle to remember what we ate last week let alone what went into our mouths over the last six months.

That's not the only problem with food frequency questionnaires.

Equally as vexing is the well-documented fact that people tend to underestimate their intake of foods like processed meats, eggs, butter, high-fat dairy products, mayonnaise and creamy salad dressings, refined grains, and sweets and desserts, and overestimate most of the vegetable and fruit groups, nuts, high-energy and low-energy drinks, and condiments.[3]

It's also known that, whether due to the pressure of social norms or something else, women tend to be less accurate in their food reporting than men.[4]

The point here is that studies based on food frequency questionnaires, including the ones hijacking news headlines every few months, are a roll of the dice.

Another thing you have to keep in mind when looking at observational research is how other factors like lifestyle choices play into and influence the bigger picture.

For example, when you review the data in the Harvard study on the lifestyles of the subjects, you find that the people that were, according to their food reports, eating the most red meat were the most physically inactive, the most likely to smoke, and the least likely to take a multivitamin supplement. Their daily calorie intake was also higher, and they were more overweight, drank more alcohol, and tended to eat less healthy foods in general.

Little-to-no exercise, being overweight, smoking, drinking alcohol regularly, and eating too much junk food? That's a pretty darn good recipe for dying young, with or without red meat.

Now, the Harvard study is only one of several such studies used to stoke the flames of red meat hysteria, but we don't need to review them all here. The long story short is that it's just more of the same. Observational research, design and execution flaws, and the rest of it.

So where does all this leave us, then? Should we thumb our noses and eat all the red meat we want?

Not necessarily.

Research shows that some people (myself included) have a genetic polymorphism that may increase the risk of colorectal cancer from meats that are cooked at very high temperatures, like frying or grilling to the point of being well-done.[5] When meat is cooked in this way, several types of compounds are created that may contribute to cancer.

The association isn't conclusive yet, but I'm playing it safe and eating very little grilled or overcooked meat.

There's also some valid controversy over the health of processed meat products like hot dogs, hams, bacon products, pre-packaged deli meats, and other products that are pink, cured, and preserved with sodium nitrate.

There's good evidence that two substances found in these foods—nitrates and heme—contribute to the formation of carcinogenic compounds known as nitrosamines in the body, which increases the risk of cancer.[6]

So, it's reasonable to assume that eating too much processed meat can cause cancer. That said, without controlled interventions, which would never pass an ethics board due to the possibility of actually giving someone cancer, we can't say whether this finding is conclusive.

Personally, I treat processed meats the same way I treat grilled or overcooked meat. I'm not afraid to have a hot dog or some chicken nuggets and then, but I eat very little of these types of foods and recommend you do the same.

Here's the real take-home message of this chapter:

◆ Don't be overweight
◆ Exercise regularly
◆ Don't smoke
◆ Limit your alcohol intake
◆ Eat several servings of fruits and vegetables per day
◆ Avoid processed meats
◆ Avoid overcooked meats
◆ Do all that and you'll be in the best possible position to live a long, vital, and disease-free life.

UNDERSTANDING BEEF LABELS

Organic... grass-fed... locally grown... all-natural...

Which are just buzzwords and which actually mean something? Let's find out.

BEEF GRADES

The "grade" associated with a cut of beef refers to the quality of its marbling, which is how the fat is interlaced with the meat.

"Prime" is the highest grade, though these cuts are rarely found in grocery stores. Restaurants typically buy them at wholesale before they make their way to the consumer.

"Choice" and "select" represent the next two tiers, while "standard" and "commercial" grade beef are often sold without specific labels.

"Utility," "cutter," and "canner" grades aren't typically sold as-is in grocery stores but may be purchased as commercial ground beef, such as hamburger patties, or processed meat products, including hot dogs and frankfurters.

CERTIFICATION

The USDA doesn't certify beef on its own. Instead, the term "certified" is used to modify other labels as specified by the USDA (e.g. "certified choice" beef).

It is, however, legal for beef to be certified by other organizations' certification processes, as long as the organization is clearly identified (e.g. "Triple 888 Ranch's Certified Beef").

ORGANIC

Beef can only be labeled as "organic" under USDA protocols if it is raised without the use of antibiotics, growth hormones, genetically modified feed, or feed that contains animal by-products.

It is important to note, though, that this standard does not address the treatment of the animals, a consideration that's critical for many meat eaters.

GRASS-FED

Some studies suggest that cattle raised primarily on grass produce beef that contains more nutrients and less saturated fat than those that are raised and finished on grain.[7]

The USDA has a grass-fed labeling program, but it's voluntary and lacks third-party certification, which basically means the label may or may not mean anything, depending on the integrity of the farm.

If you want grass-fed beef that you can trust, look for beef certified as "100% grass-fed" or "grass-finished" by the American Grassfed Association.

NATURAL

According to the USDA, the labels "natural" and "all-natural" can be given to beef that's been minimally processed and contains no artificial ingredients or preservatives, but since these criteria apply to nearly all fresh meat, the phrases are relatively meaningless.

LOCALLY GROWN

This is another label of dubious value, thanks to the USDA's vague standards on where and when "locally grown" can be added to beef packaging.

To find out if the beef you're buying really was locally grown, ask your butcher for details or go straight to the source by buying direct from a local farm.

HUMANELY RAISED

Different groups have set their own criteria and certification processes for designating beef as "humanely raised."

The HFAC/Certified Humane, Animal Welfare Approved (AWA), American Humane Certified, and Global Animal Partnership organizations have the strictest standards and the greatest transparency.

KOSHER/HALAL

Kosher and Halal designations signify that the beef has been prepared in accordance with either Jewish ("Kosher") or Muslim ("Halal") religious practices.

ANGUS, WAGYU, AND KOBE

These labels indicate the type of cow the beef comes from.

Angus beef comes from Angus cows, which are the most popular beef breed of cattle in the U.S. because of the superior flavor and tenderness of their meat.

Look for the Certified Angus Beef label given by the American Angus Association. Only 8% of beef meets the organization's stringent ten-point certification criteria.

Wagyu beef, unsurprisingly, comes from Japanese Wagyu cows, which are genetically predisposed to high marbling and a high percentage of unsaturated fat.

"Kobe" refers to a specific strain of Japanese Waygu beef that's prized for its flavor and texture and famous for its cultivation, which includes feeding the animals beer and massaging them with sake.

THE BOTTOM LINE

As you can see, beef labeling is more marketing hocus-pocus than anything else.

Don't pay more for "natural" beef, because the claim means nothing.

Don't give "grass-fed" and "locally grown" special value either, because in many cases they, too, mean nothing.

Many people feel that "choice" and "select" cuts of beef tend to taste better than "standard" and "commercial" grades.

Personally I eat mainly organic meat, simply to reduce my exposure to pesticides and other potentially unhealthy chemicals.

I don't give much weight to the "locally grown" label unless I can verify the actual farm the meat came from.

And, if budget permits, treat yourself to a good Wagyu steak sometime. They're absolutely delicious.

ADOBO SIRLOIN

SERVES **4** | PREP TIME **5 MINUTES**, PLUS **2 HOURS** TO MARINATE | COOKING TIME **10 MINUTES**, PLUS **10 MINUTES** RESTING
237 CALORIES | **39** GRAMS PROTEIN | **2** GRAMS CARBOHYDRATES | **7** GRAMS FAT

Juice of 1 lime

1 tablespoon minced garlic

1 teaspoon dried oregano

1 teaspoon ground cumin

2 tablespoons finely chopped canned chipotle chiles in adobo sauce plus 2 tablespoons sauce

4 (6-ounce) sirloin steaks, trimmed of fat

Salt and ground black pepper, to taste

1 In a small bowl, combine lime juice, garlic, oregano, cumin, chiles, and adobo sauce. Mix well to combine.

2 Season meat with salt and pepper. Place steaks into a large Ziploc bag with adobo marinade. Seal tightly and shake to coat. Refrigerate for at least 2 hours, shaking occasionally.

3 Prepare a grill to high heat. Lightly coat the grill grates with cooking spray. Once the grill is hot, cook steaks until desired doneness, about 4 to 5 minutes on each side. Let the steaks rest for 10 minutes and serve

BEEF STROGANOFF

SERVES **4** | PREP TIME **10 MINUTES** | COOKING TIME **20 MINUTES**, PLUS **5 MINUTES** RESTING

519 CALORIES | **37** GRAMS PROTEIN | **47** GRAMS CARBOHYDRATES | **19** GRAMS FAT

Salt and ground black pepper, to taste

8 *ounces egg noodles*

1 *pound beef tenderloin, trimmed of fat and sliced*

2 *tablespoons extra-virgin olive oil*

½ *medium onion, sliced*

4 *ounces white mushrooms, sliced*

1 *tablespoon cornstarch*

1 *(10.5-ounce) can condensed beef broth, divided*

1 *teaspoon Dijon mustard*

1 *clove garlic, peeled and minced*

3 *tablespoons white wine*

½ *tablespoon Worcestershire sauce*

2 *tablespoons low-fat sour cream*

2 *tablespoons reduced-fat cream cheese*

1 Bring a large pot of lightly salted water to a boil over high heat. Cook noodles according to package instructions. Drain and reserve.

2 Meanwhile, season meat with salt and pepper. Warm oil in a large skillet over medium heat. Add beef; brown on all sides and then push to one side of the pan.

3 Add onion and mushrooms, cooking until tender, about 3 to 5 minutes. Push to the side with beef. In a small bowl, combine cornstarch with 2 tablespoons cold beef broth. Add to the skillet and mix with juices in the pan to deglaze.

4 Pour in remaining beef broth. Bring to a boil, stirring frequently. Reduce the heat to low and stir in mustard, garlic, wine, and Worcestershire sauce. Cover with a tight-fitting lid and simmer for 10 minutes.

5 Two minutes before beef is done, stir in sour cream and cream cheese. Stir well and allow beef to finish cooking in the sauce. Let meat rest 5 minutes and serve.

MIKE'S SAVORY BURGERS

SERVES **4** | PREP TIME **5 MINUTES** | COOKING TIME **12 MINUTES**
516 CALORIES | **42** GRAMS PROTEIN | **29** GRAMS CARBOHYDRATES | **26** GRAMS FAT

1½ *pounds 92% lean ground beef*

4 *tablespoons Dijon mustard*

Salt and ground black pepper, to taste

½ *cup low-carb ketchup*

½ *cup light mayonnaise*

1 *tablespoon red wine vinegar*

2 *teaspoons Worcestershire sauce*

4 *whole-grain hamburger buns*

4 *sandwich slice pickles, halved*

1 Prepare a grill to high heat. Lightly coat the grill grates with cooking spray.

2 In a large bowl, combine beef, mustard, salt, and pepper. Shape into 4 equal-sized patties and grill the patties for 5 to 6 minutes per side.

3 Meanwhile, in a small bowl, mix ketchup, mayonnaise, vinegar, and Worcestershire sauce.

4 Slice the buns in half and place cut side down on the grill to toast until light golden brown, about 10 seconds.

5 Place hamburgers onto buns and top with pickles and sauce. Serve.

BEEF LO MEIN

SERVES **1** | PREP TIME **10 MINUTES** | COOKING TIME **15 MINUTES**
524 CALORIES | **49** GRAMS PROTEIN | **50** GRAMS CARBOHYDRATES | **14** GRAMS FAT

Salt, to taste

2 *ounces whole-grain spaghetti*

1 *teaspoon sesame oil*

1 *(6-ounce) sirloin steak, trimmed of fat and sliced into strips*

¼ *cup fresh snow pea pods, trimmed*

¼ *cup broccoli florets*

¼ *cup shredded carrots*

1 *scallion, chopped*

⅛ *teaspoon red pepper flakes*

½ *clove garlic, peeled and minced*

2 *tablespoons less-sodium soy sauce*

½ *teaspoon peeled and grated fresh ginger*

1 *teaspoon toasted sesame seeds*

1 Bring a medium pot of lightly salted water to a boil over high heat. Cook spaghetti according to package instructions. Drain and reserve.

2 Meanwhile, warm oil in a wok or large skillet over medium-high heat. Add beef and stir-fry until browned, about 4 to 6 minutes. Remove from pan and set aside.

3 Add snow peas, broccoli, carrots, scallion, red pepper flakes, and garlic. Continue stir-frying for 2 to 3 minutes.

4 Stir in soy sauce, ginger, reserved noodles, and beef. Mix well and cook until hot.

5 Remove wok from heat and garnish stir-fry with sesame seeds. Serve.

BEEF LASAGNA FOR TWO

SERVES **2** | PREP TIME **10 MINUTES** | COOKING TIME **60 MINUTES**, PLUS **10 MINUTES** RESTING

624 CALORIES | **41** GRAMS PROTEIN | **65** GRAMS CARBOHYDRATES | **19** GRAMS FAT

1 teaspoon extra-virgin olive oil

½ pound 92% lean ground beef

½ small onion, chopped

½ teaspoon dried oregano

　Pinch of ground black pepper

2 cups tomato sauce

1 cup low-fat ricotta cheese

1 tablespoon grated Parmesan cheese

6 no-boil lasagna noodles

1 zucchini, thinly sliced

1 Preheat the oven to 350°F.

2 Warm oil in a large nonstick skillet over medium-high heat. Into the skillet, add beef, onion, oregano, and pepper, using a wooden spoon to break the meat into small pieces. Cook for 6 to 8 minutes, stirring frequently, until the meat is fully cooked. Stir in tomato sauce, bring to a boil, and then remove from heat.

3 In a small bowl, mix ricotta and Parmesan.

4 To build lasagna, layer ingredients in a 9-inch by 13-inch baking dish: start with ½ cup sauce, 2 noodles, and ½ cup cheese mixture. Add another ½ cup sauce and half the zucchini slices. Continue by layering with 2 noodles, remaining ½ cup cheese mixture, ½ cup sauce, and remaining zucchini slices. Top with remaining ½ cup sauce and remaining 2 noodles.

5 Cover the dish with foil and bake in the oven for 30 minutes. Remove foil and continue to bake for 15 more minutes.

6 Remove from oven and let lasagna sit for at least 10 minutes before cutting to serve.

TERIYAKI SIRLOIN STEAKS

SERVES **4** | PREP TIME **5 MINUTES**, PLUS **2 HOURS** TO MARINATE | COOKING TIME **10 MINUTES**, PLUS **10 MINUTES** RESTING
279 CALORIES | **40** GRAMS PROTEIN | **10** GRAMS CARBOHYDRATES | **7** GRAMS FAT

⅓ cup less-sodium soy sauce

2 tablespoons molasses

2 teaspoons Dijon mustard

3 cloves garlic, peeled and minced

2 teaspoons peeled and grated fresh ginger

4 (6-ounce) sirloin steaks, trimmed of fat

Salt and ground black pepper, to taste

1 In a small bowl, add soy sauce, molasses, Dijon mustard, garlic, and ginger. Whisk together until mixed.

2 Place steaks into a large Ziploc bag, season with salt and pepper, and pour in marinade. Seal tightly, shake to coat, and refrigerate steaks for at least 2 hours, shaking occasionally.

3 Prepare a grill to high heat. Lightly coat the grill grates with cooking spray. Once the grill is hot, grill steaks for 4 minutes undisturbed. Then use tongs to flip the steaks and grill another 4 to 6 minutes, depending on preferred doneness. Let the steaks rest for 10 minutes and serve.

SALISBURY STEAK

SERVES **5** | PREP TIME **10 MINUTES** | COOKING TIME **15 MINUTES**
216 CALORIES | **24** GRAMS PROTEIN | **11** GRAMS CARBOHYDRATES | **8** GRAMS FAT

3 cups sliced white mushrooms, divided

1 pound 92% lean ground beef

¼ cup plain breadcrumbs

2 egg whites or 6 tablespoons liquid egg white substitute

¼ cup 2% milk

¼ teaspoon dried thyme

3 tablespoons low-carb ketchup, divided

1 (12-ounce) jar fat-free beef gravy

1 Finely chop 1 cup of mushrooms, reserving the remaining sliced mushrooms for later.

2 In a medium bowl, combine chopped mushrooms, ground beef, breadcrumbs, egg whites, milk, thyme, and 1 tablespoon ketchup. Mix until thoroughly combined. Shape into 5 oval patties, about ½-inch thick.

3 Coat a large nonstick skillet with cooking spray and warm over medium-high heat. Add patties, cooking until browned on both sides, about 2 to 3 minutes per side.

4 Into the skillet, add the remaining 2 cups mushrooms, remaining 2 tablespoons ketchup, and gravy into the skillet. Bring the mixture to a boil; reduce heat to low. Cover and let simmer for 5 to 10 minutes until patties are fully cooked. Serve patties with gravy.

BEEF AND CHICKEN SAUSAGE-STUFFED MINI PEPPERS

SERVES **4** | PREP TIME **35 MINUTES** | COOKING TIME **40 MINUTES**

279 CALORIES | **16** GRAMS PROTEIN | **35** GRAMS CARBOHYDRATES | **10** GRAMS FAT

1 tablespoon extra-virgin olive oil

1 cup chopped onion

¼ pound 92% lean ground beef

¼ pound chicken sausage, casing removed

½ cup cooked medium-grain rice

¼ cup chopped scallions

1 teaspoon sweet paprika

½ teaspoon ground cayenne pepper

1 teaspoon dried oregano

Salt and ground black pepper, to taste

24 mini bell peppers, tops and seeds removed

1 Preheat the oven to 400°F.

2 Warm oil in a large skillet over medium heat. Add onion, stirring occasionally, and cook until translucent and lightly brown.

3 Remove from heat and transfer onion to a medium bowl. Into the bowl, add beef, sausage, rice, scallions, paprika, cayenne, oregano, salt, and pepper. Mix well.

4 Use a spoon to stuff the mixture into the cavity of each pepper. Add peppers to a shallow pan and cover with aluminum foil.

5 Bake peppers for 30 minutes or until their tops are crusty and brown. Serve hot.

GRILLED ROSEMARY LAMB CHOPS

SERVES **4** | PREP TIME **15 MINUTES**, PLUS **1 HOUR** TO MARINATE | COOKING TIME **8 MINUTES**, PLUS **10 MINUTES** RESTING

269 CALORIES | **20** GRAMS PROTEIN | **2** GRAMS CARBOHYDRATES | **19** GRAMS FAT

1 tablespoon extra-virgin olive oil

Juice of 1 lemon

3 cloves garlic, peeled and minced

1 tablespoon chopped fresh rosemary leaves

Salt and ground black pepper, to taste

8 (4-ounce) lamb chops, trimmed of fat

1 In a small bowl, combine olive oil, lemon juice, garlic, and rosemary.

2 Place lamb chops into a large Ziploc bag, season with salt and pepper, and pour in marinade. Seal tightly, shake to coat, and refrigerate lamb for at least 1 hour and up to overnight, shaking occasionally.

3 Prepare a grill to medium-high heat. Lightly coat the grill grates with cooking spray.

4 Discard marinade. Once the grill is hot, grill lamb for 4 minutes on each side. Let the lamb chops rest for 10 minutes and serve 2 chops per person.

EASY HONEY-MUSTARD LEG OF LAMB

SERVES **8** | PREP TIME **10 MINUTES** | COOKING TIME **1 HOUR 5 MINUTES**, PLUS **10 MINUTES** RESTING
441 CALORIES | **54** GRAMS PROTEIN | **12** GRAMS CARBOHYDRATES | **35** GRAMS FAT

¼ cup honey

5 tablespoons Dijon mustard

2 tablespoons chopped fresh thyme leaves

3 cloves garlic, peeled and minced

Salt and ground black pepper, to taste

5 pounds whole leg of lamb

1 Preheat the oven to 450°F.

2 In a small bowl, add honey, mustard, thyme, garlic, salt, and pepper. Mix well to combine.

3 Place lamb on a rack in a roasting pan. Rub honey-mustard mixture onto lamb. Roast in the oven for 20 minutes.

4 Reduce the heat to 400°F and roast lamb an additional 45 minutes. For medium-rare doneness, the internal temperature should be at least 140°F on a meat thermometer.

5 Let lamb rest for 10 minutes before carving.

PORK CHOPS BRAISED WITH ORANGES

SERVES **4** | PREP TIME **5 MINUTES** | COOKING TIME **25 MINUTES**

247 CALORIES | **38** GRAMS PROTEIN | **13** GRAMS CARBOHYDRATES | **4** GRAMS FAT

4 *(6-ounce) boneless pork chops, trimmed of fat*

Salt and ground black pepper, to taste

1 *(11-ounce) can mandarin oranges, drained*

½ *teaspoon ground cloves*

1 Season pork chops with salt and pepper, pressing seasoning into meat.

2 Spray a large skillet with cooking spray and warm over medium-high heat. Add each pork chop into the pan and sauté until golden brown on both sides. Pour oranges over the top and sprinkle the pork chops with cloves.

3 Cover the pan with a tight-fitting lid and reduce heat to low. Braise until meat is cooked through, about 20 to 25 minutes. Serve.

PLUM SAUCE-GLAZED PORK CHOPS

SERVES **4** | PREP TIME **5 MINUTES** | COOKING TIME **10 MINUTES**

229 CALORIES | **39** GRAMS PROTEIN | **8** GRAMS CARBOHYDRATES | **4** GRAMS FAT

4 *(6-ounce) boneless pork chops, trimmed of fat*

¼ *teaspoon salt*

¼ *teaspoon ground black pepper*

¼ *cup Chinese plum sauce*

4 *teaspoons yellow mustard*

1 Season pork chops with salt and pepper. Coat a large nonstick skillet with cooking spray and warm over medium-high heat.

2 Add pork chops into the skillet, cooking until no longer pink in the center, about 3 minutes per side.

3 In a small bowl, combine plum sauce and mustard. Brush the mixture on top of each pork chop and serve.

DIJON AND SAGE-COATED PORK TENDERLOIN

SERVES **4** | PREP TIME **5 MINUTES** | COOKING TIME **25 MINUTES**, PLUS **10 MINUTES** RESTING

172 CALORIES | **26** GRAMS PROTEIN | **1** GRAM CARBOHYDRATES | **6** GRAMS FAT

1 pound pork tenderloin, trimmed of fat

1 tablespoon extra-virgin olive oil

Salt and ground black pepper, to taste

2 tablespoons Dijon mustard

2 cloves garlic, peeled and minced

1 tablespoon finely chopped fresh sage

1 Preheat the oven to 375°F. Coat a shallow baking pan with cooking spray and set aside.

2 Use paper towels to pat the pork dry and season it with salt and pepper.

3 Warm oil in a large nonstick skillet over high heat. Once the pan is hot but not yet smoking, add pork, turning occasionally until browned on all sides, about 4 minutes. Transfer to the prepared baking pan.

4 Spread mustard, garlic, and sage over pork. Roast in the middle rack of the oven until an instant-read thermometer diagonally inserted 2 inches into the meat registers 145°F, about 20 minutes

5 Transfer pork to a cutting board and cover with aluminum foil. Let pork rest for 10 minutes before slicing and serving.

SMOTHERED CAJUN PORK CHOPS WITH TOMATOES

SERVES **4** | PREP TIME **10 MINUTES** | COOKING TIME **15 MINUTES**

190 CALORIES | **32** GRAMS PROTEIN | **6** GRAMS CARBOHYDRATES | **3** GRAMS FAT

4 *(5-ounce) boneless pork chops, ½-inch thick and trimmed of fat*

2 *teaspoons salt-free extra-spicy seasoning blend*

½ *medium yellow onion, sliced*

1 *jalapeño pepper, seeded and finely chopped*

1 *(14.5-ounce) can diced tomatoes, undrained*

1 Rub both sides of pork chops with spicy seasoning blend.

2 Coat a large nonstick skillet with cooking spray and warm the pan over medium-high heat. Add onion and jalapeño, sautéing until slightly tender, about 2 minutes. Push the mixture to one side of the skillet.

3 On the other side of the skillet, add pork chops. Cook pork chops for 3 minutes, turning once so both sides are evenly browned.

4 Add tomatoes into the pan. When liquid begins to boil, reduce the heat to low, and cover with a lid. Cook until pork chops are no longer pink in the center, about 6 to 8 minutes. Serve chops, spooning sauce over them.

PARMESAN-CRUSTED PORK CHOPS

SERVES **4** | PREP TIME **5 MINUTES** | COOKING TIME **22 MINUTES**

256 CALORIES | **42** GRAMS PROTEIN | **6** GRAMS CARBOHYDRATES | **6** GRAMS FAT

¼ *cup 2% milk*

¼ *cup grated Parmesan cheese*

¼ *cup seasoned breadcrumbs*

¼ *teaspoon salt*

⅛ *teaspoon pepper*

¼ *teaspoon garlic powder*

4 *(6-ounce) boneless pork chops, ½-inch thick and trimmed of fat*

1 Preheat the oven to 375°F. Coat a baking sheet with cooking spray.

2 Place milk into a shallow dish. Into another shallow dish, add cheese, breadcrumbs, salt, pepper, and garlic powder; mix to combine.

3 Dip each pork chop into milk and then coat in the breadcrumb mixture. Place breaded chops onto the prepared baking sheet.

4 Bake chops in the oven until done, about 9 to 11 minutes on each side.

PORK TENDERLOIN AND BOK CHOY NOODLE STIR-FRY

SERVES **4** | PREP TIME **5 MINUTES** | COOKING TIME **15 MINUTES**

413 CALORIES | **28** GRAMS PROTEIN | **54** GRAMS CARBOHYDRATES | **8** GRAMS FAT

Salt, to taste

8 *ounces rice noodles*

⅓ *cup water*

¼ *cup Shao Hsing rice wine
or dry sherry*

2 *tablespoons less-sodium soy sauce*

2 *teaspoons cornstarch*

1 *tablespoon peanut oil
or canola oil*

1 *onion, thinly sliced*

1 *pound bok choy, cored and
cut into long, thin strips*

1 *pound pork tenderloin, trimmed
of fat and cut into thin strips*

2 *cloves garlic, peeled and minced*

1 *tablespoon chili garlic sauce
(sambal oelek)*

1 Bring a large pot of lightly salted water to a boil over high heat. Cook rice noodles according to package instructions. Drain and reserve.

2 In a small bowl, whisk together water, rice wine, soy sauce, and cornstarch.

3 Warm oil in a Dutch oven over medium heat. Once hot, add onion and cook until softened, about 2 to 3 minutes. Add bok choy and cook, stirring occasionally, until it begins to soften, about 5 minutes.

4 Add the pork, garlic, and chili garlic sauce. Stir occasionally until pork is just cooked through, about 1 minute.

5 Give the cornstarch mixture a quick whisk and pour into the Dutch oven. Bring to a boil, stirring frequently for 2 minutes until the sauce thickens. Serve pork stir-fry on top of noodles.

Poultry

In many people's minds, poultry lacks the flair of steak, veal, or pork.

Poultry is seen as the quintessential "blue collar" protein: affordable, humble, and, well, bland.

It doesn't have to be, though. As you'll see, poultry is a blank slate that you can craft into a vast number of flavorful dishes.

Apart from simply being a red-meat alternative, poultry can offer a number of health benefits:

- Chicken is both rich in protein and low in fat and calories. Just 100 grams of chicken breast provides 23 grams of protein and 1 gram of fat.
- Chicken is packed full of micronutrients. Chicken's phosphorous and calcium levels benefit bone health. Plus, it's rich in selenium, which has been associated with a reduced risk of arthritis, as well as vitamin B5 and tryptophan, both of which have calming, anti-anxiety effects.
- Chicken promotes heart health. Chicken is a great source of vitamin B6, which works within the body to reduce levels of homocysteine, a molecule linked to an increased risk of heart attack. The niacin found in chicken also helps lower cholesterol, further reducing heart attack risk.
- Chicken can help bolster the immune system. There's a reason your parents always served you chicken noodle soup when you were sick. Besides feeling soothing and providing steam to help clear congestion, the broth itself can help reduce the inflammation that makes the common cold so miserable.[1]

The benefits of poultry aren't limited to just chicken breast, either. Darker meats like turkey and duck offer many of chicken's health benefits with a wider variety of flavors to experiment with.

Now, before we dive into poultry recipes, let's talk sourcing and labels.

Generally speaking, you're going to get the highest-quality meat from locally sourced, humanely treated, and naturally raised poultry. If that isn't an option, however, use the following label information to choose the best option you can afford.

Officially, the USDA's Agricultural Marketing Service (AMS) oversees the language used to sell and market meat in the U.S. Here are a few of their terms that you need to know:

POULTRY GRADES

The AMS assigns grades based on the physical pre- and post-slaughter features of the bird, such as its plumpness, bone structure, and distribution of fat. Grades of A, B, or C can be assigned, with Grade A being the highest of the rankings.

FREE RANGE

Though this phrase is often thrown around to mean chickens raised in humane settings, the strict AMS definition implies only that the birds have "continuous and confined access to pasture throughout their lifecycle."

In practice, this covers everything from fully pastured birds to mass-production warehouses that have outdoor access but little to no opportunity to take advantage of it.

CAGE FREE

Another similarly misleading term, "cage free" only applies to egg-laying hens and requires that birds are able to "freely roam a building, room, or enclosed area."

What you might not know, however, is that commercial chicken production rarely involves the use of cages in the first place (rather, all birds are housed in large open barns), making this term pretty much meaningless.

NO ANTIBIOTICS ADMINISTERED

Finally, one marketing phrase that actually means what it implies!

Chicken advertised as having no antibiotics administered must, according to the AMS, have gone without antibiotics from birth to harvest.

NO HORMONES

Administering growth hormones or steroids to chickens has been illegal in the U.S. since 1959, but many producers still include this marketing message on their packaging.

NATURALLY RAISED

Distinct from "natural" poultry, naturally raised chickens have been given only vegetarian feed, eliminating contamination from the slaughter by-products occasionally found in chicken feed; have never received antibiotics; and have never been given hormones.

ORGANIC.

To qualify as "organic," chickens must be naturally raised, allowed to range freely, and given certified organic feed that's free from pesticides and chemical fertilizer.

POLLO FAJITAS

SERVES **4** | PREP TIME **5 MINUTES**, PLUS **30 MINUTES** TO MARINATE | COOKING TIME **12 MINUTES**
445 CALORIES | **46** GRAMS PROTEIN | **44** GRAMS CARBOHYDRATES | **9** GRAMS FAT

1 tablespoon Worcestershire sauce

1 tablespoon apple cider vinegar

1 tablespoon less-sodium soy sauce

1 teaspoon chili powder

1 clove garlic, peeled and minced

Dash of hot sauce

4 (6-ounce) boneless, skinless chicken breasts trimmed of fat and cut into strips

1 tablespoon vegetable oil

1 medium onion, thinly sliced

1 green bell pepper, seeded and sliced

Salt and ground black pepper, to taste

8 (6-inch) whole-wheat tortillas

Juice of ½ lemon

1 In a large Ziploc bag, add Worcestershire sauce, vinegar, soy sauce, chili powder, garlic, and hot sauce. Add chicken strips into the Ziploc bag. Seal tightly and shake to coat. Let chicken marinate at room temperature for 30 minutes (or refrigerate for several hours), shaking them occasionally.

2 Warm oil in a large skillet over high heat. Add the chicken strips and marinade to the pan; sauté for 5 to 6 minutes.

3 To the pan, add onion and green pepper, season with salt and pepper, and continue to sauté until chicken is fully cooked, about another 3 to 4 minutes. Remove from heat.

4 Warm tortillas in a nonstick pan or in the microwave. Top tortillas with the fajita mixture and squeeze with lemon juice before serving.

CHUNKY CHICKEN QUESADILLA

SERVES **2** | PREP TIME **5 MINUTES** | COOKING TIME **15 MINUTES**
315 CALORIES | **30** GRAMS PROTEIN | **28** GRAMS CARBOHYDRATES | **9** GRAMS FAT

1 (6-ounce) boneless, skinless chicken breast, trimmed of fat

1 tablespoon low-fat sour cream

2 (8-inch) whole-wheat tortillas

⅓ cup salsa

1 cup shredded lettuce

⅓ cup shredded low-fat cheddar cheese

1 Coat a medium nonstick skillet with cooking spray and warm over medium heat. Add chicken and cook for 3 to 5 minutes per side. Once fully cooked, transfer chicken to a cutting board.

2 Spread sour cream onto 1 tortilla. Slice chicken breast and layer it over sour cream, topping with salsa and lettuce. Sprinkle with cheese and top with the other tortilla.

3 Recoat skillet with cooking spray and warm over low heat. Cook quesadilla until golden, about 3 minutes per side, using a large spatula to carefully flip it. Remove from the skillet, slice, and serve.

CHICKEN FETTUCCINE WITH SHIITAKE MUSHROOMS

SERVES **4** | PREP TIME **10 MINUTES** | COOKING TIME **20 MINUTES**
444 CALORIES | **33** GRAMS PROTEIN | **43** GRAMS CARBOHYDRATES | **13** GRAMS FAT

Salt and ground black pepper, to taste

8 *ounces whole-grain fettuccine*

2 *tablespoons extra-virgin olive oil*

2 *(6-ounce) boneless, skinless chicken breasts, trimmed of fat and cut into strips*

3 *cloves garlic, peeled and minced*

2 *ounces stemmed and sliced shiitake mushrooms (around 1 to 1½ cups)*

2 *teaspoons lemon zest*

2 *tablespoons lemon juice*

½ *cup grated Parmesan cheese*

½ *cup chopped fresh basil*

1 Bring a large pot of lightly salted water to a boil over high heat. Cook fettuccine according to package instructions. Drain the pasta, reserving ½ cup of pasta water.

2 Meanwhile, warm oil in a large nonstick skillet over medium heat. Add chicken strips, sautéing for 3 to 4 minutes.

3 Add garlic and mushrooms. Cook, stirring occasionally, until mushrooms are tender, 4 to 5 minutes. Stir in lemon zest, lemon juice, salt, and pepper. Remove from the heat.

4 Into the skillet, add pasta, reserved pasta water, Parmesan, and basil. Toss well and serve.

HARVEST CHICKEN STEW

SERVES **6** | PREP TIME **15 MINUTES** | COOKING TIME **1 HOUR 10 MINUTES**

324 CALORIES | **44** GRAMS PROTEIN | **31** GRAMS CARBOHYDRATES | **3** GRAMS FAT

6 *(6-ounce) boneless, skinless chicken breasts trimmed of fat and cut into cubes*

1 *pound eggplant, peeled and cut into 1-inch cubes (about 4 cups)*

10 *to 12 small red potatoes, cut into ⅛-inch slices (about 4 cups)*

4 *carrots, peeled and sliced*

3 *medium onions, cut into quarters*

3½ *cups low-sodium chicken broth*

¾ *cup chopped fresh parsley*

2 *tablespoons chopped fresh thyme leaves*

¼ *teaspoon salt*

¼ *teaspoon ground black pepper*

½ *cup cold water*

2 *tablespoons whole-wheat flour*

1 Preheat the oven to 350°F.

2 Add chicken, eggplant, potatoes, carrots, onions, broth, parsley, thyme, salt, and pepper to an ovenproof Dutch oven. Cover with lid and bake in the oven for 50 minutes.

3 Place water and flour into a tightly covered container or small Ziploc bag. Seal tightly and shake. Pour the flour mixture into the stew and stir well.

4 Cover and place the Dutch oven back into the oven until potatoes are tender and chicken is fully cooked, about 20 more minutes. Remove from oven and serve.

CHICKEN YAKITORI

SERVES **4** | PREP TIME **5 MINUTES** | COOKING TIME **15 MINUTES**
225 CALORIES | **41** GRAMS PROTEIN | **5** GRAMS CARBOHYDRATES | **2** GRAMS FAT

½ cup less-sodium soy sauce

½ cup sherry or white cooking wine

½ cup low-sodium chicken broth

½ teaspoon ground ginger

Pinch of garlic powder

½ cup chopped scallions

4 (6-ounce) boneless, skinless chicken breasts, trimmed of fat and cut into 2-inch cubes

1 If using bamboo skewers versus metal skewers, soak in water for 30 minutes to prevent the wood from burning.

2 Into a small pot, add soy sauce, sherry, chicken broth, ginger, garlic powder, and scallions. Bring ingredients to a boil over medium-high heat and immediately remove from heat. Reserve.

3 Preheat the oven's broiler. Start threading chicken onto skewers.

4 Coat a broiler pan with cooking spray and place chicken skewers on the pan. Brush each skewer with sherry sauce.

5 Place the pan under the broiler until chicken is browned, about 3 minutes. Remove the pan from the oven to turn each chicken skewer over, brushing sauce onto chicken again.

6 Return the pan to the broiler until chicken is cooked through and nicely browned. Serve.

MUSCLE MEATBALLS

SERVES **4** (4 MEATBALLS PER SERVING) | PREP TIME **10 MINUTES** | COOKING TIME **20 MINUTES**
316 CALORIES | **40** GRAMS PROTEIN | **10** GRAMS CARBOHYDRATES | **13** GRAMS FAT

1½ *pounds 93% ground turkey*

2 *egg whites or 6 tablespoons liquid egg white substitute*

½ *cup toasted wheat germ*

¼ *cup quick-cooking oats*

1 *tablespoon whole flaxseed*

1 *tablespoon grated Parmesan cheese*

½ *teaspoon all-purpose seasoning*

¼ *teaspoon ground black pepper*

1 Preheat the oven to 400°F. Coat a 9-inch by 13-inch baking dish with cooking spray.

2 In a large bowl, add all of the ingredients and gently mix together to combine.

3 Form mixture into 16 meatballs and place them into the baking dish.

4 Bake for 7 minutes and use a spatula to flip each meatball. Return to oven and cook until meatballs are no longer pink in the center, about 8 to 13 minutes. Serve.

ORANGE AND HONEY-GLAZED CHICKEN

SERVES 4 | PREP TIME 5 MINUTES | COOKING TIME 25 MINUTES

216 CALORIES | 39 GRAMS PROTEIN | 10 GRAMS CARBOHYDRATES | 2 GRAMS FAT

4 (6-ounce) boneless, skinless chicken breasts, trimmed of fat

2 tablespoons orange juice

2 tablespoons honey

1 tablespoon lemon juice

⅛ teaspoon salt

1 Preheat the oven to 375°F.

2 Coat a 9-inch by 13-inch baking dish with cooking spray and add chicken.

3 In a small bowl, mix orange juice, honey, lemon juice, and salt. Baste each piece of chicken with the orange juice mixture.

4 Cover the dish with foil and bake for 10 minutes. Remove the foil and flip chicken. Bake chicken another 10 to 15 minutes until cooked through and juices run clear.

THAI BASIL CHICKEN

SERVES 4 | PREP TIME 5 MINUTES | COOKING TIME 15 MINUTES
220 CALORIES | 40 GRAMS PROTEIN | 5 GRAMS CARBOHYDRATES | 4 GRAMS FAT

4 (6-ounce) boneless, skinless chicken breasts, trimmed of fat

3 cloves garlic, peeled and minced

2 jalapeño peppers, minced

1 tablespoon fish sauce

1 tablespoon granulated sugar

¼ cup chopped fresh basil

1 tablespoon chopped fresh mint

1 tablespoon chopped unsalted dry-roasted peanuts

1 Cut each chicken breast into about 8 strips. Set aside.

2 Coat a large nonstick skillet with cooking spray and warm over medium-high heat. Add garlic and jalapeños. Sauté, stirring constantly, until garlic is just golden.

3 Add chicken strips and cook, stirring frequently, until chicken is fully cooked, about 8 to 10 minutes.

4 Add fish sauce and sugar. Sauté for 30 seconds and remove from heat. Garnish with basil, mint, and peanuts before serving.

CURRY CHICKEN

SERVES 4 | PREP TIME **10 MINUTES** | COOKING TIME **25 MINUTES**
213 CALORIES | **40** GRAMS PROTEIN | **7** GRAMS CARBOHYDRATES | **3** GRAMS FAT

CURRY CONTAINS TURMERIC, TURMERIC CONTAINS CURCUMIN, AND CURCUMIN IS AWESOME. Turmeric gets its distinct yellow color from a pigment known as curcumin, and scientists around the world are investigating applications for it to fight a variety of diseases, such as cancer, cardiovascular disease, osteoporosis, arthritis, diabetes, Alzheimer's, and more.[2]

TURMERIC HELPS KEEP YOUR BLOOD SUGAR LEVELS STABLE. Research shows that turmeric can decrease blood glucose levels and improve insulin sensitivity in obese and overweight men and women with type 2 diabetes.[3]

FENUGREEK, ANOTHER COMPONENT FOUND IN CURRY, CAN IMPROVE BLOOD GLUCOSE MANAGEMENT. In one study of 24 type 2 diabetic patients, the consumption of powdered fenugreek seeds over a period of eight weeks was correlated with a 25 to 31% improvement in measures of blood glucose control.

---

1 small onion, chopped

1 clove garlic, peeled and minced

3 tablespoons curry powder

1 teaspoon sweet paprika

1 bay leaf

1 teaspoon ground cinnamon

½ teaspoon peeled and grated fresh ginger

Salt and ground black pepper, to taste

4 (6-ounce) boneless, skinless chicken breasts, trimmed of fat and cut into 1-inch cubes

1 tablespoon tomato paste

½ cup water

Juice of ½ lemon

½ teaspoon Indian chili powder

1 cup 2% Greek yogurt

1 Coat a large skillet with cooking spray and warm over medium heat. Sauté onion until translucent, about 5 minutes.

2 Into the skillet, add garlic, curry powder, paprika, bay leaf, cinnamon, ginger, salt, and pepper; stir for 2 minutes.

3 Add chicken to the pan, along with tomato paste and water; stir to combine. Bring liquid to a boil, reduce the heat to low, and simmer for 10 minutes.

4 Stir in lemon juice and chili powder. Simmer until chicken is cooked through, about 5 more minutes. Take off the heat and remove and discard bay leaf. Stir in yogurt and serve.

SIMPLE ITALIAN PARMESAN CHICKEN

SERVES **4** | PREP TIME **5 MINUTES** | COOKING TIME **25 MINUTES**
290 CALORIES | **42** GRAMS PROTEIN | **6** GRAMS CARBOHYDRATES | **11** GRAMS FAT

2 tablespoons extra-virgin olive oil

2 teaspoons minced garlic

¼ cup seasoned breadcrumbs

¼ cup grated Parmesan cheese

4 (6-ounce) boneless, skinless chicken breasts, trimmed of fat

1 Preheat the oven to 425°F.

2 In a medium heatproof bowl, add olive oil and garlic. Warm in the microwave for 30 to 60 seconds to blend flavors. In a separate medium bowl, combine breadcrumbs and cheese.

3 Coat chicken breast in the oil mixture, letting the excess run off. Then, coat in the breadcrumb mixture and place in a shallow baking dish. Repeat until all chicken breasts are breaded.

4 Place chicken in the oven for 10 minutes, then flip and cook until chicken is no longer pink in the center and juices run clear, about another 10 to 15 minutes. Remove from oven and serve.

CHICKEN AND BROCCOLI STIR-FRY

SERVES **4** | PREP TIME **5 MINUTES** | COOKING TIME **15 MINUTES**
233 CALORIES | **41** GRAMS PROTEIN | **10** GRAMS CARBOHYDRATES | **3** GRAMS FAT

2 *tablespoons red wine*

1 *tablespoon less-sodium soy sauce*

½ *teaspoon cornstarch*

1 *tablespoon granulated sugar*

1 *teaspoon salt*

2 *cups broccoli florets*

1 *red bell pepper, seeded and chopped*

½ *onion, sliced*

4 *(6-ounce) boneless, skinless chicken breasts, trimmed of fat and cut into thin strips*

1 In a small bowl, combine red wine, soy sauce, cornstarch, sugar, and salt. Whisk well with a fork until cornstarch has dissolved.

2 Coat a large nonstick skillet with cooking spray and warm over medium-high heat. Sauté broccoli, bell pepper, and onion until tender.

3 Add chicken and stir-fry until browned, about 2 to 3 more minutes.

4 Pour soy sauce mixture over chicken and vegetables. Continue to stir-fry until sauce thickens and chicken is cooked through, about 2 to 4 minutes. Remove from heat and serve.

GREEK PITA PIZZA

SERVES **1** | PREP TIME **5 MINUTES** | COOKING TIME **15 MINUTES**
461 CALORIES | **49** GRAMS PROTEIN | **38** GRAMS CARBOHYDRATES | **14** GRAMS FAT

1   *(6-ounce) boneless, skinless chicken breast, trimmed of fat*

1   *whole-grain pita bread*

½   *tablespoon extra-virgin olive oil*

2   *tablespoons sliced olives*

1   *teaspoon red wine vinegar*

½   *clove garlic, peeled and minced*

¼   *teaspoon dried oregano*

¼   *teaspoon dried basil*

Salt and ground black pepper, to taste

¼   *cup fresh spinach*

2   *tablespoons crumbled low-fat feta cheese*

½   *tomato, seeded and chopped*

1 Preheat the oven's broiler to high.

2 Coat a small skillet with cooking spray and warm over medium heat. Add chicken to the skillet and cook 3 to 5 minutes per side. Remove chicken from the heat once juices run clear; set aside. Let cool and then chop chicken breast into small pieces.

3 Meanwhile, place pita bread on a baking sheet and lightly brush with oil. Broil 4 inches from the heat for 2 minutes.

4 In a small bowl, add olives, vinegar, garlic, oregano, basil, salt, pepper, and any remaining oil. Mix well to combine.

5 Spread the olive mixture over the pita. Layer pita with spinach, feta, tomato, and chicken.

6 Broil until feta is warmed and softened, about 3 more minutes. Remove from broiler and serve.

CHICKEN CACCIATORE

SERVES **4** | PREP TIME **5 MINUTES** | COOKING TIME **45 MINUTES**
440 CALORIES | **44** GRAMS PROTEIN | **44** GRAMS CARBOHYDRATES | **7** GRAMS FAT

1 tablespoon extra-virgin olive oil

4 (6-ounce) boneless, skinless chicken breasts, trimmed of fat and cut into strips

½ medium onion, chopped

½ cup thinly sliced mushrooms

1 clove garlic, peeled and minced

1 (28-ounce) can plum tomatoes with juice

½ cup dry red wine

1 teaspoon dried oregano

1 bay leaf

Salt, to taste

6 ounces quinoa rotelle pasta

½ cup chopped fresh parsley

1 Warm oil in a large deep skillet over medium-high heat. Add chicken and brown, cooking about 3 minutes per side. Add onion, mushrooms, and garlic; sauté until vegetables are tender.

2 Add tomatoes with juice, wine, oregano, and bay leaf. Reduce the heat to medium-low and cover with a lid. Stirring occasionally, simmer until chicken is cooked through and sauce thickens, about 30 to 35 minutes.

3 Meanwhile, bring a large pot of lightly salted water to a boil over high heat. Cook rotelle pasta according to package instructions. Drain the pasta, reserving ¼ cup of pasta water.

4 Add both the pasta and reserved pasta water to the chicken. Cook 1 to 2 minutes, mixing until sauce sticks to pasta.

5 Remove bay leaf and discard it. Garnish with fresh parsley and serve.

MEXICAN MEATLOAF

SERVES **8** | PREP TIME **10 MINUTES** | COOKING TIME **60 MINUTES**

343 CALORIES | **28** GRAMS PROTEIN | **32** GRAMS CARBOHYDRATES | **9** GRAMS FAT

2 pounds 93% lean ground turkey

1 (15-ounce) can black beans, drained and rinsed

1 (15-ounce) can whole kernel corn, drained and rinsed

½ (4-ounce) can fire-roasted diced green chiles

1 cup mild chunky salsa

1 (1-ounce) packet dry taco seasoning mix

¾ cup plain breadcrumbs

3 egg whites or ½ cup liquid egg white substitute

Salt and ground black pepper, to taste

1 (28-ounce) can enchilada sauce, divided

1 Preheat the oven to 400°F. Coat a 9-inch by 13-inch baking dish with cooking spray.

2 In a large bowl, combine turkey, black beans, corn, chiles, salsa, taco seasoning, breadcrumbs, and egg whites. Season with salt and pepper and mix thoroughly.

3 Add meat to the prepared baking dish, using clean hands or a spatula to form meat into a loaf shape. Spread half the enchilada sauce over the meat and cook in the oven for 45 minutes.

4 Remove loaf from the oven and top with remaining enchilada sauce. Return to the oven and bake until meatloaf is no longer pink inside, about 10 to 15 more minutes. A thermometer inserted into the center should read at least 165°F. Remove meatloaf from oven and serve.

BOW-TIE PASTA SALAD WITH CHICKEN AND CHICKPEAS

SERVES **6** | PREP TIME **10 MINUTES**, PLUS **4 HOURS** TO CHILL | COOKING TIME **15 MINUTES**

371 CALORIES | **28** GRAMS PROTEIN | **41** GRAMS CARBOHYDRATES | **12** GRAMS FAT

Salt, to taste

8 *ounces whole-grain bow-tie pasta*

3 *(6-ounce) chicken breasts, trimmed of fat, cooked, and shredded*

½ *(15-ounce) can chickpeas, drained and rinsed*

1 *(2.25-ounce) can sliced black olives, drained*

2 *stalks celery, chopped*

2 *cucumbers, chopped*

½ *cup shredded carrots*

½ *yellow onion, finely chopped*

2 *tablespoons shredded Parmesan cheese*

3 *tablespoons extra-virgin olive oil*

⅓ *cup red wine vinegar*

½ *teaspoon Worcestershire sauce*

½ *teaspoon spicy brown mustard*

½ *clove garlic, peeled and minced*

2 *tablespoons chopped fresh Italian parsley*

1 *tablespoon chopped fresh basil or 1 teaspoon dried basil*

¼ *teaspoon ground black pepper*

1 Bring a large pot of lightly salted water to a boil over high heat. Cook pasta according to package instructions. Drain and run pasta under cold water for about 30 seconds or until it is completely cool.

2 Transfer pasta to a large bowl and add remaining ingredients. Use tongs to mix thoroughly to combine.

3 Cover the bowl with plastic wrap and refrigerate for at least 4 hours or up to overnight. Toss the salad prior to serving.

LEAN TURKEY PAPRIKASH

SERVES **4** | PREP TIME **15 MINUTES** | COOKING TIME **20 MINUTES**
456 CALORIES | **35** GRAMS PROTEIN | **45** GRAMS CARBOHYDRATES | **14** GRAMS FAT

Salt and ground black pepper, to taste

8 *ounces egg noodles*

2 *teaspoons extra-virgin olive oil*

6 *ounces white mushrooms, sliced*

1 *tablespoon finely chopped onion*

1 *pound 93% lean ground turkey*

½ *cup water*

1 *cube chicken bouillon, crumbled*

1 *tablespoon sweet paprika*

⅔ *cup 2% Greek yogurt*

1 Bring a large pot of lightly salted water to a boil over high heat. Cook pasta according to package instructions and drain. Reserve.

2 Warm oil in a large skillet over medium heat. Sauté mushrooms and onion, cooking for a few minutes until tender and lightly brown.

3 Add turkey to the skillet, stirring occasionally. Once turkey is fully cooked, stir in water and bouillon cube. Season with paprika, salt, and pepper, stirring to combine.

4 Remove pan from the heat. Stir in yogurt and immediately serve turkey over pasta.

CHICKEN PESTO PASTA

SERVES **2** | PREP TIME **5 MINUTES** | COOKING TIME **20 MINUTES**

412 CALORIES | **31** GRAMS PROTEIN | **38** GRAMS CARBOHYDRATES | **17** GRAMS FAT

Salt and ground black pepper, to taste

4 *ounces whole-grain ziti*

25 *fresh basil leaves, finely chopped*

1 *clove garlic, peeled and minced*

1 *tablespoon warm water*

2 *tablespoons pine nuts, crushed*

1 *tablespoon extra-virgin olive oil*

1 *(6-ounce) boneless, skinless chicken breast, trimmed of fat and cut into small cubes*

2 *tablespoons grated Parmesan cheese*

1 Bring a medium pot of lightly salted water to a boil over high heat. Cook pasta according to package instructions. Drain and reserve.

2 Meanwhile, in a bowl, make pesto mixture: add basil, garlic, water, pine nuts, and oil; mix to combine.

3 Coat a medium pan with cooking spray and warm over medium heat. Add chicken and cook about 7 minutes per side.

4 When chicken is almost cooked through, reduce the heat to low. Stir in salt, pepper, pesto, and cheese. Cook until chicken is no longer pink inside.

5 Add pasta into the pan, stir to combine, and serve.

AUSSIE CHICKEN

SERVES **4** | PREP TIME **30 MINUTES**, PLUS **30 MINUTES** TO MARINATE | COOKING TIME **35 MINUTES**
399 CALORIES | **46** GRAMS PROTEIN | **21** GRAMS CARBOHYDRATES | **14** GRAMS FAT

4 *(6-ounce) boneless, skinless chicken breasts, trimmed of fat and pounded to ½-inch thickness*

2 *teaspoons seasoning salt*

6 *slices bacon, cut in half*

¼ *cup yellow mustard*

¼ *cup honey*

2 *tablespoons light mayonnaise*

1 *tablespoon dried onion flakes*

1 *tablespoon vegetable oil*

1 *cup sliced white mushrooms*

½ *cup reduced-fat shredded Monterey Jack cheese*

2 *tablespoons chopped fresh parsley*

1 After pounding chicken breasts, rub them with seasoning salt. Cover and refrigerate for 30 minutes.

2 Preheat the oven to 350°F.

3 Cook bacon in a large skillet over medium-high heat until crisp. Transfer bacon to a paper towel-lined plate and set aside. Leave bacon fat in skillet.

4 In a medium bowl, mix mustard, honey, mayonnaise, and onion flakes.

5 Warm bacon fat over medium heat. Add chicken and cook until browned, about 3 to 5 minutes per side.

6 Transfer chicken to a 9-inch by 13-inch baking dish. Brush chicken with honey-mustard sauce, followed by adding a layer of mushrooms and bacon. Sprinkle with cheese.

7 Bake until cheese melts and the chicken juices run clear, about 15 minutes. Garnish with parsley and serve.

5 DELICIOUS CHICKEN MARINADES

MARINADES ARE A SIMPLE AND FLAVORFUL WAY TO SPICE UP an otherwise bland meal or to change up the taste of just about any chicken recipe.

THE BEST WAY TO MARINATE CHICKEN IS TO PUT THE MARINADE AND CHICKEN INTO A LARGE ZIPLOC BAG, seal it tightly, shake it to fully coat the chicken, and let sit overnight in the fridge.

THESE RECIPES produce enough marinade for 3 to 5 chicken breasts.

TERIYAKI

81 CALORIES | **2** GRAMS PROTEIN |
7 GRAMS CARBOHYDRATES | **5** GRAMS FAT

- ½ cup less-sodium soy sauce
- 2 tablespoons Worcestershire sauce
- 1½ tablespoons distilled white vinegar
- 1½ tablespoons vegetable oil
- 1½ tablespoons onion powder
- 1 teaspoon garlic powder
- ½ teaspoon ground ginger

LEMON-WINE

84 CALORIES | **0** GRAMS PROTEIN |
4 GRAMS CARBOHYDRATES | **7** GRAMS FAT

- 2 tablespoons extra-virgin olive oil
- ¼ cup white wine
- 2 teaspoons lemon zest
- 2 tablespoons lemon juice
- 1 tablespoon brown sugar, unpacked
- 1 tablespoon fresh thyme leaves
- 1 tablespoon fresh rosemary leaves
- 2 cloves garlic, peeled and minced

PINEAPPLE-SOY

135 CALORIES | **2** GRAMS PROTEIN |
34 GRAMS CARBOHYDRATES | **0** GRAMS FAT

- 1 cup canned crushed pineapple
- ⅓ cup less-sodium soy sauce
- ⅓ cup honey
- ¼ cup apple cider vinegar
- 2 cloves garlic, peeled and minced
- 1 teaspoon ground ginger
- ¼ teaspoon ground cloves

JALAPEÑO-LIME

50 CALORIES | **0** GRAMS PROTEIN |
13 GRAMS CARBOHYDRATES | **0** GRAMS FAT

- ½ cup orange juice
- ⅓ cup finely chopped onion
- 1 teaspoon lime zest
- ¼ cup lime juice
- 2 tablespoons honey
- 1 clove garlic, peeled and minced
- ½ jalapeño pepper, seeded and finely chopped
- 1 teaspoon ground cumin
- ¼ teaspoon garlic salt

CARNE ASADA

70 CALORIES | **0** GRAMS PROTEIN |
2 GRAMS CARBOHYDRATES | **7** GRAMS FAT

- ¼ cup red wine vinegar
- 2 tablespoons extra-virgin olive oil
- 2 tablespoons steak sauce
- 1 clove garlic, peeled and minced
- 1 teaspoon dried crumbled sage
- 1 teaspoon dried oregano
- ½ teaspoon salt
- ½ teaspoon dry mustard
- ½ teaspoon sweet paprika

═ ═ Seafood ═ ═

If seafood rarely finds its way to your plate, I would like to change that.

These recipes will not only introduce your palate to new, delicious vistas of flavor and possibility, they'll also benefit your health. Here's why.

Seafood is a great source of protein. More than 3.5 billion people rely on seafood as a primary food source. Globally, more protein is consumed in the form of seafood than in cattle, sheep, or poultry.[1]

It's also a rich source of various vitamins and minerals, such as magnesium, phosphorus, selenium, and vitamins A and D.

Seafood is a great source of omega-3 fatty acids, too. Research shows that human beings evolved on a diet that had a ratio of omega-6 to omega-3 fatty acids of about 1:1.[2] Modern Western diets, however, have a ratio of about 10:1 to 25:1, and this imbalance causes many unwanted health effects and conditions.

Well, you can increase your intake of omega-3 fatty acids either with supplementation or by eating more fatty fish. The latter has more benefits than popping another pill with your daily multivitamin: it will likely reduce your intake of omega-6 fatty acids as well. This is helpful because other sources of protein like chicken, pork, and red meat are quite high in these fats.

Now, if you dismiss seafood for the common reasons—"too fishy," too hard to prepare, too expensive, and so forth—I understand. I used to be the same way.

As you'll soon see, though, no matter your taste preferences, cooking skills, or budget, there's a seafood option for you.

For example:

SALMON
There are many types of salmon that you can buy, ranging from Atlantic to Chinook to chum, from coho to pink to sockeye, and each variety can deliver a rather different gustatory experience.

Furthermore, the texture and fullness of flavor vary based on whether the fish was wild caught or farm raised, and fresh salmon is quite different from the packaged variety.

TUNA
Tuna has just as much variety as salmon because "tuna" is more of a broad classification than an individual fish. There are albacore, bluefin, and yellowfin varieties.

Moreover, fresh tuna has a steak-like, meaty texture and a rich taste, while canned tuna tends to be white or pink in color and have faintly acidic or citrus flavors.

MAHI MAHI
"Mahi mahi" is the Hawaiian name for a fish known elsewhere as the dolphinfish. Food marketers wisely changed the name for obvious reasons (no, it's not a species of dolphin).

When raw, mahi mahi has a pinkish-white color, a moist, velvety texture, and a clean citrus flavor.

COD

Cod comes from the family of fish that includes pollock, haddock, hake, and hoki.

It's typically pink or white in color, generally moist in texture, and has earthy and herbal tones, making it a versatile choice for many different dishes.

TILAPIA

As the world's second-most farmed group of fish in the world—exceeded only by carp—tilapia is a popular ingredient on both home and restaurant menus.

The fish's small, close flakes and neutral flavor, reminiscent of chicken, give it the flexibility required to pair well with a number of different cooking methods and sauces.

HALIBUT

Though you might not know it from the small fillets you purchase at the market, halibut can reach 8 feet in length and weigh more than 600 pounds in the wild.

In the kitchen, however, this fish is prized for its moist, meaty texture, subtle oily flavor, and light pink flesh.

SHRIMP

You can enjoy a number of varieties, including black tiger, Chinese white, freshwater, gulf, Pacific white, pink, and rock shrimp.

Shrimp are a particularly versatile type of seafood whose mild, sweet flavor stands up well to poaching, steaming, deep-frying, and sautéing.

SCALLOPS

Both bay and sea scallops are popular shellfish choices. Harvested fresh from the East Coast or raised in fisheries, scallops have a pleasantly squishy texture and a flavor that's described as being fishy, sweet, buttery, and slightly nutty.

So, now that I've (hopefully) done a good job whetting your appetite for some seafood, let's get to the recipes!

LEMON-GARLIC SHRIMP WITH ASPARAGUS

SERVES **4** | PREP TIME **10 MINUTES** | COOKING TIME **10 MINUTES**

255 CALORIES | **30** GRAMS PROTEIN | **17** GRAMS CARBOHYDRATES | **8** GRAMS FAT

2 *red bell peppers, seeded and chopped*

2 *pounds asparagus, trimmed and cut into 1-inch pieces*

2 *teaspoons lemon zest*

½ *teaspoon salt, divided*

2 *teaspoons extra-virgin olive oil*

5 *cloves garlic, peeled and minced*

1 *pound raw large shrimp, shelled and deveined*

1 *cup low-sodium chicken broth*

1 *teaspoon cornstarch*

2 *tablespoons lemon juice*

2 *tablespoons chopped fresh parsley*

1 Coat a large nonstick skillet with cooking spray and warm over medium-high heat. Add bell peppers, asparagus, lemon zest, and ¼ teaspoon salt. Sauté until vegetables begin to soften, about 6 minutes. Transfer vegetables to a bowl, cover, and reserve.

2 Add oil and garlic to the pan and sauté for 30 seconds. Stir in shrimp. In a small bowl, combine broth and cornstarch with a whisk. Into the pan, stir in the broth mixture and the remaining ¼ teaspoon salt.

3 Cook, stirring frequently, until sauce thickens and shrimp are pink and cooked through, about 2 to 3 minutes. Remove the pan from the heat, adding lemon juice and parsley. Mix and serve the shrimp over the reserved vegetables.

CREAMY FETTUCCINE WITH SCALLOPS

SERVES **5** | PREP TIME **10 MINUTES** | COOKING TIME **25 MINUTES**
402 CALORIES | **31** GRAMS PROTEIN | **56** GRAMS CARBOHYDRATES | **5** GRAMS FAT

Salt and ground black pepper, to taste

8 *ounces whole-grain fettuccine*

1 *pound large sea scallops*

1 *(8-ounce) bottle clam juice (the lowest sodium available)*

1 *cup 2% milk*

3 *tablespoons cornstarch*

3 *cups frozen peas*

⅓ *cup chopped chives*

½ *teaspoon lemon zest*

1 *teaspoon lemon juice*

½ *cup grated Parmesan cheese*

1 Bring a large pot of lightly salted water to a boil over high heat. Cook fettuccine according to package instructions. Drain the pasta and reserve.

2 Meanwhile, dry scallops with a paper towel and sprinkle with salt. Coat a large nonstick skillet with cooking spray and warm over medium-high heat. Add scallops and cook until golden brown, about 2 to 3 minutes per side. Remove from pan and reserve.

3 Add clam juice to the pan. In a medium bowl, add milk, cornstarch, salt, and pepper; whisk until smooth. Pour milk mixture into the pan and whisk with clam juice. Once the mixture is simmering, stir constantly until sauce thickens, about 1 to 2 minutes.

4 Add reserved scallops and peas to clam sauce and bring to a simmer. Stir in reserved fettuccine, chives, lemon zest, lemon juice, and most of the cheese; mix well. Remove pan from the heat and top pasta with remaining cheese. Serve.

LEMON-ROSEMARY SALMON STEAKS

SERVES **4** | PREP TIME **5 MINUTES**, PLUS **15 MINUTES** TO MARINATE | COOKING TIME **15 TO 20 MINUTES**

226 CALORIES | **34** GRAMS PROTEIN | **0** GRAMS CARBOHYDRATES | **9** GRAMS FAT

1 tablespoon lemon juice

½ teaspoon dried rosemary

1 tablespoon extra-virgin olive oil

4 (6-ounce) wild Pacific salmon fillets

Salt and ground black pepper, to taste

1 Preheat the oven to 350°F. In a medium baking dish, combine lemon juice, rosemary, and olive oil.

2 Season salmon fillets with salt and pepper. Add fillets to the baking dish, turn to coat, and let marinate for 10 to 15 minutes.

3 Cover dish with foil and bake until fish easily flakes with a fork, about 20 minutes. Remove from oven and serve.

GRAHAM CRACKER-CRUSTED TILAPIA

SERVES **4** | PREP TIME **10 MINUTES** | COOKING TIME **10 MINUTES**
222 CALORIES | **24** GRAMS PROTEIN | **10** GRAMS CARBOHYDRATES | **10** GRAMS FAT

4 (4-ounce) tilapia fillets, about ¾-inch thick

½ cup plain graham cracker crumbs

1 teaspoon lemon zest

¼ teaspoon salt

¼ teaspoon ground black pepper

¼ cup 2% milk

1 tablespoon canola oil

2 tablespoons chopped pecans, toasted

1 Position the oven rack to slightly above the middle and preheat the oven to 500°F. Coat a 13-inch by 9-inch baking dish with cooking spray.

2 Cut fillets crosswise into 2-inch wide pieces.

3 In a small bowl, add graham cracker crumbs, lemon zest, salt, and pepper. Stir to combine. Pour milk into a separate small bowl.

4 Add each fish piece into the milk mixture and then coat in graham crackers. Place fish into the prepared baking dish, continuing until each piece is breaded.

5 Drizzle oil and pecans over fillets. Bake until fish easily flakes with a fork, about 10 minutes. Remove from oven and serve.

GINGER AND SOY SAUCE-MARINATED HALIBUT WITH LEEKS

SERVES **4** | PREP TIME **15 MINUTES**, PLUS **1 HOUR** TO MARINATE | COOKING TIME **20 MINUTES**
283 CALORIES | **37** GRAMS PROTEIN | **9** GRAMS CARBOHYDRATES | **11** GRAMS FAT

2 tablespoons extra-virgin olive oil

2 tablespoons less-sodium soy sauce

2 tablespoons lemon juice

2 tablespoons white wine

2 cloves garlic, peeled and minced

2 (quarter-sized) fresh ginger pieces, peeled and minced

Salt and ground black pepper, to taste

4 (6-ounce) halibut fillets

3 medium leeks (white part only), thinly sliced

2 red bell peppers, seeded and thinly sliced

1 In a large Ziploc bag, add olive oil, soy sauce, lemon juice, white wine, garlic, ginger, salt, and pepper. Add fillets into the Ziploc bag. Seal tightly and shake to coat. Refrigerate fillets for at least 1 hour, shaking them occasionally.

2 Preheat the oven's broiler to high. Remove fillets from marinade and place in a baking dish.

3 Add marinade to a large skillet and warm over medium heat. Add leeks and red bell pepper. Cook for 15 minutes or until tender.

4 Meanwhile, place fillets under the broiler, 4 to 6 inches from the heat. Broil 4 to 5 minutes; flip with a spatula and cook until fish easily flakes with a fork, about another 4 minutes. Top fillets with vegetables and sauce; serve.

GRILLED MAHI-MAHI WITH MANGO-AVOCADO SALSA

SERVES **4** | PREP TIME **20 MINUTES** | COOKING TIME **10 MINUTES**
358 CALORIES | **33** GRAMS PROTEIN | **15** GRAMS CARBOHYDRATES | **19** GRAMS FAT

4 *(6-ounce) mahi-mahi fillets*

3 *tablespoons avocado oil, divided*

Salt and ground black pepper, to taste

1 *medium avocado, peeled, pitted, and diced*

1 *medium mango, peeled, pitted, and diced*

4 *sprigs fresh cilantro, leaves thinly sliced*

3 *tablespoons lime juice, divided*

1 *teaspoon Sriracha hot sauce*

4 *lime wedges*

1 Prepare a grill to medium-high heat. Lightly coat the grill grates with cooking spray.

2 Add fish fillets into a 13-inch by 9-inch glass baking dish. Drizzle with 2 tablespoons oil and season with salt and pepper. Let fillets marinate at room temperature for 10 minutes, turning occasionally.

3 Meanwhile, in a medium bowl, prepare salsa by gently combining avocado, mango, cilantro, remaining 1 tablespoon avocado oil, and lime juice. Season with salt, pepper, and Sriracha. Reserve.

4 Grill fillets until they are just opaque in the center, about 5 minutes per side. Transfer fillets to plates.

5 Garnish fillets with mango-avocado salsa. Serve with lime wedges.

SEARED COD WITH NO-COOK MUSTARD-CAPER SAUCE

SERVES **4** | PREP TIME **15 MINUTES** | COOK TIME **15 MINUTES**

296 CALORIES | **31** GRAMS PROTEIN | **5** GRAMS CARBOHYDRATES | **17** GRAMS FAT

2 tablespoons whole-grain mustard

1 tablespoon capers, drained

1 tablespoon chopped fresh tarragon

4 tablespoons plus 1 teaspoon extra-virgin olive oil, divided

2 tablespoons water

4 (6-ounce) skinless cod fillets

1 large head Bibb lettuce, torn (about 6 cups)

½ English cucumber, thinly sliced

¼ small red onion, thinly sliced

2 tablespoons lemon juice

Salt and ground black pepper, to taste

1 In a small bowl, stir together mustard, capers, tarragon, 2 tablespoons oil, and water. Reserve.

2 Warm 1 teaspoon oil in a large nonstick skillet over medium-high heat. Add cod and season with salt and pepper. Cook until fish is opaque throughout, 4 to 7 minutes per side. Remove from heat and plate cod.

3 Meanwhile, in a large bowl, toss lettuce, cucumber, onion, lemon juice, remaining 2 tablespoons oil, salt, and pepper.

4 Drizzle reserved mustard-caper sauce over cod and serve with salad.

SEARED TUNA AND CORN PURÉE WITH WASABI

SERVES **4** | PREP TIME **10 MINUTES** | COOK TIME **30 MINUTES**
290 CALORIES | **50** GRAMS PROTEIN | **15** GRAMS CARBOHYDRATES | **4** GRAMS FAT

1¾ cups water, plus more as needed

2 cups corn kernels cut from cobs (about 3 large ears), divided

Salt, to taste

1 teaspoon wasabi paste

4 (6-ounce) tuna steaks, about ¾-inch thick

1 In a small pot, combine water, 1½ cups corn, and salt. Bring to a boil over medium-high heat. Reduce the heat and simmer until corn is very soft, about 20 minutes. Transfer corn mixture to a blender and purée until smooth. Transfer puréed corn into a small bowl, add wasabi paste, and mix thoroughly.

2 Return the small pot over medium heat. Add remaining ½ cup corn and just enough water to cover it. Cook until corn is soft, about 10 minutes, and drain.

3 Meanwhile, season both sides of tuna with salt. Coat a large nonstick skillet with cooking spray and warm over medium-high heat. Once the pan is hot, sear each side of the tuna about 3 minutes each.

4 Add corn purée to each plate; top with corn kernels and seared tuna. Serve.

Vegetarian

CHILE RELLENO CASSEROLE

SERVES **4** | PREP TIME **15 MINUTES** | COOKING TIME **40 MINUTES**
226 CALORIES | **18** GRAMS PROTEIN | **10** GRAMS CARBOHYDRATES | **13** GRAMS FAT

2 (7-ounce) cans whole green chile peppers, drained

2 cups shredded reduced-fat Monterey Jack cheese, divided

2 egg whites or 6 tablespoons liquid egg white substitute

1 cup 2% milk

1 (8-ounce) can tomato sauce

1 Preheat the oven to 350°F.

2 Layer half the chiles evenly into the bottom of a medium baking dish and top with 1 cup cheese.

3 In a bowl, beat egg whites and mix with milk. Pour the mixture over chiles.

4 Top the mixture with remaining chiles, pour tomato sauce evenly over the top, and sprinkle with remaining 1 cup cheese.

5 Bake until golden brown, about 40 minutes. Remove from oven and serve.

VEGETARIAN BIBIMBAP

SERVES 4 | PREP TIME **30 MINUTES** | COOKING TIME **20 MINUTES**
473 CALORIES | **16** GRAMS PROTEIN | **80** GRAMS CARBOHYDRATES | **10** GRAMS FAT

1 *tablespoon sesame oil*

1 *cup carrots, cut into matchsticks*

1 *cup zucchini, cut into matchsticks*

½ *(14-ounce) can bean sprouts, drained*

1 *(8-ounce) can bamboo shoots, drained*

6 *ounces white mushrooms, sliced*

Salt and ground black pepper, to taste

2 *cups cooked long-grain rice, cooled*

2 *scallions, sliced*

2 *tablespoons less-sodium soy sauce*

¼ *teaspoon ground black pepper*

4 *large eggs*

Sriracha hot sauce, to taste

1 Warm oil in a large skillet over medium heat. Sauté carrots and zucchini in the hot oil until they begin to soften, about 5 minutes. Stir in bean sprouts, bamboo shoots, and mushrooms. Cook and stir until carrots are tender, about 5 more minutes. Season with salt and transfer vegetables to a medium bowl.

2 Add rice, scallions, soy sauce, and pepper into the same skillet, stirring and cooking over medium heat until rice is hot. Remove from heat.

3 Meanwhile, in a separate nonstick skillet over medium heat, gently cook eggs sunny-side up, turning them once, until they are firm, about 3 minutes.

4 To serve, divide the rice mixture between 4 bowls and top each bowl with ¼ of the vegetable mixture and an egg. Serve Sriracha on the side for mixing into the bibimbap.

BUTTERNUT SQUASH AND MOZZARELLA BAKE

SERVES **4** | PREP TIME **20 MINUTES** | COOKING TIME **30 MINUTES**

433 CALORIES | **20** GRAMS PROTEIN | **59** GRAMS CARBOHYDRATES | **18** GRAMS FAT

1 *(4-pound) butternut squash, peeled, seeded, and cubed*

½ *yellow onion, chopped*

1 *tablespoon extra-virgin olive oil*

1 *tablespoon chopped fresh thyme leaves*

Salt and ground black pepper, to taste

8 *ounces fresh mozzarella, diced*

¼ *cup whole flaxseed*

1 Preheat the oven to 425°F. Prepare a large baking dish by coating it with cooking spray.

2 In a large bowl, toss squash, onion, olive oil, thyme, and cheese together. Season the mixture with salt and pepper; toss again to combine.

3 Transfer mixture to the baking dish and top with flaxseed.

4 Bake until the casserole is lightly browned on top, about 30 minutes. Remove from oven and serve.

TOFU AND PARMESAN-STUFFED PORTOBELLO MUSHROOMS

SERVES **2** | PREP TIME **25 MINUTES** | COOKING TIME **40 MINUTES**

438 CALORIES | **26** GRAMS PROTEIN | **51** GRAMS CARBOHYDRATES | **16** GRAMS FAT

8 whole portobello mushrooms

1 tablespoon extra-virgin olive oil

1 clove garlic, peeled and minced

1 (12-ounce) package soft tofu

¼ cup grated Parmesan cheese

¼ teaspoon onion powder

¼ cup chopped fresh parsley

¼ teaspoon sweet paprika

¼ teaspoon ground cayenne pepper

Salt and ground black pepper, to taste

1½ cups cooked brown rice, to serve

1 Preheat the oven to 350°F. Lightly coat a baking sheet with cooking spray and set aside.

2 Clean mushrooms with a damp paper towel. Carefully break off stems, chopping, and adding into a bowl to reserve. Use a spoon to scrape and remove the gills from each mushroom cap, discarding the gills.

3 Warm oil in a large skillet over medium heat. Sauté garlic with reserved chopped mushroom stems. Continue until any moisture has disappeared, taking care not to burn the garlic. Set the mixture aside to cool.

4 When the mushroom mixture is cool, stir in tofu, Parmesan, onion powder, parsley, paprika, cayenne, salt, and pepper. Mix well.

5 Using clean hands, fill each mushroom cap with a generous amount of stuffing. Arrange caps onto the prepared baking sheet.

6 Bake caps until mushrooms are piping hot and liquid starts to form under caps, about 30 minutes.

7 Serve at once with brown rice.

BLACK BEAN AND CORN QUESADILLA

SERVES **4** | PREP TIME **10 MINUTES** | COOKING TIME **30 MINUTES**
347 CALORIES | **19** GRAMS PROTEIN | **52** GRAMS CARBOHYDRATES | **10** GRAMS FAT

2 teaspoons extra-virgin olive oil

½ cup finely chopped onion

1 (15-ounce) can black beans, drained and rinsed

1½ cups frozen corn

¼ cup tomato sauce

¼ teaspoon red pepper flakes

8 (6-inch) corn tortillas

1 cup shredded low-fat Monterey Jack cheese

1 Warm oil in a large skillet over medium heat. Stir in onion and cook until softened, about 2 minutes.

2 Stir in beans, corn, tomato sauce, and pepper flakes. Mix well and cook until heated through, about 3 minutes. Transfer to a dish and reserve.

3 Use a paper towel to wipe the skillet clean and lay a tortilla in it. Sprinkle cheese evenly over the tortilla, top with about ¼ of the bean mixture, and place another tortilla on top.

4 Cook quesadilla until golden, flip it with a spatula, and cook the other side until golden too. Transfer quesadilla to a plate.

5 Repeat with remaining tortillas and filling. Serve.

QUINOA AND BLACK BEAN CASSEROLE

SERVES **4** | PREP TIME **15 MINUTES** | COOKING TIME **35 MINUTES**
402 CALORIES | **21** GRAMS PROTEIN | **77** GRAMS CARBOHYDRATES | **5** GRAMS FAT

1 teaspoon extra-virgin olive oil

1 medium onion, chopped

3 cloves garlic, peeled and minced

1 cup dry quinoa, rinsed

1¾ cups low-sodium vegetable broth

1 teaspoon ground cumin

¼ teaspoon ground cayenne pepper

Salt and ground black pepper, to taste

1 cup frozen corn kernels

2 (15-ounce) cans black beans, rinsed and drained

½ cup chopped fresh cilantro

1 Warm oil in a large skillet over medium heat. Sauté onion and garlic, stirring occasionally, until lightly browned, about 10 minutes.

2 Stir quinoa and vegetable broth into the onion mixture. Season with cumin, cayenne, salt, and pepper. Bring the mixture to a boil.

3 Cover the pan with a lid and reduce the heat to low; simmer until quinoa is tender and broth is absorbed, about 20 minutes.

4 Stir corn and black beans into quinoa and continue to simmer until heated through, about 5 minutes. Garnish with cilantro and serve.

Sides

GREEN BEANS ALMONDINE

SERVES **4** | PREP TIME **10 MINUTES** | COOKING TIME **10 MINUTES**
79 CALORIES | **3** GRAMS PROTEIN | **10** GRAMS CARBOHYDRATES | **5** GRAMS FAT

Salt and ground black pepper, to taste

1 *pound fresh green beans, trimmed*

½ *teaspoon extra-virgin olive oil*

¼ *cup slivered almonds*

1 Bring a large pot of lightly salted water to a boil over high heat. Add green beans and boil until tender, about 2 to 4 minutes.

2 Drain beans and transfer them to a large bowl. Drizzle with olive oil and season with salt and pepper; toss.

3 Warm a large nonstick skillet over medium-high heat. Coat almonds with cooking spray and add to the hot skillet. Stir frequently until toasted, about 2 to 3 minutes.

4 Reduce heat to medium and add the green beans. Cook for another 2 minutes, stirring occasionally. Remove from heat and serve.

GRILLED BALSAMIC VEGETABLE PLATTER WITH SHAVED PARMESAN

SERVES **4** | PREP TIME **25 MINUTES**, PLUS **45 MINUTES** TO MARINATE | COOKING TIME **15 MINUTES**

382 CALORIES | **8** GRAMS PROTEIN | **26** GRAMS CARBOHYDRATES | **29** GRAMS FAT

½ cup extra-virgin olive oil

2 tablespoons balsamic vinegar

Salt and ground black pepper, to taste

2 eggplants, cut into ½-inch slices

3 zucchini, cut into ½-inch slices

2 yellow squash, cut into ½-inch slices

2 red bell peppers, seeded and cut into ½-inch slices

¼ cup shaved Parmesan cheese

1 In a large bowl, whisk together olive oil, vinegar, salt, and pepper. Add eggplant, zucchini, squash, and bell peppers. Toss to coat and set aside for about 45 minutes to marinate.

2 Prepare a grill to medium heat. Lightly coat the grill grates with cooking spray. Using tongs, remove vegetables from marinade, shaking off the excess. Turning occasionally, grill vegetables until tender, 10 to 15 minutes, brushing them with the excess marinade every few minutes as they cook.

3 Transfer grilled vegetables to a platter. Garnish with Parmesan and serve.

CRISPY SQUASH FRIES

SERVES **4** | PREP TIME **5 MINUTES** | COOKING TIME **15 MINUTES**
143 CALORIES | **8** GRAMS PROTEIN | **21** GRAMS CARBOHYDRATES | **3** GRAMS FAT

SQUASH CAN KEEP EYES HEALTHY. Varieties of winter squash, in particular, are packed with beta-carotene—a compound our bodies use to make vitamin A, which is critically important for vision, bone growth, and reproduction. As a rule, the brighter the squash's flesh, the more beta-carotene it has. Butternut squash, for instance, contains 4,684 mcg per half-cup, while spaghetti squash contains just 45 mcg.

CONSUMING SQUASH MAY PREVENT CANCER CELL GROWTH. Beta-carotene, along with other molecules found in squash known as carotenoids, may limit the ability of cancer cells to communicate with each other and to act autonomously, according to studies conducted by the Cancer Research Center of Hawaii.[1]

PUMPKIN, ANOTHER MEMBER OF THE SQUASH FAMILY, MAY HELP PREVENT CATARACTS. A 2008 study that followed more than 35,000 women for 10 years found that participants who consumed the most lutein and zeaxanthin—two antioxidants found abundantly in pumpkins—had an 18% lower risk of developing cataracts.[2]

---

1 teaspoon extra-virgin olive oil

2 egg whites or 6 tablespoons liquid egg white substitute

½ cup skim milk

⅔ cup breadcrumbs

1 tablespoon grated Parmesan cheese

½ teaspoon onion powder

½ teaspoon sweet paprika

½ teaspoon dried parsley

½ teaspoon garlic powder

¼ teaspoon ground black pepper

2 large yellow squash, quartered lengthwise and then cut in half widthwise

1 Preheat the oven to 450°F. Prepare a large baking dish by greasing with oil.

2 In a medium bowl, add egg whites and milk. Lightly whisk together.

3 In a separate medium bowl, combine breadcrumbs, cheese, onion powder, paprika, parsley, garlic powder, and pepper.

4 Add each squash piece into the egg mixture and then coat in breadcrumbs. Place breaded squash cut-side-up into the prepared baking pan. Continue until all the squash has been breaded.

5 Bake squash in the oven until browned, about 15 minutes. Serve.

SWEET POTATO CHIPS

SERVES **6** | PREP TIME **5 MINUTES** | COOKING TIME **25 MINUTES**
61 CALORIES | **1** GRAM PROTEIN | **10** GRAMS CARBOHYDRATES | **2** GRAMS FAT

2 *medium sweet potatoes (5 ounces each), peeled and thinly sliced*

1 *tablespoon extra-virgin olive oil*

½ *teaspoon salt*

1 Position one rack in the center of the oven and one in the lower position. Preheat the oven to 400°F. Prepare 2 baking sheets by coating with cooking spray.

2 Add sweet potatoes to a large bowl and drizzle with olive oil. Toss to coat with tongs or clean hands. Spread potatoes in an even layer on both baking sheets and place in the oven.

3 Bake potatoes, flipping once halfway through cooking time, until centers are soft and edges are slightly crispy, about 22 to 25 minutes. Sprinkle with salt and serve.

ROASTED BRUSSELS SPROUTS

SERVES **4** | PREP TIME **15 MINUTES** | COOKING TIME **45 MINUTES**
164 CALORIES | **6** GRAMS PROTEIN | **16** GRAMS CARBOHYDRATES | **11** GRAMS FAT

BRUSSELS SPROUTS ARE CHOCK-FULL OF VITAMINS AND MINERALS. A single half-cup of cooked Brussels sprouts contains half of the RDA of vitamin C in addition to significant amounts of vitamin A, vitamin K, potassium, and folate.

BRUSSELS SPROUTS MAY REDUCE THE RISK OF CANCER. Research suggests a strong association between a high intake of brassica vegetables (including Brussels sprouts) and a decreased risk of various types of cancer, including lung, stomach, colon, and rectal cancer.[3]

BRUSSELS SPROUTS CAN MAKE FORHEALTHY PREGNANCIES. Pregnant women are advised to consume extra folate, typically in the form of folic acid, because this compound plays an important role in the creation of DNA and helps prevent birth defects like cleft palate and spina bifida. A half-cup serving of Brussels sprouts offers 12% of the average adult's recommended daily allowance of folate.

1½ pounds Brussels sprouts, ends trimmed and yellow leaves removed

3 tablespoons extra-virgin olive oil

Salt and ground black pepper, to taste

¼ cup chopped fresh cilantro

1 Preheat oven to 400°F.

2 Place Brussels sprouts, olive oil, salt, and pepper into a large Ziploc bag. Seal tightly and shake to coat.

3 Pour onto a baking sheet and roast in the oven for 30 to 45 minutes. Shake the pan halfway through cooking for even browning. Brussels sprouts should be dark brown, almost black, when done.

4 Garnish with a sprinkling of chopped cilantro and serve immediately.

BROWN RICE PILAF

SERVES **4** | PREP TIME **5 MINUTES** | COOKING TIME **45 MINUTES**, PLUS **10 MINUTES** RESTING

218 CALORIES | **5** GRAMS PROTEIN | **39** GRAMS CARBOHYDRATES | **4** GRAMS FAT

BROWN RICE CONSUMPTION IS ASSOCIATED WITH A LOWERED RISK OF HEART DISEASE. A 1999 study tracked 75,521 women over 10 years and discovered that high whole-grain intake, including consumption of brown rice, was correlated with a 30% reduction in cardiovascular disease risk compared to those who consumed fewer whole grains.[4]

BROWN RICE CONTAINS MORE FIBER THAN WHITE RICE. Compared to white rice's 0.3% fiber content, brown rice contains 1.8% fiber.

BROWN RICE IS A GREAT SOURCE OF VITAMINS AND MINERALS. A one-cup serving of cooked brown rice contains more than 10% of your RDA of thiamin, niacin, vitamin B6, magnesium, phosphorus, copper, manganese, and selenium. Manganese, in particular, is the big winner, as a single serving of brown rice contains 88% of the recommended daily allowance.

---

1 tablespoon unsalted butter

1 shallot, peeled and finely chopped

1 cup long-grain brown rice, rinsed

Salt and ground black pepper, to taste

2 cups low-sodium chicken broth

1 clove garlic, peeled and smashed

2 sprigs fresh thyme

3 tablespoons chopped fresh flat-leaf parsley

3 scallions, thinly sliced

1 Melt butter in a medium heavy-duty pot over medium heat. Add shallot and cook until tender, about 1 to 2 minutes.

2 Add rice, stirring well to coat with the butter and shallots. Cook for a few minutes until rice is glossy. Season with salt and pepper.

3 Stir in chicken broth, garlic, and thyme. Cover with a tight-fitting lid, reduce heat to low, and cook for 40 minutes. Remove from heat and let sit for 10 minutes.

4 Remove thyme sprigs and, if desired, the garlic clove. Use a fork to fluff rice and stir in parsley and scallions. Serve.

QUINOA SALAD WITH ALMONDS AND DRIED CRANBERRIES

SERVES **4** | PREP TIME **5 MINUTES**, PLUS **TIME** TO CHILL | COOKING TIME **20 MINUTES**
310 CALORIES | **9** GRAMS PROTEIN | **56** GRAMS CARBOHYDRATES | **6** GRAMS FAT

1½ cups water

1 cup dry quinoa, rinsed

½ cup grated carrots

¼ cup chopped red bell pepper

¼ cup chopped yellow bell pepper

1 small red onion, finely chopped

1½ teaspoons curry powder

¼ cup chopped fresh cilantro
    Juice of 1 lime

¼ cup almonds slivers, toasted

½ cup dried cranberries
    Salt and ground black pepper,
    to taste

1 Add water into a medium, heavy-duty pot, cover with a tight-fitting lid, and warm over high heat. Once water boils, stir in quinoa. Reduce heat to low, and cover.

2 Simmer until quinoa absorbs the water, about 15 to 20 minutes. Transfer quinoa to a large bowl and refrigerate until cool.

3 Once quinoa has chilled, stir in carrots, bell peppers, onion, curry, cilantro, lime juice, almonds, cranberries, salt, and pepper. Toss and serve.

GARLICKY ZUCCHINI AND SPINACH SAUTÉ

SERVES **6** | PREP TIME **5 MINUTES** | COOKING TIME **10 MINUTES**
46 CALORIES | **2** GRAMS PROTEIN | **5** GRAMS CARBOHYDRATES | **2** GRAMS FAT

1 *tablespoon extra-virgin olive oil*

2 *cloves garlic, peeled and minced*

2 *zucchini, cut into matchsticks*

2 *cups grape tomatoes*

3 *cups baby spinach*

1 *tablespoon lemon juice*
  Pinch of ground black pepper

1 Warm oil in a large pan over medium-low heat. Add garlic and cook until fragrant, about 1 minute. Add zucchini and increase the heat to medium. Cook for 3 to 4 minutes, stirring constantly.

2 Stir in tomatoes, cooking for 1 minute. Add spinach, stirring and sautéing for another 3 to 4 minutes until wilted. Add lemon juice and black pepper before removing from heat to serve.

ROASTED GARLIC TWICE-BAKED POTATO

SERVES **6** | PREP TIME **30 MINUTES** | COOKING TIME **1 HOUR 25 MINUTES**

242 CALORIES | **6** GRAMS PROTEIN | **43** GRAMS CARBOHYDRATES | **6** GRAMS FAT

POTATOES ARE EXTREMELY NUTRITIOUS. One potato serving provides 6.6 grams of dietary fiber and more than 20% of your RDA of vitamin C, niacin, vitamin B6, folate, magnesium, phosphorus, potassium, and manganese.

POTATOES CONTAIN A NUMBER OF COMPOUNDS THAT IMPROVE HEART HEALTH. In addition to being high in potassium, which several studies have associated with a diminished risk of high blood pressure and cardiovascular disease, potatoes are also great sources of chlorogenic acid and kukoamines, both of which can help prevent high blood pressure.[5]

POTATOES CAN HELP PREVENT OVEREATING. Potatoes are extremely filling, which is why research shows they can reduce overall calorie consumption and thus help with weight loss.[6]

---

6 *medium baking potatoes (8 ounces each), poked with a few holes*

1 *whole garlic bulb*

1 *teaspoon extra-virgin olive oil*

2 *tablespoons unsalted butter, softened*

½ *cup skim milk*

½ *cup buttermilk*

1½ *teaspoons finely chopped fresh rosemary leaves*

½ *teaspoon salt*

½ *teaspoon ground black pepper*

Sweet paprika, to taste

1 Preheat oven to 400°F. Place potatoes onto a baking sheet and cook in the oven until fork-tender, about 1 hour.

2 Meanwhile, remove the outer papery skin from garlic bulb, drizzle with oil, and wrap in 2 sheets of heavy-duty foil. Bake the garlic in the 400°F oven until softened, about 30 to 35 minutes. Allow garlic and potatoes to cool for about 10 minutes.

3 Increase the oven's temperature to 425°F.

4 Once cool enough to handle, cut a thin slice off the top of each potato and discard. Scoop out potato flesh until a thin shell remains. Add potato flesh into a large bowl along with butter; mash together.

5 Cut the top off the garlic bulb, leaving the root intact, and squeeze roasted garlic into the potato mixture. Add milk, buttermilk, rosemary, salt, and pepper. Mix well.

6 Spoon the potato mixture back into the potato skins and return to the baking sheet. Bake until heated through, about 20 to 25 minutes. Remove from oven and garnish with a dash of paprika.

BUTTERNUT SQUASH AND BROCCOLI STIR-FRY

SERVES **6** | PREP TIME **10 MINUTES** | COOKING TIME **10 MINUTES**
71 CALORIES | **2** GRAMS PROTEIN | **14** GRAMS CARBOHYDRATES | **2** GRAMS FAT

*1 pound butternut squash, peeled,
   seeded, and cut into ¼-inch slices*

1 clove garlic, peeled and minced

¼ teaspoon ground ginger

1 cup broccoli florets

½ cup thinly sliced celery

½ cup thinly sliced onion

2 teaspoons honey

1 tablespoon lemon juice

2 tablespoons sunflower seed kernels

1 Coat a large skillet with cooking spray and warm over medium-high heat. Add squash, garlic, and ginger; stir-fry for 3 minutes.

2 Add broccoli, celery, and onion and continue to stir-fry until vegetables are tender, about 3 to 4 minutes.

3 Meanwhile, in a small bowl, combine honey and lemon juice. Mix well.

4 Transfer vegetables to a large serving dish and pour the honey mixture over top. Using tongs, toss to coat. Garnish with sunflower kernels and serve.

CURRIED POTATOES AND CAULIFLOWER

SERVES **4** | PREP TIME **5 MINUTES** | COOKING TIME **25 MINUTES**
230 CALORIES | **12** GRAMS PROTEIN | **47** GRAMS CARBOHYDRATES | **1** GRAM FAT

Salt, to taste

1 (2- to 3-pound) head cauliflower, cut into florets

1 pound potatoes, peeled and cut into 1-inch cubes

1 medium onion, chopped

2 cloves garlic, peeled and minced

2 tablespoons garam masala or curry powder

1 cup low-sodium vegetable broth

2 cups frozen peas

1 Bring a pot of lightly salted water to a boil over high heat. Add the cauliflower and potatoes; cook for 4 to 5 minutes and drain.

2 Meanwhile, coat a Dutch oven with cooking spray and warm over medium heat. Add chopped onion and garlic and cook until onion softens, about 2 to 3 minutes. Add garam masala and stir for 1 minute.

3 Transfer cooked potatoes and cauliflower to the Dutch oven. Stir well, coating in the onion mixture. Add broth and deglaze the pan.

4 Cover with a lid and let mixture simmer for 10 minutes. Stir in peas, cover, and cook for another 5 to 7 minutes. Serve immediately.

Desserts

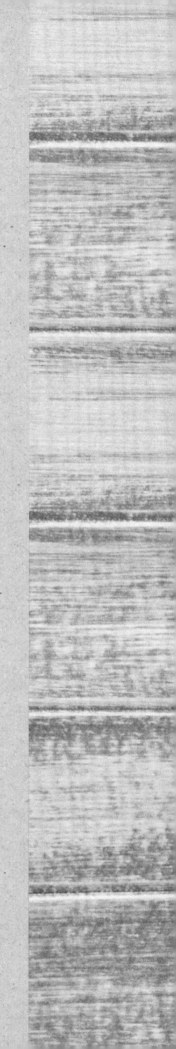

PEACH COBBLER

SERVES **6** | PREP TIME **10 MINUTES** | COOKING TIME **30 MINUTES**, PLUS **20 MINUTES** RESTING
161 CALORIES | **12** GRAMS PROTEIN | **28** GRAMS CARBOHYDRATES | **1** GRAM FAT

3 tablespoons blueberry, raspberry, strawberry, or mixed-fruit preserves

1 (15-ounce) can diced peaches in water or 100% juice, drained

½ cup 2% cottage cheese

½ cup water

2 scoops vanilla protein powder

¼ cup all-purpose flour

⅓ cup Truvia

½ cup quick-cooking oats

1 tablespoon honey

1 Preheat the oven to 350°F. Coat an 8-inch square baking dish with cooking spray.

2 Add the fruit preserves into the prepared dish and use a spatula to spread it evenly. Top with a layer of peaches and set aside.

3 In a medium bowl, add cottage cheese, water, protein powder, flour, and Truvia. Mix well and pour over the peaches.

4 In a small bowl, mix oats and honey. Spoon over the top of cobbler.

5 Bake until golden, around 30 minutes. Let sit for at least 20 minutes before serving.

KEY LIME PIE

SERVES **6** | PREP TIME **15 MINUTES**, PLUS **4 TO 6 HOURS** TO CHILL | COOKING TIME **55 MINUTES**

475 CALORIES | **11** GRAMS PROTEIN | **74** GRAMS CARBOHYDRATES | **16** GRAMS FAT

¾ *cup honey graham cracker crumbs (about 4 sheets of crackers)*

½ *cup applesauce*

1 *cup quick-cooking oats*

1 *teaspoon ground cinnamon*

3 *large egg yolks*

1 *(14-ounce) can condensed milk*

⅓ *cup key lime juice*

2 *cups frozen whipped topping, thawed in fridge for 4 to 5 hours*

1 Preheat the oven to 350°F.

2 In a large bowl, add graham cracker crumbs, applesauce, oats, and cinnamon. Mix well. Remove 1 tablespoon of the mixture and reserve in the refrigerator for later use.

3 Spread the graham cracker mixture into a 9-inch pie plate. Lightly press it along the bottom and sides to form the crust. Bake until edges are golden, about 15 minutes. When crust is done, reduce the oven temperature to 250°F.

4 In a medium bowl, whisk egg yolks, condensed milk, and lime juice until smooth. Pour the lime juice mixture into the prepared crust. Bake until the filling is firm, about 40 minutes.

5 Remove the pie from the oven and cool completely. Refrigerate for 4 to 6 hours or until fully chilled. Top with a 2-inch layer of the whipped topping, sprinkle with reserved crumb mixture, and serve.

MAPLE-RAISIN BREAD PUDDING

SERVES **4** | PREP TIME **20 MINUTES**, PLUS **TIME** TO CHILL | COOK TIME **55 MINUTES**
277 CALORIES | **10** GRAMS PROTEIN | **50** GRAMS CARBOHYDRATES | **3** GRAMS FAT

2 *cups ½-inch cubes French bread*

1 *cup skim milk*

2 *large eggs*

2½ *teaspoons vanilla extract*

4 *tablespoons pure maple syrup, divided*

⅓ *cup raisins*

1 Preheat the oven to 350°F. Spread bread pieces onto a baking sheet, ensuring pieces don't touch. Toast in the oven, stirring after a couple minutes. Bake until golden, about 5 minutes, and then let cool.

2 In a large bowl, whisk together milk, eggs, vanilla, and 3 tablespoons maple syrup. Use a spatula to stir in raisins and gently fold in toasted bread. Cover and refrigerate for at least 30 minutes and up to 4 hours.

3 Preheat the oven to 325°F. Coat 4 small ramekins with cooking spray and divide the mixture between them. Evenly space the ramekins in an 8-inch by 8-inch square baking pan and fill the pan with 1 inch of hot water.

4 Bake bread pudding until set, about 45 to 50 minutes. Drizzle the remaining 1 tablespoon maple syrup over the top and serve.

SWEET POTATO CASSEROLE

SERVES **4** | PREP TIME **15 MINUTES** | COOKING TIME **30 MINUTES**

243 CALORIES | **5** GRAMS PROTEIN | **41** GRAMS CARBOHYDRATES | **7** GRAMS FAT

3 *cups mashed sweet potatoes*

⅓ *cup skim milk*

1 *tablespoon melted unsalted butter*

1 *teaspoon vanilla extract*

½ *teaspoon salt*

2 *egg whites or 6 tablespoons liquid egg white substitute*

¼ *cup packed brown sugar*

¼ *cup all-purpose flour*

1 *tablespoon olive oil*

1 Preheat the oven to 350°F. Coat a 7-inch by 11-inch baking dish with cooking spray and set aside.

2 In a large bowl, add mashed sweet potatoes, milk, butter, vanilla, salt, and egg whites. Mix well and spread evenly into the prepared baking dish.

3 In a small bowl, add brown sugar and flour. Slowly drizzle in olive oil and stir until the mixture has the consistency of coarse crumbs.

4 Sprinkle the crumb mixture over sweet potatoes and bake for 30 minutes. Serve.

MINI CHEESECAKES

SERVES **6** (2 CHEESECAKES PER SERVING) | PREP TIME **30 MINUTES** | COOKING TIME **15 MINUTES**
567 CALORIES | **9** GRAMS PROTEIN | **79** GRAMS CARBOHYDRATES | **24** GRAMS FAT

1 (12-ounce) package vanilla wafers

2 (8-ounce) packages reduced-fat cream cheese

⅓ cup plus 1 tablespoon Truvia

2 large eggs

1 teaspoon vanilla extract

1 Preheat the oven to 350°F. Line the cups of a standard 12-cup muffin pan with paper liners.

2 Make wafers into fine crumbs by pulsing in a food processor or adding into a large Ziploc bag, sealing tightly, and crushing with a rolling pin. Spoon 2 tablespoons into each muffin liner.

3 In a large bowl, add cream cheese, Truvia, eggs, and vanilla. Using a handheld mixer, blend until light and fluffy.

4 Fill each muffin liner almost to the top with the cream cheese mixture.

5 Bake until set, around 15 minutes. Remove from the oven and let cool before serving.

TRIPLE BERRY CRISP

SERVES **6** | PREP TIME **20 MINUTES** | COOKING TIME **40 MINUTES**

524 CALORIES | **6** GRAMS PROTEIN | **92** GRAMS CARBOHYDRATES | **17** GRAMS FAT

¾ *cup blackberries*

¾ *cup raspberries*

¾ *cup blueberries*

1 *tablespoon granulated sugar*

¾ *cup Truvia*

1 *cup whole-wheat flour*

1 *cup rolled oats*

½ *teaspoon ground cinnamon*

¼ *teaspoon ground nutmeg*

½ *cup (1 stick) cold butter, cubed*

1 Preheat oven to 350°F. Coat a 9-inch by 13-inch pan with cooking spray.

2 In a large bowl, gently toss together blackberries, raspberries, and blueberries with 1 tablespoon sugar.

3 In another large bowl, combine Truvia with flour, oats, cinnamon, and nutmeg. Add cubed butter, using a fork to combine butter into mixture until crumbly.

4 Press half the oat mixture into the bottom of the prepared pan. Cover with berries and sprinkle remaining oat mixture on top.

5 Bake until fruit is bubbling and topping is golden brown, about 30 to 40 minutes.

BANANAS FOSTER

SERVES **2** | PREP TIME **5 MINUTES** | COOKING TIME **10 MINUTES**

693 CALORIES | **6** GRAMS PROTEIN | **76** GRAMS CARBOHYDRATES | **44** GRAMS FAT

¼ *cup vegetable oil*

⅓ *cup dark brown sugar, unpacked*

1 *tablespoon bourbon vanilla extract*

½ *teaspoon ground cinnamon*

2 *ripe bananas, peeled and sliced lengthwise and then crosswise*

¼ *cup coarsely chopped macadamia nuts*

1 *cup low-fat vanilla frozen yogurt*

1 Warm oil in a large skillet over medium heat. Stir in brown sugar, vanilla, and cinnamon.

2 When the sugar mixture begins to bubble, stir in bananas and nuts. Cook until bananas are hot, 1 to 2 minutes.

3 Remove bananas from the heat and serve over a small scoop of frozen yogurt.

HOMEMADE CINNAMON-SPICED APPLESAUCE

SERVES **4** | PREP TIME **10 MINUTES**, PLUS **TIME** TO CHILL | COOKING TIME **20 MINUTES**
96 CALORIES | **1** GRAM PROTEIN | **25** GRAMS CARBOHYDRATES | **0** GRAMS FAT

4 apples, peeled, cored, and chopped

½ cup water

¼ cup Truvia

½ teaspoon ground cinnamon

1 In a medium pot, combine apples, water, Truvia, and cinnamon.

2 Cover with a lid and cook over medium heat until apples are soft and break down, about 15 to 20 minutes.

3 Allow to cool and then mash with a fork or potato masher. Refrigerate until chilled and serve.

CLASSIC TIRAMISU

SERVES **8** | PREP TIME **30 MINUTES**, PLUS **TIME** TO CHILL

227 CALORIES | **5** GRAMS PROTEIN | **21** GRAMS CARBOHYDRATES | **13** GRAMS FAT

1 (8-ounce) container reduced-fat cream cheese, softened

½ (8-ounce) container mascarpone cheese

½ cup Truvia

1 tablespoon brewed espresso or Kahlúa (optional)

24 ladyfingers

1 cup espresso, brewed and cooled

1 tablespoon Kahlúa

1 tablespoon packed brown sugar

1½ teaspoons unsweetened cocoa powder

½ ounce bittersweet chocolate, grated

1 To make the filling, add cream cheese and mascarpone into a large bowl and use a handheld mixer to beat at medium speed until smooth. Add Truvia and 1 tablespoon brewed espresso or Kahlúa, if desired, beating at medium speed until blended.

2 Cut ladyfingers in half lengthwise. Arrange 24 ladyfinger halves, cut-side up, in the bottom of an 8-inch square baking dish.

3 In a small bowl, mix 1 cup espresso, 1 tablespoon Kahlúa, and brown sugar. Pour half the mixture over the ladyfingers to soak them; then spread a layer of half the cream cheese filling on top.

4 Repeat procedure with remaining 24 ladyfinger halves, soaking with the remaining espresso mixture and then topping with remaining cream cheese filling.

5 In a small bowl, combine cocoa and grated chocolate; sprinkle evenly over top of filling.

6 Cover with plastic wrap and chill for 2 hours or overnight. Cut and serve.

FLOURLESS CHOCOLATE CAKE

SERVES **4** | PREP TIME **15 MINUTES** | COOKING TIME **30 MINUTES**, PLUS **10 MINUTES** TO COOL

377 CALORIES | **9** GRAMS PROTEIN | **14** GRAMS CARBOHYDRATES | **34** GRAMS FAT

DARK CHOCOLATE (70%+ CACAO) CONTAINS MORE ANTIOXIDANTS THAN MANY "SUPERFOODS." Unprocessed cocoa beans are among the highest scoring foods ever measured by the "ORAC" (Oxygen Radical Absorbance Capacity) scale, which measures a food's ability to absorb free radicals in the body.[1]

DARK CHOCOLATE CAN IMPROVE BLOOD FLOW. Dark chocolate contains a large amount of molecules known as flavonoids that stimulate the production of nitric oxide. This, in turn, prompts arteries to relax, improving blood flow and reducing blood pressure.[2]

DARK CHOCOLATE MAY PROTECT THE SKIN AGAINST SUN DAMAGE. Interestingly, this increased blood flow may have a positive impact on your skin's ability to prevent sun damage. In one study, people that consumed dark chocolate for 12 weeks needed double the minimum amount of UVB rays needed to cause redness in the skin after sun exposure.[3]

⅓ cup unsalted butter, plus more for greasing

4 ounces 80% dark chocolate, finely chopped

½ cup Truvia

½ cup unsweetened cocoa powder

3 large eggs, beaten

1 teaspoon vanilla extract

1 Preheat the oven to 300°F. Grease an 8-inch round cake pan with butter.

2 In a heatproof medium bowl, add chocolate and butter. Gently warm in the microwave until melted. Stir in Truvia, cocoa powder, eggs, and vanilla. Pour into prepared pan.

3 Bake for 30 minutes. Remove from the oven and let cool for 10 minutes.

4 Remove cake from the pan onto a wire rack and let cool completely. Serve and enjoy.

FROM HERE,
YOUR BODY WILL CHANGE

————

"Your love for what you do and willingness to push yourself
where others aren't prepared to go is what will make you great."
LAURENCE SHAHLAEI

So…I guess this is it, right? We've reached the end…

No way.

You're in a process now—and yup, it has already begun—of proving to yourself that you can transform your body faster than you ever believed. Soon, you're going to know with absolute certainty that you can use what you've learned in this book to build the body of your dreams.

It's pretty cool to realize that you do have the power to change your body—to get lean, strong, and healthy—and that you are in complete control of how your body looks and performs.

No matter how "ordinary" you might think you are, I promise you that you can not only create an extraordinary physique but an extraordinary life as well. Don't be surprised if the confidence and pride you'll gain from your workouts ripples out to affect other areas of your life, inspiring you to reach for other goals and improve in other ways.

From here, all you have to do is walk the path I've laid out, and in 12 weeks, you'll look in the mirror and think, "I'm glad I did," not "I wish I had."

My goal is to help you reach your goal, and I hope this book helps.

If we work together as a team, we can and will succeed.

So, I'd like you to make a promise as you begin your transformation: Can you promise me—and yourself—that you'll let me know when you've reached your goal?

Here's how we can connect:

Facebook: facebook.com/muscleforlifefitness

Twitter: @muscleforlife

Instagram: instagram.com/muscleforlifefitness

G+: gplus.to/MuscleForLife

And last but not least, my website is www.muscleforlife.com. If you want to write me, my e-mail address is mike@muscleforlife.com. (Keep in mind that I get a lot of e-mails every day and answer everything personally, so if you can keep your message as brief as possible, it helps ensure that I can get back to everyone!)

Thanks again. I hope to hear from you, and I wish you the best!

WOULD YOU
DO ME A FAVOR?

———

Thank you for buying my book. I'm positive that if you just follow what I've written, you will be on your way to looking and feeling better than you ever have before.

I have a small favor to ask.

Would you mind taking a minute to write a blurb on Amazon about this book? I check all my reviews and love to get feedback (that's the real pay for my work—knowing that I'm helping people).

Also, if you have any friends or family who might enjoy this book, spread the love and lend it to them!

Thanks again. I hope to hear from you, and I wish you the best!

INTRODUCING
THE MUSCLE FOR LIFE
CUSTOM MEAL PLAN

––––––

If you want to take all the thought out of dieting and get a meal plan built specifically for you, that is guaranteed to work if you simply follow it, then you want to read this page.

The first thing I want you to know is when I say "custom" meal plan, I mean it.

Nothing is more annoying than paying for a meal plan from a ""guru" and receiving a bland, copy-and-paste job that doesn't take into account foods you like, dislike, your schedule, training times, and lifestyle.

That's why we do our custom meal plans differently.

Not only do we build each and every one from scratch, we can work with any and all budgetary and dietary needs as well: vegan vegetarian, Paleo, food availabilities, sensitivities, and allergies, and any other food preferences or restrictions.

What this means is you'll actually *enjoy* your diet. You'll look forward to every meal, every day, which works wonders for compliance. It's easy to stick to a diet full of foods you love!

We don't just shoot you a plan and send you off on your way, either. We're always available to help via email to make sure you actually get results.

HERE'S HOW THE PROCESS WORKS...

Step 1
You pay and create your account, and then fill out a detailed questionnaire that tells my team about your fitness goals, exercise schedule, food preferences, and everything else we need to make your meal plan.

Step 2
We use your answers to create your meal plan and upload it to the Website within 5 to 7 days of receiving your completed questionnaire.

Step 3
You're notified via email that your meal plan is ready and you access your account to download it.

You check it out and let us know if any tweaks are needed. If not, you get rolling.

Step 4
If, at any time along the way, you run into any issues, we're always available via email to answer any questions you might have and ensure everything goes smoothly for you.

So, how much fat would you like to lose? Or how much muscle would you like to build? Working out isn't enough. Let me show you exactly how to eat to get there!

VISIT WWW.MUSCLEFORLIFE.COM/MP NOW TO GET YOUR CUSTOM MEAL PLAN!

I WANT TO CHANGE
THE SUPPLEMENT INDUSTRY
WILL YOU JOIN ME?

———

The supplement industry could be best described by Obi-Wan Kenobi's famous words: a wretched hive of scum and villainy.

Here's the bottom-line truth of this multibillion-dollar industry:

While certain supplements can help, they do NOT build great physiques (proper training and nutrition does), and most are a complete waste of money.

Too many products are "proprietary blends" of low-quality ingredients, junk fillers, and unnecessary additives. Key ingredients are horribly underdosed. There's a distinct lack of credible scientific evidence to back up the outrageous claims made on labels and in ads. The list of what's wrong with this industry goes on and on.

And that's why I decided to get into the supplement game.

What gives? Am I just a hypocritical sell-out? Should you grab your pitchfork and run me off the Internet? Well, hear me out for a minute and then decide.

The last thing we need is yet another marketing machine churning out yet another line of hyped-up, flashy products claiming to be more effective than steroids.

I think things should be done differently, and I believe in being the change I want to see. That's why I started LEGION.

You see, I created LEGION not only to bring unique products to the supplement world but also to start a movement. Here's what sets LEGION apart from the rabble:

- 100% transparent product formulas. The only reason to use proprietary blends is fraud and deception. You deserve to know exactly what you're buying.

- 100% science-based ingredients and dosages. Every ingredient we use is backed by published scientific literature and is included at true clinically effective dosages.

- 100% naturally sweetened and flavored. Research suggests that regular consumption of artificial sweeteners can be harmful to our health, which is why we use natural sweeteners with proven health benefits. And while artificial flavors seem to be benign, they just aren't necessary, natural flavors taste equally good.

Not only are LEGION supplements a better value and better for your health...but they also deliver REAL RESULTS you can feel.

LEARN MORE AT WWW.LEGIONATHLETICS.COM AND USE THE COUPON CODE "TSC10" AND SAVE 10%!

OTHER BOOKS BY MICHAEL MATTHEWS

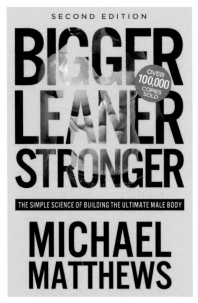

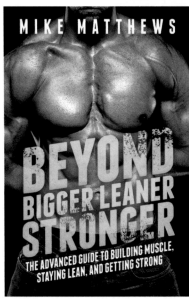

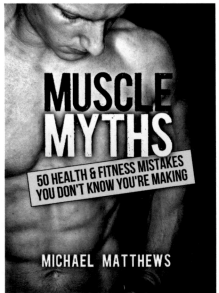

BONUS MATERIAL

Chances are you'd like to use the recipes in this book to plan out your daily meals, and I want to give you a spreadsheet that will help.

In it you'll find the calories and macros for each recipe broken down by ingredient, which makes it easy to modify recipes and portions as desired.

Thus, when you're creating your meal plan, all you have to do is skim over the spreadsheet and pick recipes that fit within your caloric and macronutritional targets. No need to browse through the entire cookbook!

Visit the link below to download this free spreadsheet today!

VISIT WWW.BIT.LY/TSC-SPREADSHEET
TO GET THIS SPREADSHEET NOW!

REFERENCES

THE GREAT "ONE TRUE DIET" HOAX

1. Gregory A. Hand, Robin P. Shook, Amanda E. Paluch, Meghan Baruth, E. Patrick Crowley, Jason R. Jaggers, Vivek K. Prasad, Thomas G. Hurley, James R. Hebert, Daniel P. O'Connor, Edward Archer, Stephanie Burgess, and Steven N. Blair, "The Energy Balance Study: The Design and Baseline Results for a Longitudinal Study of Energy Balance," *Research Quarterly for Exercise and Sport* 84, no. 3 (2013): 275–86.

2. Madison Park, "Twinkie Diet Helps Nutrition Professor Lose 27 Pounds," CNN.com, last modified November 8, 2010, http://www.cnn.com/2010/HEALTH/11/08/twinkie.diet.professor/.

3. Samuel Mettler, Nigel Mitchell, and Kevin D. Tipton, "Increased Protein Intake Reduces Lean Body Mass Loss during Weight Loss in Athletes," *Medicine and Science in Sports and Exercise* 42, no. (2010): 326–37. doi: 10.1249/MSS.0b013e3181b2ef8e.

4. John D. Bosse and Brian M. Dixon, "Dietary Protein to Maximize Resistance Training: A Review and Examination of Protein Spread and Change Theories," *Journal of the International Society of Sports Nutrition* 9, no. 1 (2012): 42. doi: 10.1186/1550-2783-9-42.

5. Eric R. Helms, Caryn Zinn, David S. Rowlands, and Scott R. Brown, "A Systematic Review of Dietary Protein during Caloric Restriction in Resistance Trained Lean Athletes: A Case for Higher Intakes," *International Journal of Sport Nutrition and Exercise Metabolism* 24, no. 2 (2014): 127–38. doi: 10.1123/ijsnem.2013-0054.

6. Anssi H. Manninen, "High-Protein Weight Loss Diets and Purported Adverse Effects: Where Is the Evidence?" *Journal of the International Society of Sports Nutrition* 1, no. 1 (2004): 45–51. doi: 10.1186/1550-2783-1-1-45; William F. Martin, Lawrence E. Armstrong, and Nancy R. Rodriguez, "Dietary Protein Intake and Renal Function," *Nutrition and Metabolism* 2 (2005): 25. doi: 10.1186/1743-7075-2-25.

7. Wieke Altorf–van der Kuil, Mariëlle F. Engberink, Elizabeth J. Brink, Marleen A. van Baak, Stephan J. L. Bakker, Gerjan Navis, Pieter van 't Veer, and Johanna M. Geleijnse, "Dietary Protein and Blood Pressure: A Systematic Review," *PLOS One* 5, no. 8 (2010): e12102. doi: 10.1371/journal.pone.0012102; Mary C. Gannon, Frank Q. Nuttall, Asad Saeed, Kelly Jordan, and Heidi Hoover, "An Increase in Dietary Protein Improves the Blood Glucose Response in Persons with Type 2 Diabetes," *American Journal of Clinical Nutrition* 78, no. 4 (2003): 734–41.

8. Jean-Philippe Bonjour, "Dietary Protein: An Essential Nutrient for Bone Health," *Journal of the American College of Nutrition* 24, suppl. no. 6 (2006): 526S–36S. doi: 10.1080/07315724.2005.10719501; Jane E. Kerstetter, Anne M. Kenny, and Karl L. Insogna, "Dietary Protein and Skeletal Health: A Review of Recent Human Research," *Current Opinion in Lipidology* 22, no. 1 (2011): 16–20. doi: 10.1097/MOL.0b013e3283419441.

9. Oliver C. Witard, Sarah R. Jackman, Arie K. Kies, Asker E. Jeukendrup, and Kevin D. Tipton, "Effect of Increased Dietary Protein on Tolerance to Intensified Training," *Medicine and Science in Sports and Exercise* 43, no. 4 (2011): 598–607. doi: 10.1249/MSS.0b013e3181f684c9.

10. Erin Gaffney-Stomberg, Karl L. Insogna, Nancy R. Rodriguez, and Jane E. Kerstetter, "Increasing Dietary Protein Requirements in Elderly People for Optimal Muscle and Bone Health," *Journal of the American Geriatrics Society* 47, no. 6 (2009): 1073–79. doi: 10.1111/j.1532-5415.2009.02285.x.

11. Mettler, Mitchell, and Tipton, "Increased Protein Intake Reduces Lean Body Mass Loss," 326–37.

12. Petra Stiegler and Adam Cunliffe, "The Role of Diet and Exercise for the Maintenance of Fat-Free Mass and Resting Metabolic Rate during Weight Loss," *Sports Medicine* 36, no. 3 (2006): 239–62.

13. Jo Smith and Lars McNaughton, "The Effects of Intensity of Exercise on Excess Postexercise Oxygen Consumption and Energy Expenditure in Moderately Trained Men and Women," *European Journal of Applied Physiology and Occupational Physiology* 67, no. 5 (1993): 420–25.

14. Tyler A. Churchward-Venne, Caoileann H. Murphy, Thomas M. Longland, and Stuart M. Phillips, "Role of Protein and Amino Acids in Promoting Lean Mass Accretion with Resistance Exercise and Attenuating Lean Mass Loss during Energy Deficit in Humans," *Amino Acids* 45, no. 2 (2013): 231–40. doi: 10.1007/s00726-013-1506-0.

15. Donald K. Layman, Richard A. Boileau, Donna J. Erickson, James E. Painter, Harn Shiue, Carl Sather, and Demtra D. Christou, "A Reduced Ratio of Dietary Carbohydrate to Protein Improves Body Composition and Blood Lipid Profiles during Weight Loss in Adult Women," *Journal of Nutrition* 133, no. 2 (2003): 411–17; Mettler, Mitchell, and Tipton, "Increased Protein Intake Reduces Lean

Body Mass Loss during Weight Loss in Athletes," 326–37.

16. Carol S. Johnston, Sherrie L. Tjonn, Pamela D. Swan, Andrea White, Heather Hutchins, and Barry Sears, "Ketogenic Low-Carbohydrate Diets Have No Metabolic Advantage over Nonketogenic Low-Carbohydrate Diets," *American Journal of Clinical Nutrition* 83, no. 5 (2006): 1055–61; Shane A. Phillips, Jason W. Jurva, Amjad Q. Syed, Amina Q. Syed, Jacquelyn P. Kulinski, Joan Pleuss, Raymond G. Hoffmann, and David D. Gutterman, "Benefit of Low-Fat over Low-Carbohydrate Diet on Endothelial Health in Obesity," *Hypertension* 51, no. 2 (2008): 376–82; Frank M. Sacks, George A. Bray, Vincent J. Carey, Steven R. Smith, Donna H. Ryan, Stephen D. Anton, Katherine McManus, Catherine M. Champagne, Louise M. Bishop, Nancy Laranjo, Meryl S. Leboff, Jennifer C. Rood, Lilian de Jonge, Frank L. Greenway, Catherine M. Loria, Eva Obarzanek, and Donald A. Williamson, "Comparison of Weight-Loss Diets with Different Compositions of Fat, Protein, and Carbohydrates," *New England Journal of Medicine* 360 (February 26, 2009): 859–73. doi: 10.1056/NEJMoa0804748; Cynthia A. Thomson, Alison T. Stopeck, Jennifer W. Bea, Ellen Cussler, Emily Nardi, Georgette Frey, and Patricia A. Thompson, "Changes in Body Weight and Metabolic Indexes in Overweight Breast Cancer Survivors Enrolled in a Randomized Trial of Low-Fat vs. Reduced Carbohydrate Diets," *Nutrition and Cancer* 62, no. 8 (2010): 1142–52. doi: 10.1080/01635581.2010.513803.

17. "Dietary Reference Intakes: Macronutrients," National Academies Institute of Medicine, accessed December 18, 2015, http://iom.nationalacademies. org/~/media/Files/Activity%20Files/ Nutrition/DRIs/DRI_Macronutrients.pdf.

18. Susan C. Wooley, "Physiologic Versus Cognitive Factors in Short Term Food Regulation in the Obese and Nonobese," *Psychosomatic Medicine* 34, no. 1 (1972): 62–68.

19. Jameason D. Cameron, Marie-Josée Cyr, and Éric Doucet, "Increased Meal Frequency Does Not Promote Greater Weight Loss in Subjects Who Were Prescribed an 8-Week Equi-Energetic Energy-Restricted Diet," *British Journal of Nutrition* 103, no. 8 (2010): 1098–101. doi: 10.1017/S0007114509992984.

20. Sigal Sofer, Abraham Eliraz, Sara Kaplan, Hillary Voet, Gershon Fink, Tzadok Kima, and Zecharia Madar, "Greater Weight Loss and Hormonal Changes after 6 Months Diet with Carbohydrates Eaten Mostly at Dinner," *Obesity* 19, no. 10 (2011): 2006–14. doi: 10.1038/oby.2011.48.

21. Alan A. Aragon and Brad J. Schoenfeld, "Nutrient Timing Revisited: Is There a Post-Exercise Anabolic Window?" *Journal of the International Society of Sports Nutrition* 10 (2013): 5. doi: 10.1186/1550-2783-10-5.

HOW TO GET THE BODY YOU WANT WITH FLEXIBLE DIETING

1. Xia Wang, Yingying Ouyang, Jun Liu, Minmin Zhu, Gang Zhao, Wei Bao, and Frank B. Hu, "Fruit and Vegetable Consumption and Mortality from All Causes, Cardiovascular Disease, and Cancer: Systematic Review and Dose-Response Meta-Analysis of Prospective Cohort Studies," *British Medical Journal* 349 (2014): g4490. doi: 10.1136/bmj. g4490.

2. Hiroyasu Mori, "Effect of Timing of Protein and Carbohydrate Intake after Resistance Exercise on Nitrogen Balance in Trained and Untrained Young Men," *Journal of Physiological Anthropology* 33, no. 1 (2014): 24; Tipton, Kevin D., Tabatha A. Elliott, Melanie G. Cree, Asle A. Aarsland, Arthur P. Sanford, and Robert R. Wolfe. "Stimulation of net muscle protein synthesis by whey protein ingestion before and after exercise." *American Journal of Physiology-Endocrinology and Metabolism* 292, no. 1 (2007): E71-E76.

3. Corby K. Martin, Leonie K. Heilbronn, Lilian de Jonge, James P. DeLany, Julia Volaufova, Stephen D. Anton, Leanne M. Redman, Steven R. Smith, and Eric Ravussin, "Effect of Calorie Restriction on Resting Metabolic Rate and Spontaneous Physical Activity," *Obesity* 15, no. 12 (2007): 2964–73. doi: 10.1038/ oby.2007.354.

4. Leanne M. Redman, Leonie K. Heilbronn, Corby K. Martin, Lilian de Jonge, Donald A. Williamson, James P. Delany, and Eric Ravussin, "Metabolic and Behavioral Compensations in Response to Caloric Restriction: Implications for the Maintenance of Weight Loss," *PLOS One* 4, no. 2 (2009): e4377.

5. James A. Levine, "Non-Exercise Activity Thermogenesis (NEAT)," *Clinical Endocrinology & Metabolism* 16, no. 4 (2002): 679–702. doi: 10.1053/ beem.2002.0227.

6. James A. Levine, Mark W. Vander Weg, James O. Hill, and Robert C. Klesges, "Non-Exercise Activity Thermogenesis: The Crouching Tiger Hidden Dragon of Societal Weight Gain," *Arteriosclerosis, Thrombosis, and Vascular Biology*, 26 (2006): 729–36. doi: 10.1161/01. ATV.0000205848.83210.73.

7. David S. Weigle, "Contribution of Decreased Body Mass to Diminished Thermic Effect of Exercise in Reduced-Obese Men," *International Journal of Obesity* 12, no. 6 (1988): 567–78.

8. David S. Weigle and John D. Brunzell, "Assessment of Energy Expenditure in Ambulatory Reduced-Obese Subjects by the Techniques of Weight Stabilization and Exogenous Weight Replacement," *International Journal of Obesity* 14, suppl. no. 1 (1990): 77–81.

HOW TO EAT RIGHT WITHOUT OBSESSING OVER EVERY CALORIE

1. Bosse and Dixon, "Dietary Protein to Maximize Resistance Training," 42.

2. Thomas L. Halton and Frank B. Hu, "The Effects of High Protein Diets on

Thermogenesis, Satiety and Weight Loss: A Critical Review," *Journal of the American College of Nutrition* 23, no. 5 (2004): 373–85; Mettler, Mitchell, and Tipton, "Increased Protein Intake Reduces Lean Body Mass Loss," 326–37.

3. Eric R. Helms, Caryn Zinn, David S. Rowlands, Ruth Naidoo, and John Cronin, "High-Protein, Low-Fat, Short-Term Diet Results in Less Stress and Fatigue Than Moderate-Protein Moderate-Fat Diet during Weight Loss in Male Weightlifters: A Pilot Study," *International Journal of Sport Nutrition and Exercise Metabolism* 25, no. 2 (2015): 163–70. doi: 10.1123/ ijsnem.2014-005.

4. David S. Weigle, Patricia A. Breen, Colleen C. Matthys, Holly S. Callahan, Kaatje E. Meeuws, Verna R. Burden, and Jonathan Q. Purnel, "A High-Protein Diet Induces Sustained Reductions in Appetite, Ad Libitum Caloric Intake, and Body Weight Despite Compensatory Changes in Diurnal Plasma Leptin and Ghrelin Concentrations," *American Journal of Clinical Nutrition* 82, no. 1 (2005): 41–48.

5. Margriet S. Westerterp-Plantenga, "The Significance of Protein in Food Intake and Body Weight Regulation," Current Opinion in *Clinical Nutrition and Metabolic Care* 6, no. 6 (2003): 635–38; Laura C. Ortinau, Heather A. Hoertel, Steve M. Douglas, and Heather J. Leidy, "Effects of High-Protein vs. High-Fat Snacks on Appetite Control, Satiety, and Eating Initiation in Healthy Women," *Nutrition Journal* 13 (2014): 97. doi: 10.1186/1475-2891-13-97.

6. John A. Batsis, Todd A. Mackenzie, Laura K. Barre, Francisco Lopez-Jimenez, and Stephen J. Bartels, "Sarcopenia, Sarcopenic Obesity, and Mortality in Older Adults: Results from the National Health and Nutrition Examination Survey III," *European Journal of Clinical Nutrition* 68 (2014): 1001–07. doi: 10.1038/ejcn.2014.117.

7. José A. Morais, Stéphanie Chevalier, and Rejeanne Gougeon, "Protein Turnover and Requirements in the Healthy and Frail Elderly," *Journal of Nutritional Health and Aging* 10, no. 4 (2006): 272–83; Dorothee Volkert and Cornel Christian Sieber, "Protein Requirements in the Elderly," *International Journal for Vitamin and Nutrition Research* 81 (2011): 109–19. doi: 10.1024/0300-9831/a000061; Michael Tieland, Marlou L. Dirks, Nikita van der Zwaluw, Lex B. Verdijk, Ondine van de Rest, Lisette C. P. G. M. de Groot, and Luc J.C. van Loon, "Protein Supplementation Increases Muscle Mass Gain during Prolonged Resistance-Type Exercise Training in Frail Elderly People: A Randomized, Double-Blind, Placebo-Controlled Trial," *Journal of Post-Acute and Long-Term Care Medicine* 13, no. 8 (2012): 713–19. doi: 10.1016/j.jamda.2012.05.020.

8. Erin Gaffney-Stomberg, Karl L. Insogna, Nancy R. Rodriguez, and Jane E. Kerstetter, "Increasing Dietary Protein Requirements in Elderly People for Optimal Muscle and Bone Health," *Journal of the American Geriatrics Society* 57, no. 6 (2009): 1073–79.

9. Eric R. Helms, Caryn Zinn, David Stephen Rowlands, and Scott Randall Brown, "A Systematic Review of Dietary Protein during Caloric Restriction in Resistance Trained Lean Athletes: A Case for Higher Intakes," *International Journal of Sport Nutrition and Exercise Metabolism* 24, no. 2 (2013): 127–38. doi: 10.1123/ ijsnem.2013-0054.

10. Joanne L. Slavin, "Dietary Fiber: Classification, Chemical Analyses, and Food Sources," *Journal of the American Dietary Association* 87, no. 9 (1987): 1164–71.

11. Alison M. Stephen and John H. Cummings, "Mechanism of Action of Dietary Fibre in the Human Colon," Nature 284, no. 5753 (1980): 283–84. doi: 10.1038/284283a0; Alfredo A. Rabassa and Arvey I. Rogers, "The Role of Short-Chain Fatty Acid Metabolism in Colonic Disorders," *American Journal of Gasteroenterology* 87, no. 4 (1992): 419–23.

12. Slavin, "Dietary Fiber," 1164–71.

13. Medical College of Georgia, "Scientists Learn More about How Roughage Keeps You 'Regular,'" *Science Daily*, Aug. 23, 2006, http://www.sciencedaily.com/ releases/2006/08/060823093156.htm.

14. Peter C. Elwood, Janet E. Pickering, D. Ian Givens, and John E. Gallacher, "The Consumption of Milk and Dairy Foods and the Incidence of Vascular Disease and Diabetes: An Overview of the Evidence," *Lipids* 45, no. 10 (2010): 925–39. doi: 10.1007/s11745-010-3412-5; Zaldy S. Tan, William S. Harris, Alexa S. Beiser, Jayandra J. Himali, Stephanie Debette, Alexandra Pikula, Charles DeCarli, Philip A. Wolf, Ramachandran S. Vasan, Sander J. Robins, and Sudha Seshadri, "Red Blood Cell Omega-3 Fatty Acid Levels and Markers of Accelerated Brain Aging," *Neurology* 78, no. 9 (2012): 658–64. doi: 10.1212/WNL.0b013e318249f6a9; Ying Bao, Jiali Han, Frank B. Hu, Edward L. Giovannucci, Meir J. Stampfer, Walter C. Willett, and Charles S. Fuchs, "Association of Nut Consumption with Total and Cause-Specific Mortality," *New England Journal of Medicine* 369 (2013): 2001–11. doi: 10.1056/NEJMoa1307352; Satoko Yoneyama, Katsuyuki Miura, Satoshi Sasaki, Katsushi Yoshita, Yuko Morikawa, Masao Ishizaki, Teruhiko Kido, Yuchi Naruse, and Hideaki Nakagawa, "Dietary Intake of Fatty Acids and Serum C-Reactive Protein in Japanese," Journal of Epidemiology 17, no. 3 (2007): 86–92. doi: 10.2188/jea.17.86.

15. Qibin Qi, Audrey Y. Chu, Jae H. Kang, Jinyan Huang, Lynda M. Rose, Majken K. Jensen, Liming Liang, Gary C. Curhan, Louis R. Pasquale, Janey L. Wiggs, Immaculata De Vivo, Andrew T. Chan, Hyon K. Choi, Rulla M. Tamimi, Paul M. Ridker, David J. Hunter, Walter C. Willett, Eric B. Rimm, Daniel I. Chasman, Frank B. Hu, and Lu Qi, "Fried Food Consumption, Genetic Risk, and Body Mass Index: Gene-Diet Interaction Analysis in Three US Cohort Studies," *BMJ* (2014): 348. doi: 10.1136/bmj.g1610; Federico Soriguer, Gemma Rojo-Martínez, M. Carmen Dobarganes, José M. García

Almeida, Isabel Esteva, Manuela Beltrán, M. Soledad Ruiz De Adana, Francisco Tinahones, Juan M. Gómez-Zumaquero, Eduardo García-Fuentes, and Stella González-Romero, "Hypertension Is Related to the Degradation of Dietary Frying Oils," *American Journal of Clinical Nutrition* 78, no. 6 (2003): 1092–97; Michael J. A. Williams, Wayne H. F. Sutherland, Maree P. McCormick, Sylvia A. de Jong, Robert J. Walker, and Gerard T. Wilkins, "Impaired Endothelial Function Following a Meal Rich in Used Cooking Fat," *Journal of the American College of Cardiology* 33, no. 4 (1999): 1050–55. doi: 10.1016/S0735-1097(98)00681-0; Carlotta Galeone, Claudio Pelucchi, Renato Talamini, Fabio Levi, Cristina Bosetti, Eva Negri, Salvatore Franceschi, and Carlo La Vecchia, "Role of Fried Foods and Oral/Pharyngeal and Oesophageal Cancers," *British Journal of Cancer* 92, no. 11 (2005): 2065–69. doi: 10.1038/sj.bjc.6602542; Rashmi Sinha, Amanda J. Cross, Barry I. Graubard, Michael F. Leitzmann, and Arthur Schatzkin, "Meat Intake and Mortality: A Prospective Study of over Half a Million People," *Archives of Internal Medicine* 169, no. 6 (2009): 562–71; Amanda MacMillan, "The 22 Worst Foods for Trans Fat," *Health*, accessed July 20, 2015, http://www.health.com/health/gallery/0,,20533295,00.html; Gary P. Zaloga, Kevin A. Harvey, William Stillwell, and Rafat Siddiqui, "Trans Fatty Acids and Coronary Heart Disease," *Nutrition in Clinical Practice* 21, no. 5 (2006): 505–12. doi: 10.1177/0115426506021005505; Jorge Salmerón, Frank B. Hu, JoAnn E. Manson, Meir J. Stampfer, Graham A. Colditz, Eric B. Rimm, and Walter C. Willett, "Dietary Fat Intake and Risk of Type 2 Diabetes in Women," *American Journal of Clinical Nutrition* 73, no. 6 (2001): 1019–26; Jorge E. Chavarro, Janet W. Rich-Edwards, Bernard A. Rosner, and Walter C. Willett, "Dietary Fatty Acid Intakes and the Risk of Ovulatory Infertility," *American Journal of Clinical Nutrition* 85, no. 1 (2007): 231–37.

16. Frank B. Hu, Meir J. Stampfer, JoAnn E. Manson, Eric Rimm, Graham A. Colditz, Bernard A. Rosner, Charles H. Hennekens, and Walter C. Willett, "Dietary Fat Intake and the Risk of Coronary Heart Disease in Women," *New England Journal of Medicine* 337 (1997): 1491–99. doi: 10.1056/NEJM199711203372102.

17. John E. Blundell and Jennie I. MacDiarmid, "Fat as a Risk Factor for Overconsumption: Satiation, Satiety, and Patterns of Eating," *Journal of the American Dietetic Association* 97, suppl. no. 7 (1997): S63–69. doi: 10.1016/S0002-8223(97)00733-5.

18. Dariush Mozaffarian, Renata Micha, and Sarah Wallace, "Effects on Coronary Heart Disease of Increasing Polyunsaturated Fat in Place of Saturated Fat: A Systematic Review and Meta-Analysis of Randomized Controlled Trials," *PLOS Medicine* 7, no. 3 (2010): e1000252; Frank B. Hu, Eunyoung Cho, Kathryn M. Rexrode, Christine M. Albert, and JoAnn E. Manson, "Fish and Long-Chain ω-3 Fatty Acid Intake and Risk of Coronary Heart Disease and Total Mortality in Diabetic Women," *Circulation* 107, no. 14 (2003): 1852–57. doi: 10.1161/01.CIR.0000062644.42133.5F; Teresa T. Fung, Kathryn M. Rexrode, Christos S. Mantzoros, JoAnn E. Manson, Walter C. Willett, and Frank B. Hu, "Mediterranean Diet and Incidence and Mortality of Coronary Heart Disease and Stroke in Women," *Circulation* 1998, no. 8 (2009): 1093–100. doi: 10.1161/CIRCULATIONAHA.108.816736; Manas Kaushik, Dariush Mozaffarian, Donna Spiegelman, JoAnn E. Manson, Walter C. Willett, and Frank B. Hu, "Long-Chain Omega-3 Fatty Acids, Fish Intake, and the Risk of Type 2 Diabetes Mellitus," *American Journal of Clinical Nutrition* 90, no. 3 (2009): 613–20. doi: 10.3945/ajcn.2008.27424; Lawrence J. Appel, Frank M. Sacks, Vincent J. Carey, Eva Obarzanek, Janis F. Swain, Edgar R. Miller, Paul R. Conlin, Thomas P. Erlinger, Bernard A. Rosner, Nancy M. Laranjo, Jeanne Charleston, Phyllis McCarron, and Louise M. Bishop, "Effects of Protein, Monounsaturated Fat, and Carbohydrate Intake on Blood Pressure and Serum Lipids: Results of the OmniHeart Randomized Trial," *JAMA* 294, no. 19 (2005): 2455–64. doi: 10.1001/jama.294.19.2455.

19. Patty W. Siri-Tarino, Qi Sun, Frank B. Hu, and Ronald M. Krauss, "Meta-Analysis of Prospective Cohort Studies Evaluating the Association of Saturated Fat with Cardiovascular Disease," *American Journal of Clinical Nutrition* 91, no. 3 (2010): 535–46. doi: 10.3945/ajcn.2009.27725.

20. Jan I. Pedersen, Philip T. James, Ingeborg A. Brouwer, Robert Clarke, Ibrahim Elmadfa, Martijn B. Katan, Penny M. Kris-Etherton, Daan Kromhout, Barrie M. Margetts, Ronald P. Mensink, Kaare R. Norum, Mike Rayner, and Matti Uusitupa, "The Importance of Reducing SFA to Limit CHD," *British Journal of Nutrition* 106, no. 7 (2011): 961–63. doi: 10.1017/S000711451100506X; Daan Kromhout, Johanna M. Geleijnse, Alessandro Menotti, and David R. Jacobs, Jr., "The Confusion about Dietary Fatty Acids Recommendations for CHD Prevention," *British Journal of Nutrition* 106, no. 5 (2011): 627–32. doi: 10.1017/S0007114511002236; Jeremiah Stamler, "Diet-Heart: A Problematic Revisit," *American Journal of Clinical Nutrition* 91, no. 3 (2010): 497–99.

ORGANIC OR CONVENTIONAL FOOD? A SCIENCE-BASED REVIEW

1. Crystal Smith-Spangler, Margaret L. Brandeau, Grace E. Hunter, J. Clay Bavinger, Maren Pearson, Paul J. Eschbach, Vandana Sundaram, Hau Liu, Patricia Schirmer, Christopher Stave, Ingram Olkin, and Dena M. Bravata, "Are Organic Foods Safer or Healthier Than Conventional Alternatives?: A Systematic Review," *Annals of Internal Medicine* 147, no. 5 (2012): 348–66. doi: 10.7326/0003-4819-157-5-201209040-00007.

2. David C. Holzman, "Organic Food Conclusions Don't Tell the Whole Story," *Environmental Health Perspectives* 120, no. 12 (2012): A458; Charles Benbrook, "Initial Reflections on the *Annals of Internal Medicine Paper* 'Are Organic Foods Safer and Healtheir Than Conventional Alternatives? A Systematic Review," accessed December 18, 2015, http://www.tfrec.wsu.edu/pdfs/P2566.pdf.

3. Kirsten Brandt, Carlo Leifert, Roy Sanderson, and Chris Seal, "Agroecosystem Management and Nutritional Quality of Plant Foods: The Case of Organic Fruits and Vegetables," *Critical Reviews in Plant Sciences* 30, no. 1–2 (2011): 177–97. doi: 10.1080/07352689.2011.554417#sthash.QGwMK1Qp.dpuf.

4. Loren Cordain, S. Boyd Eaton, Anthony Sebastian, Neil Mann, Staffan Lindeberg, Bruce A. Watkins, James H. O'Keefe, and Janette Brand-Miller, "Origins and Evolution of the Western Diet: Health Implications for the 21st Century," *American Journal of Clinical Nutrition* 81, no. 2 (2005): 341–54.

5. Benbrook, "Initial Reflections," http://www.tfrec.wsu.edu/pdfs/P2566.pdf; Brandt, et al., "Agroecosystem Management and Nutritional Quality of Plant Foods," 177–97.

6. Gidfred Darko and Samuel O. Acquaah, "Levels of Organochlorine Pesticides Residues in Meat," *International Journal of Environmental Science and Technology* 4, no. 4 (2007): 521–24.

7. Benbrook, "Initial Reflections," http://www.tfrec.wsu.edu/pdfs/P2566.pdf.

8. Laura N. Vandenberg, Theo Colborn, Tyrone B. Hayes, Jerrold J. Heindel, David R. Jacobs, Jr., Duk-Hee Lee, Toshi Shioda, Ana M. Soto, Frederick S. vom Saal, Wade V. Welshons, R. Thomas Zoeller, and John Peterson Myers, "Hormones and Endocrine-Disrupting Chemicals: Low-Dose Effects and Nonmonotonic Dose Responses," *Endocrine Reviews* 33, no. 3 (2012): 378–455. doi: 10.1210/er.2011-1050.

9. David C. Bellinger, "A Strategy for Comparing the Contributions of Environmental Chemicals and Other Risk Factors to Neurodevelopment of Children," *Environmental Health Perspectives* 120, no. 4 (2012): 501–07. doi: 10.1289/ehp.1104170.

10. Joel Forman and Janet Silverstein, "Organic Foods: Health and Environmental Advantages and Disadvantages," *Pediatrics* 130, no. 5 (2012): e1406–15. doi: 10.1542/peds.2012-2579.

11. Frank Aarestrup, "Sustainable Farming: Get Pigs Off Antibiotics," *Nature* 486 (2012): 465–66.

12. Torey Looft, Timothy A. Johnson, Heather K. Allen, Darrell O. Bayles, David P. Alt, Robert D. Stedtfeld, Woo Jun Sul, Tiffany M. Stedtfeld, Benli Chai, James R. Cole, Syed A. Hashsham, James M. Tiedje, and Thad B. Stanton, "In-Feed Antibiotic Effects on the Swine Intestinal Microbiome," *PNAS* 109, no. 5 (2011): 1691–96. doi: 10.1073/pnas.1120238109.

13. Benbrook, "Initial Reflections," http://www.tfrec.wsu.edu/pdfs/P2566.pdf.

14. European Commission, "Opinion of the Scientific Committee on Veterinary Measures Relating to Public Health: Assessment of Potential Risks to Human Health from Hormone Residues in Bovine Meat and Meat Products," accessed December 18, 2015, http://ec.europa.eu/food/fs/sc/scv/out21_en.pdf.

15. Shanna H. Swan, Fan Liu, James W. Overstreet, Charlene Brazil, and Niels E. Skakkebaek, "Semen Quality of Fertile US Males in Relation to Their Mothers' Beef Consumption during Pregnancy," *Human Reproduction* 22, no. 6 (2007): 1497–502. doi: 10.1093/humrep/dem068.

16. Pesticide Action Network North America, "Butter," What's on My Food, accessed December 18, 2015, http://www.whatsonmyfood.org/food.jsp?food=BU.

17. Frozen Food Foundation, "New Study Encourages Consumers to Think Frozen When Buying Fruits & Vegetables," accessed December 18, 2015, http://www.frozenfoodfacts.org/assets-foundation/misc/images/FINAL%20FFF%20UGA%20News%20Release.pdf.

18. Brandt, et al., "Agroecosystem Management and Nutritional Quality of Plant Foods," 177–97.

THE MINIMALIST'S GUIDE TO COOKING GREAT FOOD

1. World Health Organization, "The Top 10 Causes of Death," accessed December 18, 2015, http://www.who.int/mediacentre/factsheets/fs310/en/; Luc Djoussé, Akintunde O. Akinkuolie, Jason H.Y. Wu, Eric L. Ding, and J. Michael Gaziano, "Fish Consumption, Omega-3 Fatty Acids and Risk of Heart Failure: A Meta-Analysis," *Clinical Nutrition* 31, no. 6 (2012): 846–53. doi: 10.1016/j.clnu.2012.05.010.

2. Jyrki K. Virtanen, Dariush Mozaffarian, Stephanie E. Chiuve, and Eric B. Rimm, "Fish Consumption and Risk of Major Chronic Disease in Men," *American Journal of Clinical Nutrition* 88, no. 6 (2008): 1618–25. doi: 10.3945/ajcn.2007.25816.

3. Martha Clare Morris, Denis A. Evans, Christine C. Tangney, Julia L. Bienias, and Robert S. Wilson, "Fish Consumption and Cognitive Decline with Age in a Large Community Study," *JAMA Neurology* 62, no. 12 (2005): 1849–53. doi: 10.1001/archneur.62.12.noc50161; Lars C. Stene, Geir Joner, and the Norwegian Childhood Diabetes Study Group, "Use of Cod Liver Oil during the First Year of Life Is Associated with Lower Risk of Childhood-Onset Type 1 Diabetes: A Large, Population-Based, Case-Control Study," *American Journal of Clinical Nutrition* 78, no. 6 (2003): 1128–34; Kimberly Y. Z. Forrest and Wendy L. Stuhldreher, "Prevalence and Correlates of Vitamin D Deficiency in US Adults," *Nutrition Research* 31, no. 1 (2011): 48–54. doi: 10.1016/j.nutres.2010.12.001; William G. Christen, Debra A. Schaumberg, Robert J. Glynn, and Julie E. Buring, "Dietary ω-3 Fatty Acid and Fish Intake and Incident

Age-Related Macular Degeneration in Women," *Archives of Ophthalmology* 129, no. 7 (2011): 921–29. doi: 10.1001/archophthalmol.2011.34.

4. Gordon I. Smith, Philip Atherton, Dominic N. Reeds, B. Selma Mohammed, Debbie Rankin, Michael J. Rennie, and Bettina Mittendorfer, "Omega-3 Polyunsaturated Fatty Acids Augment the Muscle Protein Anabolic Response to Hyperaminoacidemia-Hyperinsulinemia in Healthy Young and Middle Aged Men and Women," *Clinical Science* 121, no. 6 (2011): 267–78. doi: 10.1042/CS20100597; Bakhtiar Tartibian, Behzad Hajizadeh Maleki, and Asghar Abbasi, "The Effects of Ingestion of Omega-3 Fatty Acids on Perceived Pain and External Symptoms of Delayed Onset Muscle Soreness in Untrained Men," *Clinical Journal of Sport Medicine* 19, no. 2 (2009): 115–19. doi: 10.1097/JSM.0b013e31819b51b3; Jonathan D. Buckley and Peter R. C. Howe, "Anti-Obesity Effects of Long-Chain Omega-3 Polyunsaturated Fatty Acids," *Obesity Reviews* 10, no. 6 (2009): 648–59. doi: 10.1111/j.1467-789X.2009.00584.x.

5. National Resources Defense Council, "Mercury in Fish," accessed December 18, 2015, http://www.nrdc.org/health/effects/mercury/walletcard.pdf.

BREAKFAST

1. Leah E. Cahill, Stephanie E. Chiuve, Rania A. Mekary, Majken K. Jensen, Alan J. Flint, Frank B. Hu, and Eric B. Rimm, "Prospective Study of Breakfast Eating and Incident Coronary Heart Disease in a Cohort of Male US Health Professionals," *Circulation* 128 (2013): 337–43. doi: 10.1161/CIRCULATIONAHA.113.001474.

2. Amber A. W. A. van der Heijden, Frank B. Hu, Eric B. Rimm, and Rob M. van Dam, "A Prospective Study of Breakfast Consumption and Weight Gain among U.S. Men," *Obesity* 15, no. 10 (2007): 2463–69. doi: 10.1038/oby.2007.292.

3. Rania A. Mekary and Edward Giovannucci, "Belief beyond the Evidence: Using the Proposed Effect of Breakfast on Obesity to Show 2 Practices That Distort Scientific Evidence," *American Journal of Clinical Nutrition* 99, no. 1 (2014): 232–13. doi: 10.3945/ajcn.113.077214.

4. David G. Schlundt, Tracy Sbrocco, and Christopher Bell, "Identification of High-Risk Situations in a Behavioral Weight Loss Program: Application of the Relapse Prevention Model," *International Journal of Obesity* 13, no. 2 (1989): 223–34.

5. Marge Dwyer, "Skipping Breakfast May Increase Coronary Heart Disease Risk," last modified July 23, 2013, http://www.hsph.harvard.edu/news/features/skipping-breakfast-may-increase-coronary-heart-disease-risk/.

6. David G. Schlundt, James O. Hill, Tracy Sbrocco, Jamie Pope-Cordle, and Teresa Sharp, "The Role of Breakfast in the Treatment of Obesity: A Randomized Clinical Trial," *American Journal of Clinical Nutrition* 55, no. 3 (1992): 645–51.

7. Michelle N. Harvie, Mary Pegington, Mark P. Mattson, Jan Frystyk, Bernice Dillon, Gareth Evans, Jack Cuzick, Susan A. Jebb, Bronwen Martin, Roy G. Cutler, Tae G. Son, Stuart Maudsley, Olga D. Carlson, Josephine M. Egan, Allan Flyvbjerg, and Anthony Howell, "The Effects of Intermittent or Continuous Energy Restriction on Weight Loss and Metabolic Disease Risk Markers: A Randomised Trial in Young Overweight Women," *International Journal of Obesity* 35, no. 5 (2011): 714–27. doi: 10.1038/ijo.2010.171.

8. James A. Betts, Judith D. Richardson, Enhad A. Chowdhury, Geoffrey D. Holman, Kostas Tsintzas, and Dylan Thompson, "The Causal Role of Breakfast in Energy Balance and Health: A Randomized Controlled Trial in Lean Adults," *American Journal of Clinical Nutrition* 100, no. 2 (2014): 539–47. doi: 10.3945/ajcn.114.083402.

9. K. Sreekumaran Nair, Paul D. Woolf, Stephen L. Welle, and Dwight E. Matthews, "Leucine, Glucose, and Energy Metabolism after 3 Days of Fasting in Healthy Human Subjects," *American Journal of Clinical Nutrition* 46, no. 4 (1987): 557–62.

10. Christian Zauner, Bruno Schneeweiss, Alexander Kranz, Christian Madl, Klaus Ratheiser, Ludwig Kramer, Erich Roth, Barbara Schneider, and Kurt Lenz, "Resting Energy Expenditure in Short-Term Starvation Is Increased as a Result of an Increase in Serum Norepinephrine," *American Journal of Clinical Nutrition* 71, no. 6 (2000): 1511–15.

11. George F. Cahill, "Starvation in Man," *New England Journal of Medicine* 282 (1970): 668–75. doi: 10.1056/NEJM197003192821209.

12. Ibid.

13. Khaled Trabelsi, Stephen R. Stannard, Zohra Ghlissi, Ronald J. Maughan, Choumous Kallel, Kamel Jamoussi, Khaled M. Zeghal, and Ahmed Hakim, "Effect of Fed- Versus Fasted State Resistance Training during Ramadan on Body Composition and Selected Metabolic Parameters in Bodybuilders," *Journal of the International Society of Sports Nutrition* 10 (2013): 23. doi: 10.1186/1550-2783-10-23.

14. Ying Rong, Li Chen, Tingting Zhu, Yadong Song, Miao Yu, Zhilei Shan, Amanda Sands, Frank B. Hu, and Liegang Liu, "Egg Consumption and Risk of Coronary Heart Disease and Stroke: Dose-Response Meta-Analysis of Prospective Cohort Studies," *BMJ* 346 (2013): e8539. doi: 10.1136/bmj.e8539; Christopher N. Blesso, Catherine J. Andersen, Jacqueline Barona, Jeff S. Volek, and Maria Luz Fernandez, "Whole Egg Consumption Improves Lipoprotein Profiles and Insulin Sensitivity to a Greater Extent Than Yolk-Free Egg Substitute in Individuals with Metabolic Syndrome," *Metabolism* 62, no. 3 (2013): 400–10; Gisella Mutungi, David Waters, Joseph Ratliff, Michael Puglisi, Richard M. Clark, Jeff S. Volek, and Maria Luz Fernandez, "Eggs Distinctly Modulate Plasma Carotenoid and Lipoprotein Subclasses in Adult Men Following a

Carbohydrate-Restricted Diet," *Journal of Nutritional Biochemistry* 21, no. 4 (2010): 261–67. doi: 10.1016/j.jnutbio.2008.12.011.

15. Michelle Wien, Ella Haddad, Keiji Oda, and Joan Sabaté, "A Randomized 3x3 Crossover Study to Evaluate the Effect of Hass Avocado Intake on Post-Ingestive Satiety, Glucose and Insulin Levels, and Subsequent Energy Intake in Overweight Adults," *Nutrition Journal* 12 (2013): 155. doi: 10.1186/1475-2891-12-155.

16. Nancy J. Aburto, Sara Hanson, Hialy Gutierrez, Lee Hooper, Paul Elliott, and Francesco P. Cappuccio, "Effect of Increased Potassium Intake on Cardiovascular Risk Factors and Disease: Systematic Review and Meta-Analyses," *BMJ* 346 (2013): f1378. doi: 10.1136/bmj.f1378.

17. R. López Ledesma, A. C. Frati Munari, B. C. Hernández Domínguez, S. Cervantes Montalvo, M. H. Hernández Luna, C. Juárez, and S. Morán Lira, "Monounsaturated Fatty Acid (Avocado) Rich Diet for Mild Hypercholesterolemia," *Archives of Medical Research* 27, no. 4 (1996): 519–23.

18. Candida J. Rebello, William D. Johnson, Corby K. Martin, Wenting Xie, Marianne O'Shea, Anne Kurilich, Nicolas Bordenave, Stephanie M. Andler, B. Jan Willem van Klinken, Yi Fang Chu, and Frank L. Greenway, "Acute Effect of Oatmeal on Subjective Measures of Appetite and Satiety Compared to a Ready-to-Eat Breakfast Cereal: A Randomized Crossover Trial," *Journal of the American College of Nutrition* 32, no. 4 (2013): 272–79. doi: 10.1080/07315724.2013.816614.

19. Rgia A. Othman, Mohammed H. Moghadasian, and Peter J. H. Jones, "Cholesterol-Lowering Effects of Oat ⌧-Glucan," *Nutrition Reviews* 69, no. 6 (2011): 299–09. doi: 10.1111/j.1753-4887.2011.00401.x.

20. Alexander Lammert, Jüergen Kratzsch, Jochen Selhorst, Per M. Humpert, Angelika Bierhaus, Rainer Birck, Klaus Kusterer, and Hans-Peter Hammes,

"Clinical Benefit of a Short Term Dietary Oatmeal Intervention in Patients with Type 2 Diabetes and Severe Insulin Resistance: A Pilot Study," *Experimental and Clinical Endocrinology & Diabetes* 116 (2008): 132–34.

21. Peter T. Res, Bart Groen, Bart Pennings, Milou Beelen, Gareth A. Wallis, Annmie P. Gijsen, Joan M. Senden, and Luc J. C. van Loon, "Protein Ingestion before Sleep Improves Postexercise Overnight Recovery," *Medicine and Science of Sports and Exercise* 44, no. 8 (2012): 1560–69. doi: 10.1249/MSS.0b013e31824cc363.

22. "Vitamin A," U.S. National Library of Medicine, last modified February 2, 2015, https://www.nlm.nih.gov/medlineplus/ency/article/002400.htm.

23. "Beta-Carotene," U.S. National Library of Medicine, last modified June 3, 2015, https://www.nlm.nih.gov/medlineplus/druginfo/natural/999.html.

24. "National Nutrient Database for Standard Reference Release 28," U.S. Department of Agriculture, accessed December 18, 2015, http://ndb.nal.usda.gov/ndb/foods/show/3667.

25. Michelle Wien, David Bleich, Maya Raghuwanshi, Susan Gould-Forgerite, Jacqueline Gomes, Lynn Monahan-Couch, and Keiji Oda, "Almond Consumption and Cardiovascular Risk Factors in Adults with Prediabetes," *Journal of the American College of Nutrition* 29, no. 3 (2010): 189–97.

26. Sze Yen Tan and Richard D. Mattes, "Appetitive, Dietary and Health Effects of Almonds Consumed with Meals or as Snacks: A Randomized, Controlled Trial," *European Journal of Clinical Nutrition* 67, no. 11 (2013): 1205–14.

SALADS

1. Ian A. Prior, Flora Davidson, Clare E. Salmond, and Z. Czochanska, "Cholesterol, Coconuts, and Diet on Polynesian Atolls: A Natural Experiment: The Pukapuka and Tokelau Island Studies," *American Journal of Clinical Nutrition* 34, no. 8 (1981): 1552–61.

2. Barbara J. Rolls, "Carbohydrates, Fats, and Satiety," *American Journal of Clinical Nutrition* 61, no. 4 (1995): 960S–67S; John E. Bludell, Clare L. Lawton, Jacqui R. Cotton, and Jennie I. Macdiarmid, "Control of Human Appetite: Implications for the Intake of Dietary Fat," *Annual Review of Nutrition* 16 (1996): 285–319. doi: 10.1146/annurev.nu.16.070196.001441.

3. R. James Stubbs and Chris G. Harbron, "Covert Manipulation of the Ratio of Medium- to Long-Chain Triglycerides in Isoenergetically Dense Diets: Effect on Food Intake in Ad Libitum Feeding Men," *International Journal of Obesity-Related Metabolic Disorders* 20, no. 5 (1996): 435–44.

4. Monica L. Assunção, Haroldo S. Ferreira, Aldenir F. dos Santos, Cyro R. Cabral, Jr., and Telma M. M. T. Florêncio, "Effects of Dietary Coconut Oil on the Biochemical and Anthropometric Profiles of Women Presenting Abdominal Obesity," *Lipids* 44, no. 7 (2009): 593–601. doi: 10.1007/s11745-009-3306-6.

5. Mary Ann S. van Duyn and Elizabeth Pivonka, "Overview of the Health Benefits of Fruit and Vegetable Consumption for the Dietetics Professional," *Journal of the Academy of Nutrition and Dietetics* 100, no. 12 (2000): 1511–21. doi: 10.1016/S0002-8223(00)00420-X; "Foods That Fight Cancer," American Institute for Cancer Research, accessed December 18, 2015, http://www.aicr.org/foods-that-fight-cancer/foodsthatfightcancer_leafy_vegetables.html.

6. Stuart Richer, "ARMD—Pilot (Case Series) Environmental Intervention Data," *Journal of the American Optometric Association* 70, no. 1 (1999): 24–36.

SANDWICHES & SOUPS

1. Judith Rodin, "Insulin Levels, Hunger, and Food Intake: An Example of Feedback Loops in Body Weight Regulation," *Health Psychology* 4, no. 1 (1985): 1–24.

2. Susanna H. Holt, Jennie C. Miller, Peter Petocz, and Efi Farmakalidis, "A Satiety Index of Common Foods," *European*

Journal of Clinical Nutrition 49, no. 9 (1995): 675–90.

3. Tawfeq Al-Howiriny, Abdulmalik Alsheikh, Saleh Alqasoumi, Mohammed Al-Yahya, Kamal El Tahir, and Syed Rafatullah, "Gastric Antiulcer, Antisecretory and Cytoprotective Properties of Celery (Apium graveolens) in Rats," *Pharmaceutical Biology* 48, no. 7 (2010): 786–93. doi: 10.3109/13880200903280026.

4. Jodee L. Johnson and Elvira Gonzalez de Mejia, "Interactions between Dietary Flavonoids Apigenin or Luteolin and Chemotherapeutic Drugs to Potentiate Anti-Proliferative Effect on Human Pancreatic Cancer Cells, in Vitro," *Food and Chemical Toxicology* 60 (2013): 83–91.

SHAKES & SNACKS

1. David J. Weiss and Christopher R. Anderton, "Determination of Catechins in Matcha Green Tea by Micellar Electrokinetic Chromatography," *Journal of Chromatography A* 1011, no. 1–2 (2003): 173–80; Elaine J. Gardner, Carrie H. S. Ruxton, and Anthony R. Leeds, "Black Tea—Helpful or Harmful? A Review of the Evidence," *European Journal of Clinical Nutrition* 61 (2007): 3–18. doi: 10.1038/sj.ejcn.1602489; Piwen Wang, William J. Aronson, Min Huang, Yanjun Zhang, Ru-Po Lee, David Heber, and Susanne M. Henning, "Green Tea Polyphenols and Metabolites in Prostatectomy Tissue: Implications for Cancer Prevention," *Cancer Prevention Research* 3, no. 8 (2010): 985–93; Silvia A. Mandel, Tamar Amit, Orly Weinreb, Lydia Reznichenko, and Moussa B. H. Youdim, "Simultaneous Manipulation of Multiple Brain Targets by Green Tea Catechins: A Potential Neuroprotective Strategy for Alzheimer and Parkinson Diseases," *CNS Neuroscience & Therapeutics* 14, no. 4 (2008): 352–65. doi: 10.1111/j.1755-5949.2008.00060.x.

2. Sonia Bérubé-Parent, Catherine Pelletier, Jean Doré, and Angelo Tremblay, "Effects of Encapsulated Green Tea and Guarana Extracts Containing a Mixture of Epigallocatechin-3-Gallate and Caffeine on 24 H Energy Expenditure and Fat Oxidation in Men," *British Journal of Nutrition* 94, no. 3 (2005): 432–36. doi: : 10.1079/BJN20051502; Michelle C. Venables, Carl J. Hulston, Hannah R. Cox, and Asker E. Jeukendrup, "Green Tea Extract Ingestion, Fat Oxidation, and Glucose Tolerance in Healthy Humans," 87, no. 3 (2008): 778–84.

3. Anna C. Nobre, Anling Rao, and Gail N. Owen, "L-Theanine, a Natural Constituent in Tea, and Its Effect on Mental State," *Asia Pacific Journal of Clinical Nutrition* 17, suppl. 1 (2008): 167–68; John J. Foxe, Kristen P. Morie, Peter J. Laud, Matthew J. Rowson, Eveline A. de Bruin, and Simon P. Kelly, "Assessing the Effects of Caffeine and Theanine on the Maintenance of Vigilance during a Sustained Attention Task," *Neuropharmacology* 62, no. 7 (2012): 2320–27. doi: 10.1016/j.neuropharm.2012.01.020; Crystal F. Haskell, David O. Kennedy, Anthea L. Milne, Keith A. Wesnes, and Andrew B. Scholey, "The Effects of L-Theanine, Caffeine and Their Combination on Cognition and Mood," *Biological Psychology* 77, no. 2 (2008): 113–22.

LEAN MEAT

1. An Pan, Qi Sun, Adam M. Bernstein, Matthias B. Schulze, JoAnn E. Manson, Meir J. Stampfer, Walter C. Willett, and Frank B. Hu, "Red Meat Consumption and Mortality: Results from Two Prospective Cohort Studies," *Archives of Internal Medicine* 172, no. 7 (2012): 555–63.

2. Adam Drewnowski, "Diet Image: a New Perspective on the Food-Frequency Questionnaire," *Nutrition Reviews* 59, no. 11 (2001): 370–72. doi: 10.1111/j.1753-4887.2001.tb06964.x.

3. Frank B. Hu, Eric Rimm, Stephanie A. Smith-Warner, Diane Feskanich, Meir J. Stampfer, Albert Ascherio, Laura Sampson, and Walter C. Willett, "Reproducibility and Validity of Dietary Patterns Assessed with a Food-Frequency Questionnaire," *The American Journal of Clinical Nutrition* 69, no. 2 (1999): 243–49.

4. Jose J. Lara, Jane Anne Scott, and Michael E. J. Lean, "Intentional Mis-Reporting of Food Consumption and Its Relationship with Body Mass Index and Psychological Scores in Women," *Journal of Human Nutrition and Dietetics* 17, no. 3 (2004): 209–18.

5. Dominik D. Alexander and Colleen A. Cushing, "Red Meat and Colorectal Cancer: A Critical Summary of Prospective Epidemiologic Studies," *Obesity Reviews* 12, no. 5 (2011): e472–93. doi: 10.1111/j.1467-789X.2010.00785.x.

6. Michelle H. Lewin, Nina Bailey, Tanya Bandaletova, Richard Bowman, Amanda J. Cross, Jim Pollock, David E. G. Shuker, and Sheila A. Bingham, "Red Meat Enhances the Colonic Formation of the DNA Adduct O6-Carboxymethyl Guanine: Implications for Colorectal Cancer Risk," *Cancer Research* 66, no. 3 (2006): 1859. doi: 10.1158/0008-5472.CAN-05-2237; Roisin Hughes, Amanda J. Cross, Jim R. A. Pollock, and Sheila Bingham, "Dose-Dependent Effect of Dietary Meat on Endogenous Colonic N-Nitrosation," *Carcinogenesis* 22, no. 1 (2001): 199–02. doi: 10.1093/carcin/22.1.199.

7. Eric N. Ponnampalam, Neil J. Mann, and Andrew J. Sinclair, "Effect of Feeding Systems on Omega-3 Fatty Acids, Conjugated Linoleic Acid and Trans Fatty Acids in Australian Beef Cuts: Potential Impact on Human Health," *Asia Pacific Journal of Clinical Nutrition* 15, no. 1 (2006): 21–29.

POULTRY

1. Barbara O. Rennard, Ronald F. Ertl, Gail L. Gossman, Richard A. Robbins, and Stephen I. Rennard, "FCCP Chicken Soup Inhibits Neutrophil Chemotaxis in Vitro," *CHEST Journal* 118, no. 4 (2000): 1150–57. doi: 10.1378/chest.118.4.1150.

2. Bharat B. Aggarwal, Chitra Sundaram, Nikita Malani, and Haruyo Ichikawa,

"Curcumin: The Indian Solid Gold," in *The Molecular Targets and Therapeutic Uses of Curcumin in Health and Disease*, ed. Bharat B. Aggarwal, et al. (New York: Springer, 2007), 1–75.

3. Li-Xin Na, Ying Li, Hong-Zhi Pan, Xian-Li Zhou, Dian-Jun Sun, Man Meng, Xiao-Xia Li, and Chang-Hao Sun, "Curcuminoids Exert Glucose-Lowering Effect in Type 2 Diabetes by Decreasing Serum Free Fatty Acids: A Double-Blind, Placebo-Controlled Trial," *Molecular Nutrition and Food Research* 57, no. 9 (2013): 1569–77. doi: 10.1002/mnfr.201200131. Kassaian, Nazila, Leila Azadbakht, Badrolmolook Forghani, and Masud Amini. "Effect of fenugreek seeds on blood glucose and lipid profiles in type 2 diabetic patients." *International journal for vitamin and nutrition research* 79, no. 1 (2009): 34-39.

SEAFOOD

1. Emily Oken, "Seafood Health Benefits & Risks,"Harvard T. H. School of Public Health, accessed December 18, 2015, http://www.chgeharvard.org/topic/seafood-health-benefits-risks.

2. Artemis P. Simopoulos, "Evolutionary Aspects of Diet: The Omega-6/Omega-3 Ratio and the Brain," *Molecular Neurobiology* 44, no. 2 (2011): 203–15. doi: 10.1007/s12035-010-8162-0.

SIDES

1. Li-Xin Zhang, Robert V. Cooney, and John S. Bertram, "Carotenoids Enhance Gap Junctional Communication and Inhibit Lipid Peroxidation in C3H/10T1/2 Cells: Relationship to Their Cancer Chemopreventive Action," *Carcinogenesis* 12, no. 11 (1991): 2109–114.

2. William G. Christen, Simin Liu, Robert J. Glynn, J. Michael Gaziano, and Julie E. Buring, "A Prospective Study of Dietary Carotenoids, Vitamins C and E, and Risk of Cataract in Women," *Archives of Ophthalmology* 126, no. 1 (2008): 102–09. doi: 10.1001/archopht.126.1.102.

3. Geert van Poppel, Dorette T. H. Verhoeven, Hans Verhagen, and R. Alexandra Goldbohm, "Brassica Vegetables and Cancer Prevention: Epidemiology and Mechanisms," *Advances in Experimental Medicine and Biology* 472 (1999): 159–68.

4. Simin Liu, Meir J. Stampfer, Frank B. Hu, Edward Giovannucci, Eric Rimm, JoAnn E. Manson, Charles H. Hennekens, and Walter C. Willett, "Whole-Grain Consumption and Risk of Coronary Heart Disease: Results from the Nurses' Health Study," *American Journal of Clinical Nutrition* 70, no. 3 (1999): 412–19.

5. Paul Whelton and Jiang He, "Health Effects of Sodium and Potassium in Humans," *Current Opinion in Lipidology* 25, no. 1 (2014): 75–79. doi: 10.1097/MOL.0000000000000033; Igho J. Onakpoya, Elizabeth A. Spencer, Matthew J. Thompson, and Carl J. Heneghan, "The Effect of Chlorogenic Acid on Blood Pressure: A Systematic Review and Meta-Analysis of Randomized Clinical Trials," *Journal of Human Hypertension* 29 (2015): 77–81. doi: 10.1038/jhh.2014.46.

6. Johannes Erdmann, Yvonne Hebeisen, Florian Lippl, Stefan Wagenpfeil, and Volker Schusdziarra, "Food Intake and Plasma Ghrelin Response during Potato-, Rice- and Pasta-Rich Test Meals," *European Journal of Nutrition* 46, no. 4 (2007): 196–03.

DESSERTS

1. Stephen J. Crozier, Amy G. Preston, Jeffrey W. Hurst, Mark J. Payne, Julie Mann, Larry Hainly, and Debra L. Miller, "Cacao Seeds Are a 'Super Fruit': A Comparative Analysis of Various Fruit Powders and Products," *Chemistry Central Journal* 5 (2011): 5. doi: 10.1186/1752-153X-5-5.

2. Helmut Sies, Tankred Schewe, Christian Heiss, and Malte Kelm, "Cocoa Polyphenols and Inflammatory Mediators," *American Journal of Clinical Nutrition* 81, no. 1 (2005): 304S–12S.

3. Stefanie Williams, Slobodanka Tamburic, and Carmel Lally, "Eating Chocolate Can Significantly Protect the Skin from UV Light," *Journal of Cosmetic Dermatology* 8, no. 3 (2009): 169–73. doi: 10.1111/j.1473-2165.2009.00448.x.